Talking to Writers

Talking to Writers

The Craft of Fiction

Dean Nelson

BLOOMSBURY ACADEMIC
NEW YORK • LONDON • OXFORD • NEW DELHI • SYDNEY

BLOOMSBURY ACADEMIC
Bloomsbury Publishing Inc
Bloomsbury Publishing Inc, 1359 Broadway, New York, NY 10018, USA
Bloomsbury Publishing Plc, 50 Bedford Square, London, WC1B 3DP, UK
Bloomsbury Publishing Ireland, 29 Earlsfort Terrace, Dublin 2, D02 AY28, Ireland

BLOOMSBURY, BLOOMSBURY ACADEMIC and the Diana logo are trademarks of Bloomsbury Publishing Plc

First published in the United States of America 2025

Cover design: Dustin Watson

Cover image © Writer's Symposium by the Sea / University of California Television

Library of Congress Cataloging-in-Publication Data

Names: Nelson, Dean, 1954- author interviewer
Title: Talking to writers : the craft of fiction / Dean Nelson.
Description: New York : Bloomsbury Publishing, 2025. | Includes index. |
Summary: "Dean Nelson embraces the questions that plague writers by turning to some of the best-known authors of our time. With encouragement, advice, and refreshing honesty, writers discuss their own beginnings, struggles, and victories in a manner that will make readers say, "I can do that.""-- Provided by publisher.
Identifiers: LCCN 2025015498 (print) | LCCN 2025015499 (ebook) | ISBN 9798881803506 hardback | ISBN 9798881803513 epub | ISBN 9798881867980 pdf
Subjects: LCSH: Authors--20th century--Interviews | Authors--21st century--Interviews | Fiction--Authorship | Poetry--Authorship | LCGFT: Interviews
Classification: LCC PN452 .N45 2025 (print) | LCC PN452 (ebook)
LC record available at https://lccn.loc.gov/2025015498
LC ebook record available at https://lccn.loc.gov/2025015499

ISBN: HB: 979-8-8818-0350-6
ePDF: 979-8-8818-6798-0
eBook: 979-8-8818-0351-3

Typeset by Deanta Global Publishing Services, Chennai, India

To find out more about our authors and books visit www.bloomsbury.com and sign up for our newsletters.

To the memory of Joe Wambaugh, friend and inspiration.

Contents

Acknowledgments ix

Introduction 1

1 A Reason to Write Fiction: Why Do Stories Matter? 19

2 Awakening to the Art: How Did You Know You Wanted to Write? 51

3 Subject Matter: Where Do Ideas Come From? 77

4 The Voices Outside Your Head: Where Did You Receive Encouragement? 135

5 Emerging Path: When Did You First Think You Were a Success? 143

6 Growing, Changing, Improving: How Have You Evolved as a Writer? 157

7 Worldview, Pessimism, and Optimism: How Does Your Mindset Affect Your Writing? 185

8 When the World Says No: How Do You Handle Rejection and Criticism? 199

9 More Than Words on a Page: What Do We Mean By "Craft"? 221

10 When Enthusiasm Fades: How Important Is Discipline? 255

11 Consider the Reader: Who Is Your Audience, Really? 287

12 What You Believe: How Does Faith Affect Your Writing? 291

13 The Importance of Reading: What Writers Inform Your Own Writing? What Role Do Libraries Play? **313**

14 Words of Wisdom: What Advice Do You Have for Aspiring Authors? **337**

Index **365**

About the Author **375**

Acknowledgments

The format for these discussions started when Joe Wambaugh told me no.

I was trying to bring writers to our campus to inspire our students and give them a picture of what the writing life could be. I knew that Joe lived nearby, and his book *Lines and Shadows* helped shape me when I was writing about the US/Mexico border for the *Boston Globe*. He wrote fiction and nonfiction. He was a role model.

A mutual friend told me that Joe didn't like to talk on the phone, so the friend gave me Joe's fax number. Some of you have no idea what that previous sentence means. I faxed my request to Joe, told him how much I admired him, asked if he would come to our campus to give a talk or a reading. His faxed response was a swift and brief "No." Then, he said, almost as an afterthought, "But if someone wants to ask me questions, I guess I could do that."

I read every one of his books and prepared as if I was going to write his biography. We hired a video crew from the University of California-San Diego (UCSD-TV), and had a gathering in a conference room with about eighty people. The interview was a great success, Joe had a good time, and the Writer's Symposium By The Sea style was born.

The writers who have come over the past thirty or so years have been generous, forthcoming and helpful. They hung out with our students, did writing workshops with them, and encouraged them. Just by reading their works in preparation for the interviews I felt like they were teaching me how to write better. Then the interviews were a master class in the craft. So thank you to all who let me butt into your lives and practice. You've made us better storytellers. I look at you, then say to our students, "Aspire to this."

The Symposium has evolved over the years, with the help of Rachel Mournian, Edie Chapman, Randy Meza, Charlie Merritt, and especially Ashley Reynolds-Montano. Ashley's dream for the Symposium is at least as big as mine. My migraines abated when she started running things. She should rule the world.

Many students and department assistants got roped into transcribing these interviews. I experimented with AI and other technology to give an accurate representation for what was said in the interviews, but I spent as much time correcting inaccurate sentences and words from certain breakneck conversations (looking at you, Cornel West!), as it would have taken for a human being to do it in the first place. No bots were used or harmed or exploited in these transcriptions—only students. So thank you Aliah Fabros, Madi Bucci, Amanda Rasing, Ashley Reynolds-Montaño, Meghan Coley, Melanie Coffman, Noah Harrel, Tony Le Calvez, Reyna Huff, Toby Franklin, Vicky Gonzalez, and Zach Dinsmore. Anyone who has done transcriptions knows they can be a pain. Most of these students thanked me, because it forced them to consider at an even deeper level the wisdom being revealed. Thanks also to Nate Eaton, who gave us the original art for the cover of these books. And thank you to my friend and colleague Karl Martin, who did a few of these interviews—I am grateful for his expertise and friendship

A big thank you to Kelly Mitchell at Point Loma Nazarene University, who saw the value of these conversations, and found people who wanted to help support them financially. Also thanks to Jim Daichendt, our university provost, Lindsey Lupo and Mark Maddix, two of our university deans, who helped me carve out time for this book.

UCSD-TV has recorded and posted these interviews from the very beginning. The executive producer Shannon Bradley saw the value right from the start. The current executive producer Natalie Walsh sees the Symposium similarly. She even let me take her crew to the home of N. Scott Momaday in Santa Fe when he became too frail to travel. We brought the Symposium to him. The UCSD-TV bunch are a dream to work with.

I am proud to call Elise Capron of the Sandra Dijkstra Literary Agency my agent. Elise helped shape my thinking and this manuscript, and my earlier book on interviewing, *Talk To Me: How to Ask Better Questions, Get Better*

Answers, and Interview Anyone Like a Pro. If you have ever wondered what an ideal relationship between an agent and writer should be, you would only have to look at Elise. She's professional, tireless, visionary, and knows how to get a project to completion. I am so grateful for her.

And finally, thank you to my wife Marcia, son Blake, daughter Vanessa, and their spouses Amy and Evan. When I first started doing the Writer's Symposium, my family organized their lives around it as much as I did. Even now, our yearly family calendar has the notation "BWS and AWS"—Before Writer's Symposium and After Writer's Symposium. During preparation time, nothing else gets done. Thank you for enabling this to happen, and for making it seem as fun for you as it is for me!

Introduction

Do you want to be a writer, or do you want to write?

CHRISTOPHER BUCKLEY

Are You a Writer?

Have you ever wanted to be a writer? Do you think you *might* be a writer, but it sounds pretentious to say it to anyone? What does "being a writer" even mean? Are you a writer if you've written a novel that has won awards and sold enough copies so you can buy a beach house? Are you a writer if you write your own posts about your kids or pets or recipes or house cleaning tips that only your family reads? Are you a writer if you never get out of your pajamas, write fantasy fiction at your computer for hours, and the only way you know when morning has moved into afternoon is that at some point you stopped reaching for your coffee mug and reached for the wine bottle instead?

Are you a writer if you wrote a couple of poems in high school and now, years later, you're thinking about "getting back into writing?" Are you a writer if you have written a screenplay that has been accepted and green-lit for production by someone in the film industry? Are you a writer if you wrote a screenplay that got rejected by everyone, and, when you get the resources, you'll make it with your friends and post it online?

Are you a writer if you write stories for your kids to read before they go to bed, and no one else will read them?

Are you a writer if you have a degree in some aspect of writing, like a Master's in Fine Arts (MFA) from a prestigious writing school, or a creative writing program, or a journalism school?

Are you a writer?

This is going to sound really simple and condescending, but the answer is this: You are a writer if you write. Actually, I want to qualify that a little. In my opinion, a writer is someone who wrote *today.*

I didn't say that the writing today had to be any good, or that anyone would be interested in reading it. In fact, most of what we write isn't very good, and should never see the light of day. But that's not the point. The point is that everyone can be a writer, and everyone has something to say, and everyone has a story to tell, and there are some ways you can get better at it. And they are writers if they wrote today.

I had a student recently who severely tested my hypothesis that everyone can be a writer. It was class with a mix of talent and experience, as are most writing classes. One had won awards as a student journalist and had done a semester-long internship as a member of the press corps in Washington D.C. Another was just intuitively good at the craft, maybe because she had been near death in her younger years, and it created a seriousness about the big questions in her mind. She told stories that brought tears to my eyes. Another was brought into this country as a child when her family fled a civil war, and spent the first few years of her life in a refugee camp on another continent. One had a rough start in the class because his autism made it hard for him to concentrate, but once he started telling stories in voices of dinosaurs, his writing became quite good.

But this student—let's call her Clare—just wasn't getting it. I had never thought about writing the way we might consider math or physics, where some people feel like they just don't "get it." Writing never struck me that way. For Clare, it seemed that the "writing gene" had skipped her. The stories she wrote were technically okay—she knew how to spell and how to construct a sentence—but they were pointless and boring. She was clearly intimidated by the other students in the class. Their writing was interesting. Hers was not. We met in my office privately a few times to talk about her progress, or lack of, in the class.

I was a firm believer in the Flannery O'Connor line that said anyone who had survived childhood had plenty of material to write about.

Except for maybe Clare.

"I just don't have anything to say," she told me.

"That's hard for me to believe," I replied, but silently wondered if she was correct.

We talked about her life, her interests, her passions (more on these things later), and after a couple of meetings I started to conclude that maybe the reason her stories were so boring and pointless was that SHE was boring, and nothing really was going on in that head of hers. I hated the comparison I made (just to myself, thankfully. I'm pretty sure, anyway) during one of our conversations. The way she described herself reminded me of my Airedale Terrier dog. Sometimes he would just walk into a room and stare at my wife or kids or me. In these moments, his tail didn't wag, he didn't paw at his food or water dish, he didn't pant or yawn or stretch. He just stood there. I would take on what I thought his voice would sound like if he could speak, a Homer Simpson voice, and I would say, "There is nothing in my head right now." My kids thought it was hilarious. My wife, not so much.

But as Clare sat in my office, I saw that same thought bubble appear over her head: "There is nothing in my head right now." No wonder she couldn't write.

Of course I was wrong.

Halfway through the semester she made another appointment to see me after class. It had been a couple of weeks since she had turned anything in. She was falling behind, and this was her senior year. Nothing seemed to work as far as getting her to write.

She came into my office and sat down, as she had several times before.

"What's going on, Clare?"

She stared at me for several seconds. I could tell she was thinking something this time. Her face became red, then almost purple, and she burst into tears. It took her several minutes to get control of her emotions before she could speak.

"I hate school," she said. "I don't want to be here. I hate all of my classes. I hate my dorm and my roommate. I hate my life."

I let that settle for a few moments, and quietly asked, "Then why are you here? If you hate everything so much, why do you stay in school?"

"My parents won't let me quit," she said, between bouts of angry sobs. "They're making me stay in school. They say I should just tough it out. But I just want to go home."

"Can I make a suggestion for your next story in my class?" I softly asked.

She nodded.

"I would like to see a story about a girl named Clare who feels trapped. She's trapped by her circumstances. She wants to live her own life and pursue her own dreams, which do not include college, but she can't overcome this pressure from her family to live according to their understanding of success in our society. The Clare character wants to break free from those rules, but something is holding her back. Do you think that might be a story you could tell?"

Clare calmed down and nodded again.

I think you can predict what happened. Her next story was good. It had passion and rage and a character who wanted something, but had to face all of these impediments to get what she wanted. And her next story was better, and the next one was better.

She didn't think she had anything to say. And she was on the brink of convincing me that she didn't have anything to say.

But something was roiling beneath the surface. She felt like it was unspeakable. It was too personal and painful to put language on. It was like when I hiked on a glacier in Iceland, and how my guide described the volcano that was beneath the crust—right where we were walking—waiting for just enough of the ice to melt before it before it emptied its deeply buried contents into the land, sea and sky, creating a brand new surface.

Once she had permission and encouragement, Clare's story emerged. She became a writer.

I received a note from her a couple of years after she graduated. She had gone to South Korea to teach school. For a couple of years she taught English and—you guessed it—writing. She was returning to the United States and was applying to grad school. She asked if I'd write a letter of recommendation for her. Turns out she was a writer after all. That glacier in her needed to melt just a little more for her to see it.

In my role as director of an annual event called the Writer's Symposium By The Sea, I have interviewed dozens of great writers, as you'll see in the following chapters, and we talk about what it takes to be a writer.

One statement that has stuck with me, by the great political satirist, Christopher Buckley (son of William F. Buckley), is that he sees a big difference between people who say they want to be a writer, and people who want to write. "When a person says he wants to be a writer, he is tapping into a myth," Buckley told me. "He has this idea that 'being a writer' means living a romantic ideal, where the words and images flow freely and people see him as a fascinating, mysterious character. When people tell me they want to 'be a writer,' I don't take them very seriously."

On the other hand, people who want to write, simply write, he said. It's not the "idea" of writing that appeals to them. They just simply write.

Which reminds me of being at a concert where the jazz pianist and singer Diana Krall was performing. As she was introducing her next song, a guy yelled out, "I love you Diana!" She smiled sweetly and leaned into the microphone and said, "Actually, you don't. You love the *idea* of me."

That's how some people think about writing, too.

So, can anyone be a writer? Or maybe I should ask, can anyone write? The answer is "probably."

The reason many people don't write is that they don't think they have anything to say.

Or maybe, like Clare, they're afraid to really say what they are thinking.

Or maybe some people think that writing is some mysterious gift—you either "have it" or you don't.

Or maybe they think no one would be interested in anything they have written.

Everyone should write something, because I believe that everyone has a story to tell. And our stories matter.

Should You Write?

Everyone knows that the reason you should write is that it will do at least one or more of the following:

- Make you a lot of money. Think John Grisham, Stephen King, Danielle Steele. They're like ATMs! They write (easily, for about a half-hour a day), and money flows to them like it's coming out of a fire hose. There aren't enough offshore accounts—or islands, for that matter—to hold all of their cash. It's crazy!

- Make you famous. In addition to the names above, think about, well. . ., uhhhh . . ., hmmm. I'm sure there are others.
- Make everyone admire you and ask you to hang out with them.
- Make you win a Nobel Prize for Literature, a Pulitzer Prize, a Genius Grant, or an invitation to my Writer's Symposium By The Sea.
- Make Greta Gerwig want to make a movie about your life.

The above list is why some people write. I haven't actually met any of those people, but I'm told they exist.

Here are some other reasons why you should write, and I have met people who do it for these reasons.

You should write because:

- You have something to say. You may not know what it is yet, like Clare, but my observation is that everyone feels something, is bothered by something, is moved by something that they want to talk about it and share it with others. Putting language on an incident or a thought or an experience is part of being human. We may not all have major proclamations to make about race ("I have a dream") or love or war or violence or kindness, but we all have a point of view, and it's worth expressing. Clare really did have something to say. She just needed permission, and maybe some tools, to say it. We'll talk about tools later.

Here are some more reasons why you should write.

- You need to bear witness. Ray Bradbury said it best when I interviewed him. He said that we should write because we are "witnesses to the miraculous." It sounds better when you hear him say it, almost shouting, gesturing to the heavens, filling his sentences with profanity. He and I talked about the love and mystery and wonder of life in this world and in whatever other worlds there might be. And someone needs to tell about it. "Now get the hell out of here and do it!" he proclaimed to the cheering audience. Even my wife, a lifelong accountant, said after that interview, "I think I might want to write."

- You should write because you want to. The fact that you're reading this book means that you're interested in learning how to write better, or in exploring what it means to write. That's worth paying attention to. Related to that, maybe you should write because you're good at it. That talent, that desire, that curiosity came from somewhere.
- You should write because the idea keeps coming back to you, whether through other people suggesting it, or through your own thoughts. If it keeps returning to you that "I should write about that," well, then you should.
- You should write because the world is looking for a way to feel less alone. People read not only because they want a good story, but because they also want to be able to identify with characters in stories, or experiences told by others. Laura Hillenbrand's book Unbroken was read by millions in part because it was so well-written, and because she is a superb storyteller. But it was also popular because readers could identify with the main character in their own personal ways. Very few of the readers were shot down over the ocean, taken prisoner, and tortured. But most readers have asked similar questions as the main character, Louis Zamperini, about suffering, destiny, overcoming odds, cruelty, and kindness. We read a book like that and, even though the circumstances are much different from ours, we say, "I have felt that way, too," or "I hope I respond this same way when I face insurmountable odds."

When you write something and it resonates with someone else, that's worth something. When people say "Mary Oliver's poetry saved me," they're saying "She put into words what I was feeling, only she said it better." My daughter read every book in Robin Jones Gunn's The Christy Miller Series because the Christy Miller character, as a middle school teenager, was facing the very kind of things that my daughter was facing—body image issues, peer pressure, romantic feelings, awkwardness, the sense of being alone, or not fitting in, or being a freak. The details and circumstances were different, of course, but the thoughts, the feelings, the questions that Christy Miller experienced resonated with my daughter.

I had a student several years ago who was an excellent writer, and she seemed deeper than most students her age. She also had these sad eyes that looked like were always on the verge of tears, even when she laughed. I assumed she had experienced something about the world that made her see beyond the surface things that many of her peers concentrated on. In the college cafeteria one day I saw her sitting by herself and I asked if I could sit at her table. We got to talking about writing.

"Did I ever tell you why I wanted to write?" she asked. "I read the book Ordinary People in high school. That's when I knew I wanted to write."

I had seen the movie, but hadn't read the book. The movie moved me very deeply, and I was surprised that someone considerably younger than me had also been moved by the story. When she was done telling me about it, I asked her to write her account in a few paragraphs and send it to me.

Here's what she sent:

> I was fourteen when my older sister died. I let grief dictate life for a year. I did not give in and grieve, rather, I shoved everything to the shelves of my mind. I pretended I was OK. But for a year, I was dying inside. I was convinced that no one could know what I was feeling or experiencing. No one. No one could possibly understand. Until one night, I was up late reading my literature assignment for my tenth grade English class—a novel by Judith Guest called Ordinary People—and there was a simple, two-page scene that wrecked me. In the story, the protagonist is a high school student whose older brother has died. The protagonist is in a therapy session, believing no one can understand him when his therapist says, "Let me tell you a short story."
>
> The therapist goes on to tell this hypothetical story about a perfect kid who had a younger brother, the not-so-perfect kid. The perfect kid dies. The not-so-perfect kid is left reeling—it should've been him. He's not so perfect, after all. Where's the justice? So he tries to become the perfect kid for everyone, even for himself. It works OK—they're similar to begin with, being brothers and all, and the not-so-perfect kid is a good actor. But this is

the thing—the not-so-perfect kid—he's dying inside. Because deep down, he knows he'll always fail, because he will always be not so perfect.

I read in the middle of the night as I was trying to cram and finish the book for a test the next day so that I could ace it and be the perfect kid. I sat on my bed, in the room I had shared with my sister, and I felt like someone was telling me my story.

I wept. It was like a grenade had just unleashed the waters of grief my self-made dam had been diligently holding back. Because there in front of me was proof that someone understood. A stranger writing a fictional book understood *exactly* what I was feeling. And the fact that I wasn't alone—that changed everything. The story saved my life.

This is why stories matter. And it's why YOUR story matters. As Flannery O'Connor said, the life you save may be your own.

- In the Old Testament of the Bible, Adam was put in charge of naming the animals. That's what writers do. You get to name the animals that are roaming the earth. You get to identify what's happening. You have a say in what the world is like.
- Related to the above point, you also get to tame those same animals. It's a lot harder to be afraid of the things you're writing about. Putting language on your experiences and issues and fears is a way to reduce their power over you. In Maurice Sendak's beautiful children's book Where the Wild Things Are, each of the characters experienced by the boy represented relatives who came to visit while Sendak was little. The relatives seemed so strange, bizarre, foreign to the young Sendak that he was able to name them, and even tame them, by making them characters in his story.
- Writing is one of the few places in life where you don't have to play it safe. This is where you can explore your motives, create characters who do bizarre things, be the hero, be the goat. If you're writing nonfiction, you have permission to explore what your inner life is doing, and perhaps speculate on what else your story might be about. If you're writing fiction, it's wide open—your characters can be superheroes,

criminals, Don Juans, girls with dragon tattoos, and you can explore the world as it was, is, or could be. Remember, no one HAS to see what you've written. But you have had a chance to let your freak flag fly.

- Writing is a way of becoming more whole. There are a lot of thoughts, dreams, fears, joys, bubbling beneath the surface of your conscious self. Sometimes we don't know those things are even there until we put them in a story or an essay or a poem. Remember Clare? I believe she became more whole—more engaged with her true self—when she started writing about a girl who was trapped by her surroundings and forces she had no control over. Writing about those circumstances didn't change the circumstances. But she was at least able to identify why she was so locked up inside.
- Writing is an act of creation, and we are co-creators. Think about it. Human beings are constantly creating. We're creating new businesses, new products, new children, new ideas, new methods, new inventions. Writing is a continuation of that primal activity. Unless we're extensively plagiarizing, what we write has never existed before in that particular form. You get to arrange the letters, the words, the sentences, the paragraphs, the pages. You get to tell a story from your unique perspective.
- Writing is a way to express outrage. A lot of powerful poetry has been written about slavery, injustice, war, corrupt governments, etc. Sometimes it comes out in the form of songs, like some of Pete Seeger's music, or Bob Dylan's, Iris DeMent's, and in songs like "Four Dead in Ohio," and "Sunday Bloody Sunday." It puts language on what we typically think is inexpressible because the emotions are so raw.

Why You Don't Write

In the pages above, I have listed some of the reasons why we could, and should, write.

And yet we don't, because of some unnamed force that keeps us rooted to anywhere except for in front of our notebooks and computer screens.

That force takes many shapes, so let's talk about them one at a time. Whether we're writing fiction or nonfiction, the reasons for avoiding writing are often the same, so I am putting this list in both volumes of *Talking to Writers.*

- You don't write because you don't have time. This is a legitimate statement for some, but think about it. Do you have time for checking social media? Then you have time to write. Do you have time to watch cat videos on YouTube? Then you have time to write. Do you watch television or movies or sports? Do you ride a train or a bus to work? Scott Turow wrote his first few novels while riding the train to his law office in the morning. Do your kids take naps? Do you? How much sleep do you need? Have you tried getting up 30 minutes earlier than you're used to, just so you get a few pages done?

  Do you need to have breakfast ready for everyone at 7:00 a.m.? What are you doing at 5:00 a.m.? Maybe writing for an hour? There are some days when I have gaps between the classes I teach. I could stand in the doorway of a colleague and complain about our dumb bosses and the state of education today and the lack of time for writing, or I could hole up in a library cubicle or an unused office and write a few more pages. Some people are under the illusion that they need a whole day free in order to be a little bit productive in their writing. If they have a hair appointment later in the afternoon, or have to pick up their kids at a certain hour, then they can't produce anything. If being a journalist taught me nothing else, it at least taught me that you can learn how to write on demand, no matter the time of day or night, no matter the time you have available. You have an hour today? How are you going to spend it?

- You don't write because you have been locked up inside ever since a long time ago someone told you that you were a lousy writer. I had a student in a freshman writing class who acted like writing was an exercise in torture. I'd give in-class assignments and he would sweat and strain and grimace like this was his daily experience on the rack. It was his personal Golgotha. I knew he was bright, just judging by conversations I'd had with him. But his assignments were minimal. If an essay was supposed to be three pages long, he would turn in two paragraphs. I finally met with him and asked why he was so inhibited. He told me that, when he was in high school he liked to write. He said he wasn't particularly good at it, but it wasn't a chore. Then he got an assignment on a topic he loved, and he wrote about it with great enthusiasm. His teacher gave him an F for it and accused him of plagiarizing. She told him that, since he had never done anything that well before, the only explanation for the quality of this particular essay was that he must have stolen it and put his own name on it. Boom. That was it. He was afraid to express himself after that. For the rest of the semester I tried to convince him that he had a new voice to listen to—mine—that would replace the voice of that teacher who said he was no good and that he was a fraud. I've had other students who were stifled by their parents, siblings, friends, teammates, and others, who told them that their writing was bad. You don't forget those voices. But you can quiet them down.

I had the opposite experience of many of my students. I was actually encouraged in my writing. When I was in high school, one of my friends from church and I got to thinking about writing reviews on the Sunday worship service, including the sermon, and publishing it as an underground newspaper. Every time we referred to the pastor, we spelled his name differently. We gave him suggestions on where he could find better anecdotes than the tired ones he used, the length of his sermons, the attire of the ushers, the quality of bread during communion (it was tough prying it off the roof of my mouth), the musicians—you name it, we had a commentary for it. Think about that. If there ever was an opportunity for some adult to come down harshly and squash a kid's creativity, that was the time. But the pastor didn't complain. He loved it. He encouraged it. He let us use the photocopier in the church office to make copies for early Sunday morning distribution. He even quoted from it occasionally in his sermons.

But not everyone has an experience like that. A lot of young people experience being laughed at for their writing, or having their work called inappropriate, lame, weird, derivative, or worse. When they read something out loud in class, sometimes no one "gets it." Peers don't know how to communicate their confusion without sarcasm or vicious judgment. The criticism often takes the form of, "I didn't understand your story, so you suck." Then the writer crawls into his or her shell muttering, "Never again."

- You don't write because you're too self-conscious. Writing is an act of vulnerability. Don't let anyone tell you differently. Every time you write something and let someone see it, whether it's a post, an article published, a memoir, whatever, you are inviting judgment. But you can ease yourself into a certain comfort level here, if you can have some trustworthy people read what you've written and, in a safe, non-threatening environment, give you feedback. Once a year I meet with a group of guys to discuss life, big ideas, books, and whatever else we think is worth our attention at the time. The Atlantic magazine has written about our group. One year the gents agreed to read a draft of the manuscript I had written about applying the seven sacraments to everyday life, which ultimately became the book God Hides in Plain Sight. It was scary on the one hand, because I was inviting them into something very personal—my manuscript. The contents were also very personal, where I admitted to failures and fears. So I was also inviting them into my life. Their response was constructive in that they pointed out problems in logic, research, and syntax, but it was also very loving and affirming. That made an enormous difference in my confidence level as I proceeded through the formal editing and publishing process. They convinced me that the personal risks I was taking were worth it.
- You don't write because the story you want to tell might hurt people.

  I like what Anne Lamott told our audience when she was at our Symposium: "If people didn't want you to write about them, then they should have behaved better." Perhaps it is better if certain members of your family or community die before you tell your story. But that doesn't mean you can't write it now, and wait until the day after the funeral to publish or post it.

- You don't write because you've never taken a writing class. That may be a good thing. Writing classes have been known to stifle some people's creativity. But if you know how to read, then there is a good chance you have read a good story here and there.

  Before I took any writing classes I read Mark Twain voraciously and found myself trying to imitate him. That was coursework enough at first. Others have found inspiration by imitating Hunter S. Thompson, Tom Wolfe, Anne Lamott, Annie Dillard. I am not knocking writing classes, workshops, and programs—I teach in those arenas. I'm just saying that not having formal training is not a good excuse to not write. Writers write. It's not like they have to join a guild or pass a test or get a license to do it. They just write. And if they realize they are writing badly, they can get some training. But it's not a requirement.

  When I learned to ski, I stood at the bottom of a slope and watched skiers coming down the hill. I picked out several and thought, "I don't want to ski like that guy. I do want to ski like that guy. And why are those guys skiing in just their underwear?" I watched who I wanted to emulate for a little while, then took the chair lift to the top of a slope. I should have spent more time watching how skiers got off the chair lift. But once I got myself upright and the lift began moving again, I slowly made my way down the mountain. I don't need to tell you how badly I did it, and how many times I fell. But when I got to the bottom I headed for the chair lift and did it again. I'm not an expert skier now, but I do okay, all these years later. Would a class have helped? Probably. I'll never win any skiing awards. Do I have fun skiing anyway? It's one of my favorite things to do.

- Related to the above, you don't write because you know it's not going to be any good. Well, if you haven't done it much before, then of course it's not going to be any good! Expect to write shitty first drafts, as Anne Lamott calls them in her book Bird By Bird.

  Can you imagine a baby thinking to himself, as he is on his stomach on the floor, "I've been thinking about walking, but I will probably just fall a lot. I might even bump my head. So I guess I'll just stay here and crawl around on the floor where the dog has been scooting for the past few years." When a kid learns to walk, no one says, "Look at how badly that kid walks—he sure falls a lot. Just look at him, failing, failing, failing." People expect him to fall. That's part of the deal. Writing badly is part of the deal. Eventually you get better, after you've done it for a while. I am working on a novel, and have been for a couple of years. I haven't done much fiction in my life, and it shows. This novel isn't very good. But do I really think that I'm going to get better at writing novels if I wait until I'm better? Where do I think this improvement will come from? A dream? Amazon? I have to write it and write it some more and write it some more.

- You don't write because you need to get organized first. Oh boy. That's a good one. I took a quick scan around my room when I wrote that last sentence. I have a dresser that has enough loose change from a variety of recently visited countries to pay tolls around the globe, stray breath mints that have accumulated countless diseases because of what they've been touching in my pockets, scraps of paper that meant something at some point. Membership cards to pet stores, and our dog has been dead for eight years, a flash drive that I'm sure has something important on it, a miniature Stanley Cup that I took off of my kids' table hockey game years ago, business cards of people I met somewhere. And next to my dresser is my desk. Notebooks, journals, medical records, files for stories I think I might work on someday, books that I started that I think I might someday finish. And that reminds me—the workbench in my garage needs organizing. I have a lot of tools scattered around that need to be hung back on their pegs. And a lot of loose batteries that need to be checked. And that box of cigars that I brought back from the Dominican Republic. Time for a smoke break! Which leads me to the trunk of my car. Why are there folding chairs in the trunk? Was someone going to borrow them? Or did I borrow them—maybe they're not mine? And then there are all of those emails that I need to read, respond to, put in new folders, or delete. It's just out of control. If I can just get those back to a manageable level, I'll be able to write.

Here's the deal—if you wait until you have your ish together before you write, you will never write. You can write a few pages today AND clean off your dresser. It's not an either/or game.

- You don't write because you're too old to start now.

  Well, now you're just being stupid. Is there an age limit? Maybe to learn surgery or gymnastics, but not to learn to write well. If you use this as your excuse, you're just making shit up in order not to write. Cut it out and start writing.

We all have excuses to not write. The thing is, your excuses just aren't that interesting. They don't impress anyone. Everyone else has better excuses than you. I suggest you watch the movie The Diving Bell and the Butterfly, about the editor of the French Elle Magazine who suffered a stroke in 1995. The only part of his body that could move was his left eyelid. He wrote an entire book with an assistant who would recite the alphabet until she got to the letter he wanted, and then he would blink. This method produced about one word every two minutes. You're not that guy. Sit down, quit whining, blink with both eyes, and write.

Here's Steven Pressfield's advice from his book, *The War of Art*: "Let's ask ourselves, like that new mother: What do I feel growing inside me? Let me bring that forth, if I can, for its own sake and not for what it can do for me or how it can advance my standing" (p. 157).

But don't just take my word for any of this. Listen to the experts!

For more than thirty years I have been talking to writers about these very topics. What follows are excerpts from those conversations which were done in front of a live audience as part of the annual Writer's Symposium By The Sea or at author events at the public library. Some of these writers have since died, which makes these interviews even more significant. All of the writers were extraordinarily forthcoming, I thought, and engaging.

I started the Symposium to model, inspire, and celebrate great writing. Interviewing these writers was a way for me to say to our audience, and now to you, "aspire to this." If you don't consider yourself a writer now, you'll have a change of heart as you read these conversations.

Why Fiction?

The writers in this volume chose fiction and poetry as their means to tell their stories. There are the rare birds who excel in both nonfiction and fiction (Jeannette Walls, Anne Lamott, and Elizabeth Gilbert, for example), but most writers stick to one or the other. Fiction writers and poets explore ideas, thoughts, possibilities, emotions, and try to craft stories or poems around them. These writers often begin their works by asking, "What if . . .?" They see a predicament and let their imagination follow that situation to the next scene, and then the next, and the next. They are trying to articulate what their minds are creating.

For some, there is a prophetic purpose to their writing. Isaac Bashevis Singer, in his Nobel Prize speech in 1978, said, "In the history of old Jewish literature there was never any basic difference between the poet and the prophet."

Both fiction and nonfiction writers talk about writing "truth." For fiction writers it might be emotional truth, or a deeper truth that taps into the human condition, but it is not bound by actual facts or events the way a nonfiction story is. Fiction writers can make assumptions on behalf of characters, presume motives, tell what is happening inside a character's mind, all in service to the story they are telling. Stephen King said, "Fiction is the truth inside the lie."

Both approaches to storytelling are important, and both matter to our understanding of the world. But fiction writers have more freedom to create worlds than nonfiction writers. Fiction writers have more license to explore the What Ifs of a story, to explore big ideas, to create something new. While nonfiction writers are bound by things that actually happened, fiction writers and poets have the license to explore what *could* happen.

Fiction writers are also good at just spinning yarns, or entertaining, helping us escape, or explaining people's motives. The best stories, in my view, are the ones that move me, that make me forget I am sitting in a chair, that sweep me away, and make me believe that this world the writer created is actually happening in my head. The writers in this volume did this to me over and over.

The interviews have been lightly edited for clarity and brevity.

Why Fiction?

1

A Reason to Write Fiction

Why Do Stories Matter?

In writing the stories, if they're written beautifully and compellingly . . ., they become part of a community.

JOYCE CAROL OATES

The author Chaim Potok told an audience in a speech that, when he was very young, he knew he wanted to be a writer. Just before he went off to college, his mother pulled him aside and said, "I have a better idea. Why don't you be a brain surgeon? You'll keep a lot of people from dying and you'll make a lot of money."

"No mama," he said. I want to be a writer."

When he came home for a vacation he and his mother went through the same routine.

"You'll keep a lot of people from dying, and you'll make a lot of money," she said. He replied, "I want to be a writer."

Every vacation, every holiday, every visit home, the same dialogue occurred, until it finally exploded.

"Chaim, you're wasting your time! Be a brain surgeon! You'll keep a lot of people from dying and you'll make a lot of money."

"Mama," he said, "I don't want to keep people from dying. I want to show them how to live!" (Theodore Runyon, *The New Creation* [Nashville: Abingdon Press, 1998], 159.)

This is what stories can do. This is a reason to write.

How do they do this? By preserving—or perhaps challenging—our values, traditions, history, dignity, ancestry. Stories can scare us and wake us and make us feel something.

We don't always remember information or data or lessons. But we remember the stories.

In his book *The Things They Carried*, Tim O'Brien writes, "Stories are for joining the past to the future. Stories are for those late hours in the night when you can't remember how you got from where you were to where you are. Stories are for eternity, for when the memory is erased, when there is nothing to remember except the story."

Stories give shape to experience. I often don't know what something means until I try to tell a story about it. Stories are the connective tissue of the human race and the human spirit.

Madeleine L'Engle said that stories tell us something beyond the stories. "Stories are able to help us become more whole, to become Named. And Naming is one of the impulses behind all art, to give name to the cosmos we see despite all the chaos."

Stories can help us make sense of our confusing world. They help explain what has happened to us as a people and as an individual.

"I tried to heal my fear with stories, stories which gave me courage, stories which affirmed that ultimately love is stronger than hate," L'Engle wrote. "Story helped me to learn to live. Story was in no way an evasion of life, but a way of living life creatively instead of fearfully" (Walking On Water, p. 46).

This is underscored by G.K. Chesterton's statement about the value of fairy tales:

"Fairy tales do not tell children that dragons exist. Children already know that dragons exist. Fairy tales tell children that dragons can be killed."

The writers interviewed below embody these very points. You'll see the value of stories in their words, their works and their lives, and how, through stories, we can know how to live.

Peter Matthiessen

DN: From all of the places you've been, all the things you've seen, there is a common thread among all people that you've experienced, where they love to tell stories, that stories are somehow part of us. Why is that? Why do we need stories?

PM: The story tradition is everywhere. It's not just because they're entertaining; they're very valuable. Imagine before you had electricity, lights, and TV, radio, anything, and people have a long, long winter to go through. In some tribes, you're not allowed to tell stories in the good season, where there's plenty of food and plenty to eat and hunting and everything. You're supposed to save those stories for those desperate times, when you have nothing else to entertain people. So they really have value. And then of course, those stories become part of the tribe. They are manifesting and they are legends and myths that go down and down, and down the generations, and hardly change at all after they reached that mythic quality.

N. Scott Momaday

DN: You've written a lot about the concept of what words do and what stories do. A lot of us intuitively already know the value of a word or the value of a story, but you've actually thought about this, and you've articulated that words have power. I want to hear your explanation of what words are.

NSM: Words do have power. I can think of nothing more powerful. Words are sacred. Language is sacred. I'm interested in the origin of a language. We don't know when it began or where or how. Lewis Thomas has a book called *The Fragile Species*, in which there is a chapter entitled Communication, which is a bad word, bad title. But, he says, I think I know how language began. There were people living in caves and they were having a hard time communicating with each other. They were growling. But he said, one day, a neighboring tribe came across the ridge to visit. They spent the day, but they brought their children with them. Suddenly, he said we had a critical mass of children. They played all day long, and at the end of that day we had language. That makes a lot of sense because children, they're not afraid of language. They love to play with it, you know. And that's what you need. As we grow older, we have less sympathy, less appreciation of language. But it's there and it's sacred, and we don't know what the limits of language are.

DN: That story amplifies what you have said in the past where you wrote once, words are the intricate bonds of language. Words make a family, a tribe, and a civilization. Language is the context of our experience. People had experiences before they had language, though. What does language do that helps family, tribe civilization?

NSM: It interprets the feelings of people. You say there were things before language of course. But those things needed expression—the expression that language gives them. When you have that combination, that formula, you have something to build on, and it becomes the rock of civilization.

DN: You're saying language is the rock of civilization?

NSM: I think I would say that, yes. You want to fight about it?

DN: No, I want you to tell me why! I'm not interested in fighting you!

NSM: Oh, all right. People were living together before they had language, okay, that's a given. There was a time when that was true. And with the discovery of language and the cooperation of language into their lives, they were able to understand, and it sparked the imagination. They became people who were creative and communicative.

DN: They started telling stories.

NSM: Exactly. Exactly. I think maybe the first story somehow is like the beginning of language.

DN: You've got this great line that says, what is involved in storytelling is our astonishment, imagination, belief, and holy dread. Those are your words. I'd love to know what you mean by "holy dread." What's that about?

NSM: I think dread is an interesting concept and it has its place in language. We are motivated by dread. Partly. That's not the whole story, but it works well. Dread is something that is entirely human, it seems to me. We dread things. Fear is another concept that is at the root of language, I think.

DN: Maybe stories and language are a way to address fear, are a way to maybe prepare us to avoid certain things that we might otherwise have been afraid of. But as stories developed and got locked in over time, things that people said before there was actually storytelling changed over time, right? When it became story and when it became written story, that sort of locked it in. I think the book of Genesis. I think of Beowulf or things you've written about before. Those were spoken for a long time, but the writing of it has put some limits on it, hasn't it?

NSM: I've spent virtually all of my teaching career teaching the oral tradition. Spoken word. Everybody has an oral tradition. We speak. Speech and language are essential to literature. I think the greatest expression in our oral tradition of our time is drama plays, because you have living people on the stage who are talking to each other and making contact, of course, with the audience as well. But that's a wonderful example of oral tradition.

DN: Other than that, is it still part of who we are or is it all written down now?

NSM: There's a great deal of oral tradition that has not been written down. There are stories in oral tradition that are extremely inventive and we have those. We don't think about them as much as we ought to, but yes, we have examples of written literature that did come from oral tradition. Beowulf is a good example of the first poem in English, but it was recited long before it was written down. We don't know how old it is, but it's a wonderful piece of literature. So we have things like that and we need to know more about it. If you should hear Hamlet on the stage, it makes a much greater impression than reading it.

DN: You have a character in the novel *The Ancient Child* who has mythical qualities, and I love this line where what he wanted to do was to please and to astonish God with his paintings.

NSM: Can you ever have a higher ambition than that? That's a wonderful incentive and motive. To think that you have written something that might astonish God. It's overboard, of course, but it says something about the nature of ambition and how the writer ought to work I think.

DN: You're describing yourself again in that character.

NSM: Yes. I write to astonish God. And James Earl Jones.

DN: Is there a difference?

NSM: Maybe not.

DN: You've said about poetry, that at its best, poetry is an act of disinterested generosity. What in the world does that mean? I love it, it resonates, but I don't know what it means.

NSM: It means that poetry is a gift that we make and give to other people. It's an active, disinterested generosity in the sense that it's without prejudice. It's free, it's there, it's a gift.

DN: And you can interpret it and absorb it however you can.

NSM: However you will. Reading it, you can't help forming certain impressions about it. That's a gift, a disinterested generosity. If you write a political document about the statements of this party or that, it's prejudiced; it can't help being biased. But if you write a poem that has no bias, it's got a good chance of being good or great poem.

DN: I love this other line of yours about poetry where you say, the poet says, "Here, let me show you something. Let me help you see something that you have not seen before." When you're writing a poem, is that in your mind? I want to show a reader something they have not seen before?

NSM: Yeah. You want to take a subject and do something with it that has not been done before, reveal a part of it that has been excluded. That's the purpose of literature, I suppose.

DN: Let's go back to storytelling for a moment. In Man Made of Words, you said, "We have no being beyond our stories. Stories are pools of reflection in which we see ourselves through the prism of our imagination."

NSM: Wow. Did I write that?

DN: It wasn't Shakespeare, wasn't Dickinson, it wasn't Tuckerman, it was Momaday. With that in mind, is that really the best way for us to know who we are, through the stories we tell each other?

NSM: I think so. I think we express ourselves more deeply and more meaningfully in literature than in other pursuits. I'm not sure I know much about the other pursuits, I'm just guessing, but I do know that language and literature are fundamental, basic, essential to human being.

DN: You've also said that stories have moral implications. I'd love to know what you mean by that.

NSM: A story—a poem is a moral statement.

DN: What does that even mean?

NSM: It means it has to do with the best that is in us, what is right as opposed to what is wrong. It's a gift again, a charitable gift. If I write a poem in which I express my spirit and you read it, there's a good contact, there's this something between us that matters and would not be there had it not been for the poem.

DN: That puts a lot of responsibility on a writer, it seems to me.

NSM: Well, yeah. Certainly. Yes. Why write if you don't write responsibly? That is immoral.

DN: Why not just write something to entertain people? What's the matter with that?

NSM: Nothing. But it's not as high a form of expression as a poem. If you accept my definition of a poem: a poem is a statement concerning the human condition composed in verse. That last tag is the thing that distinguishes poem. Verse is another word for measure. Poetry is measured. The measure is what is finally important in the expression of the language. It has to have some form, and it can have different kinds of form. You can write in what we call blank verse or free verse. But basically, the form of the English poem developed over hundreds of years is tried and true.

DN: Who do you write for? Do you sit down and say, this is for children, or this is for people who need to love the land instead of using the land, or do you just sit down and just start writing? Do you have an audience in mind?

NSM: William Gass was asked that question, and his answer hit the nail on the head. He said, "Well, I don't write for myself because that's self gratification. I don't write for other people because that's pandering. I write for the thing that is about to be born." Yeah. That's what I should write for. Not for any visualized audience, but for the sake of the thing itself.

DN: So, for House Made of Dawn, you aren't thinking, "this is totally going to win me the Pulitzer?"

NSM: No. It came as a complete surprise, as you know.

DN: Is part of the goal of a story to erase that space between the teller and the hearer?

NSM: Yes, I would say that.

DN: You've had that experience.

NSM: Oh, yes. Indeed.

DN: Here's a quote from one of your books describing a character: "Her words were medicine, they were magic and invisible. They came from nothing into sound and meaning." I think you've described earlier, that's what language does, something that comes from nothing into sound and meaning. That's a pretty hefty responsibility, isn't it?

NSM: Absolutely, yeah. Heavy responsibility. But it comes naturally to someone who is thinking in those terms. From sound into meaning. That's a wonderful transformation. That's maybe one of the definitions of literature itself.

DN: It's just so powerful the way you've maintained a sense of the ancient myths, your ancestry, the land, you keep grounded in all of that. Is that a conscious effort on your part or is that just the prism through which you do all your work?

NSM: It's the prism that I would like to involve all my work.

I should say something about silence at this point because there is a genuine place for silence in literature. It's not always what you express but what you don't express that matters. A few years ago, I had the experience of going through the Altamira caves in Spain and seeing the pictures, the drawings, the paintings that had been on the walls there for thousands of years and never discovered until very recently. I was with my then wife, and we went through the cave. We came out of there and went to the car, and we could not speak. We could not speak for an hour, maybe. We just had to sit there and think about what we'd seen and what it meant, trying to visualize the artists who put those things on the wall. That was a great experience. You can apply that to literature. If you read something that leaves you breathless and silent, it's a good thing. That's how you measure a great heart, perhaps.

DN: That's one of the ways you know it's sacred.

NSM: Exactly. If you read Moby Dick, for example, I think it's hard to talk for a while after you read it, and that's because you are so impressed by it, moved by it. It's a great work of art. You don't come across those things too often.

Chitra Divakaruni

DN: You said in a previous interview that "dissolving boundaries is what living is all about." Is that your hope for how you write too? If so, what boundaries are we talking about?

CD: I certainly hope to do that, through my writing. One of the most obvious boundaries that I hope to dissolve is that between the writer and the reader, creating a connection. My book becomes the connection between the writer and readers of different cultures, different backgrounds, so that it gives people of South Asian origins an insight, hopefully, into themselves in their own culture. And for people of other cultures my hope is that, not only does it tell them something about the Indian context of life, but also show them some commonalities of human experience, and make them relate to and empathize with people who on the surface seem very, very different from them, but ultimately have many of the same hopes, and many of the same challenges.

DN: So you're dissolving boundaries that naturally occur between a reader and a writer. But when your characters are dissolving boundaries, your idea is to show that those things that separate us as human beings don't *have* to separate us.

CD: They don't have to. I think our differences are wonderful. But our similarities, in some ways, are even more wonderful. A character, for example, like Tilo, from *Mistress of Spices*, actively works at dissolving boundaries between herself and the people she comes to love: the people who come to her store, whom she tries to help, between herself and the new world. She is definitely placed within certain boundaries. She has been enjoined never to leave the spice store. That's the boundary. And that's one of the boundaries she dissolves as she steps into America.

DN: Early in the book, she's a bridge between these two groups, and then she steps across it herself. Is dissolving boundaries your motive for writing?

CD: I think so. It is very important in my own life. One of my hopes is that perhaps through the books, boundaries will be dissolved between my community and the many other wonderful communities that make up the American mosaic. Hopefully, through reading the books, and perhaps relating to the characters, people will come to see people who are not like themselves, not just the characters in the book, but characters out there that perhaps they didn't think about or relate to, a little differently.

Billy Collins

DN: This is from your poem Vocation, when you're looking at constellations in the night sky. You're reminded, "after many jumbled days and nights of my true vocation—keeping an eye on things, whether they existed or not, recumbent under the random stars." Are you telling us this is your vocation—to bear witness to those things?

BC: Well, that's *his* vocation in the poem, and partially, that's our job as poets, is to observe and to report. My wife used to criticize me about this—so many poems, my character is lying down. My wife said, "why don't you get them to do something?" It's like these people in Hopper paintings; they're just kind of immobilized. He's often just looking at the ceiling, or out the window, in a couch or on a field.

But my persona is fashioned out of the cloth of English romantic poetry, basically. In English romantic poetry, you have this figure of the wanderer, the dawdler, the day-dreamer, a man who has nothing to do but walk through a landscape. He's by a wayside bench, and he falls into some reverie or speculation, and that's the poem. That's all that's required. I just loved that whole idea of endless time, and staring at the constellations, and looking at the tree or something, that whole sense of slowing down.

Max Beerbohm was a great champion of wasting time—which is really not wasting time—it's spending it well. He said, "the ant sets an example for us all, but it is not a good one."

DN: You have said that we turn to poetry when we are looking for something. Is that why we have a commemoration poem for 9/11, or a centennial?

BC: The verb "turning to" is interesting, that people turn to poetry. You don't say we turn to sculpture, we don't turn to ballet. When there is a moment of crisis, which could be something national or even global like September 11th, or moments of high importance, like weddings or funerals, and lots of stuff in between, birthdays or whatever, we often turn to verse for a stabilizing influence. The verse not only reminds us that we're in a community of feeling, and we're not the only ones feeling this, but it also connects us to a history of feeling, and usually the rhythms and the sounds of poetry have a kind of stabilizing and comforting effect. Right after 9/11, there was a lot of talk about poetry. No one said, "well, you know, we've been attacked from another country and we should all go to the movies," or something. It was all about poetry. It shows you that there's some kind of powerful recognition that poetry is a great accompaniment, in a way, to important events in our personal lives or in the lives of the nation.

DN: This is going to sound like a facetious question, but it's really not. You have talked about poetry as becoming autobiography, that autobiography has taken over poetry. So how is poetry different from something like facebook, which is all autobiography?

BC: Facebook doesn't achieve metaphor. It just stays facebook. "I'm going out for a pizza." Great. Wish I could go with you. What kind of pizza are you having? Wow. I love pizza.

It's just not going anywhere. But if a poem starts autobiographically, and just stays on the level of narrative autobiography, it fails to interest me, and the writer should go down the hall to the fiction class or the memoir class. What poetry does, if it starts autobiographically, if it's any good, or if it's going to get my interest, is that it lifts itself out of the particularities of the writer's life into a condition of metaphor. And the metaphor includes the reader. Metaphor is a general language, not about a particular language. It's not about *your* uncle who goes on a fishing trip you took. It's about something greater that everybody can plug into. That's what poetry can do that other kinds of discourse are unable to do or simply is not their job to do.

Lysley Tenorio

LT: Writing is an act of empathy. You have to try to find an emotional connection to characters who are vastly different from yourself. Even though my characters are Filipino or immigrants, it's not as though they are repeating experiences that I have. I have very little in common with what these characters are going through. I strive to create an empathetic connection with them so that hopefully any reader I'm lucky enough to have will develop that sense of empathy as well.

I don't imagine many people who have read my book have been in a leper colony before, but maybe they understand what it is like or they can relate to what it's like to be in exile or to feel like you don't belong or to question what it means to be beautiful or worthy of love. Those are not questions I'm constantly grappling with while I'm writing. I'm just trying to tell the story.

It's draft after draft when I've realized there is another story that exists here. One of the best pieces of advice I got from a teacher and I repeated to my students is that a story is not a story until it's at least two different stories. It's that second story, that third story, that fourth story that I'm working to discover as I draft each one so that hopefully if I'm lucky to have it published and I'm lucky enough to have someone read it, I'm not giving them a document of absolute truth. I'm giving them a story that hopefully gives them an experience unlike any other reader's experience.

If a person were to give a thematic summary of my stories, I hope I would hear different kinds of responses. Someone could read "Super Assassin" and say this is a story about bullying. Someone could also take that story and say this is a story about a neglected kid, or this is a story about what happens when you feel as though you don't know where you belong, or this is a story about isolation and loneliness. Or someone might even say this is a story about the dark side of art or identifying too much with a make-believe character. I would like to think that all those different interpretations exist for a story like that.

Joyce Carol Oates

DN: In the book *The Faith of a Writer*, you say: "Your forbidden passions are likely to be the fuel for your writing." Your forbidden passions as the fuel. I think I know what you mean, but could you expand on that?

JCO: When we're driven to write or create a movie or paint a picture or something, the emotions for this are very deep. I don't think they can be superficial because you'll lose interest in it. So, it has to come from some deep experience. It may be one of woundedness, or that you're an outsider, and that is a drama about being on the outside and looking at people on the inside. These are stories people start to write to maybe alleviate some of this stress and tension of being in those positions. But then in writing the stories, if they're written beautifully and compellingly, they become very successful and part of a community. That's an interesting consequence of being an artist. Probably every filmmaker and every artist and every writer starts off somewhat feeling like an outsider, but as time goes on, may become part of the community, they even become a spokesperson for the community. That's a kind of wonderful development.

DN: But what do you mean about "the forbidden passions"?

JCO: Forbidden passions could be something very venal or trivial. People don't want to write about being jealous or envious; those seem like diminishing. But if you're writing a novel, you have characters doing all sorts of different things, and one of them might be experiencing envy or jealousy. And so you can give it a real spark and a real sympathy, because everyone has these emotions, and some people don't want to talk about it. But if they read a novel or see a movie about it which is dramatized in a very sympathetic way, then I think that draws us all into what I call the human predicament or human dilemma.

DN: You have said that the most powerful moral art is not the kind that preaches goodness, but the kind that shows the sickening, corrosive effect of various kinds of evil. That's the most powerful moral art?

JCO: Well, I probably went on to say that people deal with it. People confront evil, they're not annihilated by it.

DN: But what's the matter with moral art being about goodness?

JCO: Art by itself usually has some sort of conflict. Unless you're going to paint something like Mondrian's beautiful but static canvases, you must have some sense of disequilibrium. Art is about disequilibrium; it's all conflict. You can't have three really nice people sitting in a living room for your play. And they're really, really nice people. And they're nice, and they say nice things to each other. The audience is going to walk out, because the audience—I'm not saying that the audience wants blood, it doesn't necessarily have to be like a Tarantino film—but you have to have conflict. The basis of art is conflict.

DN: You've also said that art has this transgressive kind of quality to it, that it's supposed to be evocative and maybe even get you in some trouble.

JCO: It sometimes gets the artist into trouble. Many artists have gotten in a lot of trouble.

DN: But you say that's part of the deal.

JCO: It's part of what you have to accept, yes. There are parts of the world today where if you write even a fairly innocuous novel or story, you could be locked up. You could just be taken away because they don't have freedom of expression, they don't have the tradition of freedom of speech. It's considered bizarre that we have that tradition. Other parts of the world think that we're crazy to have that. I remember before the fall of the Berlin Wall, I was a part of a delegation where we met people from Soviet Russia, and some Russian satellite countries. They were translators and writers, but they were really, I think, many of them were spies. They were basic party hacks. Edward Albee was there, I think Kurt Vonnegut, Bill Styron, John Updike, Susan Sontag. We were talking about Soviet dissidents and how they should not be put in prison. They said to us, "Why would you imagine that we should have freedom, that our dissidents should have freedom?"

They thought we were actually somewhat bizarre. It was sort of looking like a reverse mirror. And it was an interesting question. I remember this person asking me seriously, "Why would you think that this person is a writer? He's a political person and he's a traitor," or something like that. And we were saying, "Well no, these are writers, these are poets and writers, you should allow them to write." But they were saying, "No, no, no, they're against the regime." It was interesting to see this clash of ideology where we definitely felt we were right. But they seemed to think they were right too. It was really, really upsetting. It comes down to the tyranny of ideology, and how people can be so cruel and so vicious to one another just armed with an ideology. In America we do have this tradition of freedom of speech. It is true that we are not always as egalitarian and open as we should be, but we have the tradition. We do have the Constitution, and some of these other countries have nothing like that.

DN: Do you think it's our job as writers to transform culture?

JCO: Writers, like all artists, are all individuals. Some people are by nature rather Messianic, and they want to preach and they want to have an effect upon a community. Others are more retiring and private like Emily Dickinson, who's the greatest poet. Between Emily Dickinson and Walt Whitman, I think that's the whole Nineteenth Century. Walt Whitman is much more somebody who would like to reach out to an audience and preach and tell people what to think. Emily Dickinson would just withdraw and write these beautiful poems and you read them and you get a strong sense of mystery and the enigmatic nature of life. But she's not preaching, she's not standing out there preaching. So, I think people have different personalities. Sometimes we have one and sometimes we have the other.

Carlos Ruiz Zafon

DN: You have a blind character saying, about a book, "It taught me that by reading, I could live more intensely. It could give me back the sight I had lost." Is that what reading does? Does it give us a chance to live more intensely?

CZ: Reading does many things. One of the things it does is it allows us to live more and to live better. It actually engages our brain, and our brain's language, our brain's software. Our brains are huge, very powerful computers that we don't use very much, and I think that different languages can be the language of science, of numbers, of music, of verbal language, but essentially, we use this as a way to articulate the only things that are. You can learn or absorb things that are put into language, a sequence of it, and usually it's a kind of a narrative sequence. That's how the brain works. Everything needs to be told as a story. A mathematical formula is a story in itself.

The whole process of language and storytelling was something that I was always very concerned about, and one of the things I wanted to do with this series of books was to write about the very essence of storytelling: *what does it mean*? This is why there are groups about books, about readers, about writers, about publishers, about librarians, and people who leave the bulk of their lives to books, and try to get to the heart of the process. Each one of the books explores something different: this is the story of a reader, how reading can change your life, how it can open doors in your mind, to the world, and to many things in your soul. The second book is the story of a writer, in this case, a writer who is going crazy and is descending into his own hell. But we essentially are seeing how stories are built from the inside out. The third novel is the book of a character. We picked one of the characters, in this case, Fermin, and we built his backstory, but essentially it is his story and is seen from the perspective of a character. So each one of those things tries to get at the nature of storytelling, because besides all the other issues, and themes, and elements in the books, that is the essential, central theme: language and storytelling.

Nikki Giovanni

DN: You have said poems have work to do. What is that work?

NG: I think inform. I try to help people think about things differently. But also, delight. I think it's key to almost everything, that people will be able to say, "oh!" Sometimes they smile, and sometimes they won't. But we have to inform and delight and leave something with the person that they will take.

You read poems when you get married, you read poems when you die, you read poems when there's a celebration. Poems do things. Poems are right there with good wine and caviar.

DN: When you were growing up you had a secret hope that someday you would be understood.

NG: I probably still do.

DN: Is that one of the reasons why we write?

NG: Any writer will tell you, I don't know if it's secret or not, but that's the hope. The chances of that happening are incredibly slim, because the older you get, the more you're going to know, the more you're going to bring to bear other things. So you're never going to be understood.

DN: Does the writing help you through that?

NG: Well, I don't know. I called Toni Morrison about a book I was working on, because I was feeling so bad. She's an old, old, old friend. And I said, "Toni, I'm not making it." She's somebody you could say that to. "I'm just not making it." We talked and talked. And she said, "Nikki, write it out." And it was good advice. Write it out. That's when I started working on *A Good Cry*. I don't know how it's gonna turn out.

Probably nobody will like the book, because I'll be the one writing about "yeah, I got it out" and everyone else will say "it's a terrible book!" It's uneven right now. It'll probably stay uneven.

Robin Jones Gunn

DN: You work with a group that provides training and encouragement to writers and publishers, in places around the world where it's difficult.

RG: The association is Media Associates International. Every three years, they have a Lit World Conference that's held internationally. I've been to one in Brazil, and Kenya, England, and writers from around the world gather, and the workshops are specific for the basics of publishing, editing, and writing. We have our Western ways of doing things, and we have our traditional ways of publishing. A recent conference was in Bulgaria. At the time, Bulgaria had a 93 percent unemployment rate, and yet, here's twenty writers who want to be able to express themselves and want the training. So MAI was going in and saying, "We'll provide the trainers and we'll go to where you are so that you can tell your stories in the language of your people." Enough of this taking all the books from the West and translating them into the languages, because it doesn't quite fit as well as a story from a person in that culture who's telling the stories of their people in a contemporary or historic way. Every time I go, I am so humbled at how the rest of the world is doing what we're doing here.

DN: In the United States you can self-publish a book, call up a designer, call up an editor, but for folks over there, it's not so easy.

RG: And some of them do it in fear of the government finding where the printing press is. I met a woman from China. She told me that she wrote children's books, because her husband preached at a registered church in China, and she had written some curriculum for the children because they didn't have any, not even translated from all the plethora that we have here. She wanted a simple copy machine so she could provide this for other churches as well. She figured out how to do that:

she could donate her blood. So she stood up in church and said, "I am going to go on Monday and donate my blood. I'm going to do that as often as I can, until we have enough money to buy a printing machine, and then we can send these little children's material home with them." She showed up at the blood bank on Monday morning, and the whole congregation was lined up behind her, and they gave their blood. It was the blood of the people in China that is getting the printing and the publishing done.

It's a completely different privilege that we get to do this art, but it's more than art, it's a lifeline for so many people in so many countries. That's the power of the story; the power of the word.

Chris Bohjalian

DN: One of the reasons why you wrote *The Sandcastle Girls* is that there is a significant number of people who say the Armenian genocide didn't happen.

CB: Yes. That is precisely it. The fact that the Armenian genocide is still denied in so many quarters is appalling, not simply as an Armenian-American, but because so many genocide scholars have said eloquently before me that the last stage in any genocide is denial, which is the first stage in the subsequent genocide.

Adolf Hitler famously said, August 22, 1939, a written order before unleashing his Panzers on Poland, "Be merciless, be merciless—after all, who remembers the annihilation of the Armenians?" That was twenty-one years after the end of the First World War, only four years longer than we had been in Afghanistan.

Jane Smiley

DN: You started out, I think you said, wanting to communicate a certain truth or a certain story when you were first writing your novels. It was you dictating, "this is the story I want to tell." But later on in your work, it was more like you would show up and say, "OK, what's going to happen next?"

JS: Well, you do learn to be more open. There are at least two kinds of writers. One is, they have a story about their own lives that they don't understand. So they get involved in writing about it in order to come to an understanding. When they come to an understanding about it, in some ways, they don't know what to do next.

There are other writers who write out of curiosity, not about their own lives, but just because they see things and they hear things, and they get curious about them. Take Charles Dickens and Anthony Trollope, for example.

DN: Two of your literary heroes.

JS: Dickens clearly had several childhood issues that he kept moving toward and finally dealt with in *David Copperfield.* But it took him a long time to get there, because he was very secretive about the embarrassments that were his childhood.

Trollope wasn't like that. As far as we know, he didn't write about his childhood. When he got to Ireland to work for the English post office, he was motivated to write by two things. One was curiosity about Ireland, which he didn't know much about, but he was traveling all over Ireland for the post office, and the other one was the habit of telling himself stories to keep himself entertained as he was riding around. And so he got very interested in Ireland and he wrote the *MacDermots of Ballycloran* and *The Kellys and the O'Kellys.* They were absolute busts. I think *The Kellys and the O'Kellys* sold eight copies. I adore *The Kellys and the O'Kellys.*

But those were his practice novels, similar to mine. When he learned how to make them, he was in Salisbury and walking around Salisbury Cathedral, and that's where he came up with the idea of *The Warden*, which was the first volume of the *Barchester* series. So by the time he got famous, he still kept his job, he still kept doing things the way he did them, and he moved smoothly along. Dickens was much more rattled by his fame and he had to screw around with his books much more in order to make them work between the time he was twenty-four and published *The Pickwick Papers* and the time, say, he was thirty.

DN: So who do you most align with?

JS: I'm more Trollope-y in terms of what I'm interested in and what I explore. He always seemed to explore what he saw and what he was curious about.

DN: But you've had these different kinds of experiences in writing novels. At one stage of your writing life, you're the one who's saying, "here's the idea I'm exploring." You've also had experiences where you *received* a story.

JS: I've had that one experience.

DN: This is *Greenlanders.*

JS: That was a big one. I knew it was going to be a really big deal, so I had to practice to get there.

One of the things when you're writing a historical novel is you have to decide, "is my style going to imitate that style of that period, or is it going to be a straightforward, modern style and maybe imitate the *dialect* in the dialogue." I fiddled around, fiddled around, fiddled around. The first fifty pages, I tried my best, I rewrote them, I rewrote them. And then once it clicked, we were off. It really was like having the story come to be from afar. I wrote it on my first computer, and I would sit down, and it was like pulling the bearskin rug over my shoulders, and I was just going into it. And it was a very uncanny experience.

DN: Do you think it's universally part of the human experience to be a storyteller?

JS: I hope so. It seems to be, because as soon as you have language, and as soon as you have a sense of the difference between the present and the past, then you're going to start communicating about things that've happened. And then as soon as you communicate about things that happened, you're going to have doubts about how it happened, why it happened, and then whether it happened. And then bingo, you're going to start telling stories, just to keep the attention of the person that you're talking to. So it does seem to be narrating stories, telling stories, making a narrative out of events seems to be inherent human character.

DN: So we're hardwired to do it?

JS: Well, language makes us do it. Are we hardwired to speak? Yeah. We're hardwired to make sentences? Yeah, I would say so. So the next step is anecdotes, and the next step after that is stories.

DN: Do you think everybody has a story to tell? Just because they have language?

JS: As long as they desire to tell it. They don't desire to tell it, they don't have a story to tell.

Anchee Min

DN: One of the things you've said about your writing is that "The Chinese government's official version of the Cultural Revolution contrasted with the life I lived. I could not let the lies be the only record. It scared me to think that my daughter would be studying false history, and I felt obligated to do something about it." Is that a reason to write? To set the record straight? To say, what you've understood is a lie, but I'm going to tell you the truth?

AM: That's what really was in me, the anger. I think I was too busy with surviving, but that's in the back of my head, all the time, all the way.

DN: That you just need to make it right.

AM: Right. People in China, they are wonderful writers. But first of all, they cannot touch the subject of Mao, still today. My books are banned in China. I go back, get killed. It's something, it's so terrible. If you don't mention it, then people *die*, people who lived it *die*, and that history got wiped. It's not just Chinese history. China has become part of the world—it's world history. You can talk about the Cultural Revolution only to a point. For example, you can't talk about the deep humanity, the sexuality, the drives, all that.

In the future, when they are given the rights, or they come to America, they are given the time and the safety to write about it, but they *can't*. You know why? Because of the self-censorship. When I was watching *Mr. Rogers' Neighborhood*, and he was saying, it's great, the best thing that you can give to anybody is your honest self. And I was sitting there—the moment I understood that thing that he was teaching the children—I was crying. I was twenty-seven years old. And I thought, gee. My best honest self is a gift. I was this bolt on a Communist running machine. So all these authors, they come and they have the same mindset. They will not be able to write *Red Azalea.* So *Red Azalea*, in a way, is a result of American education.

Nnedi Okorafor

DN: I had several "Oh my" moments when I was reading your stuff, but here is the biggest one. In your book *Shadowspeaker*, there is a storm raging, and it finally communicates why it is raging so much. Do you remember why?

NO: I wrote that book a while ago.

DN: It's not a trick question—I just thought it would be more interesting coming from you than from me. I can tell you what it was raging about, but do you remember why?

NO: Go ahead without giving things away.

DN: The storm is raging because it says it doesn't remember its own story. I wondered, isn't that the source of a lot of rage in general, that we just don't remember who we are? What our story is, who we came from, why we're here. I don't know if it struck you when you wrote that in as powerful a way as it hit me when I read it, but you just put your finger on something really profound about the rage that people, that societies, that nations, can spin off on. Did you know you were that deep in there?

NO: That was intentional, yeah.

DN: Do you think we sometimes rage because we *do* remember our stories?

NO: That would make sense. You could definitely make that argument. The forgetting or not knowing causes intense anger. That is a normal response. But also knowing and understanding, making you have to look inward and question aspects of yourself, could be disturbing. Sometimes when we are disturbed and we have no other way to respond, it's with rage.

Christian Wiman

CW: The notion of securing immortality through a work of art, of putting a kind of rock in the river of time, is not what you're after. You're after the experience of participating in reality, of salvaging reality—that's how John Berger puts it in when he talks about Van Gogh. He said, "reality has to be salvaged." That's what poetry does for me. It does for me when I'm writing on my own, because when I read a poem that I really respond to, I feel like reality has been salvaged, like I can experience it again. You're doing it for that reason, because you believe that moment of inspiration, which some people believe is the Holy Spirit, that's what survives. The work itself—that's not necessarily the most important thing.

DN: Was it Robert Frost's line about the goal is to make sure that people will remember a couple of your poems?

CW: "It lodges in the heads of a few readers so they can't get rid of it."

DN: That sounds better. I'm guessing he was a little bit wrong, too, because his stuff has—

CW: Oh, I think he had a good sense that he was going to last. And he has, you know? If you think of all the poems one writes—Randall Jarell said famously that a good poet is someone who, after standing out in lightning and thunderstorms for their lifetime gets struck five or six times. So you write five or six good poems, and meanwhile it's a destructive lightning strike. You know that metaphor, if you get hit ten or twelve, well then you're a great poet. That's what he said. Ten or twelve that a culture decides to keep makes a great poet. It's not that much.

DN: One of the things you said about poetry is that it takes you fully into the present. Not out of the present, it takes you fully into the present.

I've also heard you say something about us never being fully in the present. We're remembering things from the past, we're projecting into the future. To you, what does present mean?

CW: That's a good question. It's an illusion. Poetry does seem to make a moment of time possible for us, it seems like it's a moment of time: the present. But consciousness can't actually be present. We are always in the past. R.P. Blackmur is a critic from the middle part of the twentieth century, and he's talking about John Berryman when he says a new metaphorical impression makes reality newly available. It enlarges the available amount of reality. How does he put it? It enlarges the available scope of reality. What he means is not that it makes reality larger in the way that space is getting larger, the universe is expanding. What he means is that it makes more of it available to us. A moment of poetic perception can make the present moment of reality absolutely in front of you. Make it apparent, almost touchable. Not quite—"Joy's trick is to supply dry lips with what would cool and slake, leaving them dumbstruck also with an ache, nothing can satisfy"—that conditions seems to be ineluctable.

DN: But the poetry can get you close

CW: Poetry is almost there.

DN: You've said that we live in a world that is designed to eradicate inner life. How do we reclaim it?

CW: Poetry. I don't believe poetry is for everybody, but I couldn't live without it. I don't know how people do without it. But clearly some do. It's beyond question that we live in a society that's designed to eradicate the inner life. If you don't think that the world you're in is bent on destroying your innerness, you're not paying attention. It's designed to do that. Reading serious poetry can be an act of resistance in that regard. It doesn't have to be poetry. There are all kinds of experiences out there that can sustain the inner life, but it does take a real conscious act now.

I'm reading Emily Dickinson, and at the time there was a real fad for reverie and they would actually sit around and have reveries, detach and have these daydreams. This was something they aspired to and it was a cultural value. Now we don't have anything like that. You have to really work at it. You have to really set something in your life and say: if my inner life is going to survive I'm going to have to do something. It's a tough thing.

DN: You've talked about different ways that poems come to you, how some take you ten years and you're still not done, and then some are just bang, it's there and you just say you nailed it. Is there any way that one can create an atmosphere that can make it more likely to channel that poem?

CW: It takes dead time. That's the problem. You talk about creating an inner life and we live in a culture without it. We also live in a culture that makes the creation of poetry very difficult, at least the kind of poetry that I respond to. I have always found that if I'm going to write poems, I have to give them a chance, which means giving them vast tracts of dead time, where I have no obligations. I don't schedule a lunch, I certainly don't teach a class. It really has to be a vacancy, sort of day after day.

DN: And it still might not happen.

CW: That's the danger of poetry. There's no practical reward. It might not happen, you might create all this space and then nothing happens. In fact, *My Bright Abyss,* I started because I went down to Marfa, Texas. There's a foundation there that gives houses for writers for a while and I went down there for a couple of months and it was the first break I'd had in quite a long time and I sat there for one month, four solid weeks. Nothing. Nothing. Couldn't figure out what to do with myself. I would read, I would go on runs, I would do whatever and then one day after that month out of sheer frustration I started writing the notes that are the beginning of that book. I wrote the first paragraph and I thought: well that's kind of interesting. And then I wrote another paragraph and then it was eight years later it emerged. It emerged out of all that silence when it seemed like nothing would come.

DN: That just is so counter to how we live.

CW: I used to arrange my whole life like that. I mean, really long periods of time in solitude. But it's just not possible anymore.

DN: A lot of contemporary poetry, as you have written about, probably needed some more of that dead time. In fact, you said you've read some contemporary poetry where you felt like the poet "wrote it while eating breakfast. You can almost hear him still chewing."

CW: A lot of the contemporary poetry I read does seem to me to add to the confusion of contemporary life rather than rescuing me from it.

DN: Is that its job, to rescue you from it?

CW: That's what I'm looking for. If you want confusion, that's the poetry for you.

Alice Walker

AW: I loved the people on whom my characters are based. And they still exist all over the world in that same condition of barely getting by, being very upset with life, down at heart. I felt in myself so much love for them, and I wanted people to feel that too, because love, as you know, is the foundation of change and transformation.

DN: So you wanted me to feel a certain way?

AW: I did, I did. And not only that, I knew you could.

DN: Regarding *The Color Purple,* you've got the novel, it wins all these awards, it's a movie, it's a theatrical production, and now it's back on the stage. Can you explain why a book written long ago feels like it was written recently?

AW: One of the foundational reasons is that pedophilia is still very strong in the cultures of the world. In this story, the abuse of children is very vital. Celie is fourteen, she's a child. This is a story that's still happening as we're sitting here. We go look at our news, there it is. A lot of the subsequent movements are actually rooted in this story, and I'm so happy about that. I've seen audiences, at the end of the story in the musical, rise with such emotional connection. It's a wonderful thing to be able to feel that you can help people liberate their own lives.

DN: An academic said that one of the main themes of your writing is "the Black woman as creator and how her attempt to be whole relates to the health of her community." Is that an accurate characterization of your writing?

AW: That's pretty good. I think of my work as medicine. And I want to get the right medicine for us. That's why "The Color Purple" has lasted for so long. It's an overdue medicine. Many people are just now getting it. I've watched generations of people respond to that story because it connects to them and it's very healing. And I absolutely love that. There's nothing more wonderful than setting other people free.

DN: You're setting them free by naming it, right? By telling a story about it.

AW: By telling a story. That's what stories do. That's my culture, that's how I learned almost everything. We grew up in a rural community and we had storytelling. That taught us so much about life, and wonder, joy, and acceptance, and a certain type of fearlessness. "Br'er Rabbit" was born in my community. All of those folktales, the indigenous Native American folktales and the African folktales are practically identical and all so intertwined. They're also always about overcoming some incredible obstacle and having a good time.

DN: That's true, because "Color Purple" is about overcoming obstacles and—

AW: Joy.

DN: And the juke joint, they're having some fun too.

AW: Yeah. Because why bother to suffer if you're not going to have a good time?

DN: I think that's going to be my next tattoo. Here's another theme that I think is in a lot of your writing: change in society is directly linked to a change in the individual. There's an outer struggle, clearly, but there's also an inner struggle. Is that a fair description of the main characters in your stories? That they're struggling with both?

AW: Yeah. We have to remember that the struggle is ours. Society can only move if we do. We are individuals; we are connected to each other. But we have to think very much of freeing ourselves in terms of where we are, in our house, in our kitchen, wherever we are. We develop resistance. We say "this is what I will do" rather than "this is what we will do." Later we can say what we will do. But unless you say what you will do, and then really honor that, there isn't likely to be a we or an us. We have to work hard at this. We're at a point where if we don't take full responsibility for how we live, in our neighborhoods, our schools, our churches, there is little possibility that we will survive. And I want us to.

DN: In your book *The Way Forward Is with a Broken Heart* you say that culture promotes conformity. And yet your work really pushes against all types of conformity. Does all art do that? Is that kind of its role, to push against conformity? Is that its purpose?

AW: Well, mine is. Maybe not against all of it, because there is so much culture and so much art in my life that I love, like Van Gogh. But the kind of pressure we can feel from an unkind art and a vicious culture, that has to be resisted.

DN: Gwendolyn Brooks says, "Art hurts, art urges voyages, but it's easier to stay home."

AW: Well, not in my life. Although I love being home. I do. I can spend days on end without seeing anybody and be perfectly happy. But I've also been extremely curious about the world, and about other people. When I was eighteen years old I went to the Soviet Union, because at that time my country was trying to bomb them. They haven't given up, really. But even as an eighteen-year-old I thought, "this is just crazy, I bet there are people over there who are just like other people. I couldn't imagine that they were so different that you could just bomb them without caring. And sure enough I got there, and after I had been given numerous glasses of vodka, and danced around wherever we were, I could see that they were really just human beings. I preferred them to some of the ones I had left back home in Georgia!

DN: You've got another line in your book *The Same River Twice* where you say, "art is the mirror in which we can see our true collective face. We must honor its sacred function. We must let art help us." That's what you did with *The Color Purple*, clearly, and some of your other books too. You just held up this mirror to us. That's the function of art, right?

AW: It is, and also it's to encourage you to have courage. Have enough courage to see yourself, your real self, not your fake self. Have the courage; develop it. It's not impossible. Because we cannot move if we're not gracious in this way.

Anthony Doerr

DN: You've made some really interesting parallels between science and storytelling. What do those two things have in common?

AD: Storytelling is everything, and the best science explainers are storytellers because they lift things down from the world, out of the abstract, and you find this mule, this thing rooted in a person to carry story forward. The best way to understand whatever—new cancer research, like this amazing book by Siddhartha Mukherjee called *The Emperor of All Maladies,* the best parts in his books are when you're following one patient's journey or one scientist's journey. You picture one monk out there in the dirt with the peas, and that's how you start to understand how discoveries are made. It's that kind of oscillation between micro and macro all the time. The best science explainers are going to tell you a story.

DN: One of the things you've said about scientists and artists is that they do the same thing: they eat breakfast, they go to work, they break the ice that is formed overnight, and they start confronting problems.

AD: That's good. I wrote that?

DN: You wrote that. But is that what storytelling is to you—an attempt to solve problems?

AD: Much of the day. Of course, there are moments when you're reaching your fingers up in the stars, but almost all the time you're just down on your hands and knees in the gravel or rearranging things. You're using these really inexact tools, which are words. Even when I say the word "tree," that means a slightly different thing to every person in the room. That's why reading and writing is a collaboration. When you read a novel, you're collaborating with the writer to make something totally unique that's never existed in the world before. You're using those inexact things to try to fumble over these universal truths.

Flaubert said, "We long to make music to melt the stars, but we're really just tapping crude rhythms on pots and pans for bears to dance to." That's what you feel like when you're writing because you have this initial vision in the shower of what this scene's going to be. But then when you sit down to make it, you're just failing all the time. It's just this inarticulate porridge that you can't quite get there, and it's only through revision after revision you can start to try to approximate. But there's always going to be gaps of misunderstanding and confusion in the gaps between words and in the words themselves. So I think there is something very much like science. Science too is a series of failures as you fumble toward some kind of conclusion. You make a hypothesis. You test it. It fails. You try to reformulate your hypothesis. That's a lot of what novel writing is for me: it's a big mesh of art and engineering and faith and doubt.

——

2

Awakening to the Art

How Did You Know You Wanted to Write?

I was born to do this. I was prepared out of my own suffering to do it and do it well.

ALICE WALKER

I have a friend who writes extraordinarily well, and he remembers reading Robinson Crusoe when he was a kid.

"I read it and knew immediately that I wanted to be that guy," he told me.

"You wanted to be Robinson Crusoe and have adventures and live on an island?" I asked.

"No—I wanted to be Daniel Defoe, the guy who wrote it," he said. "I wanted to be the person who could move a reader the way he did."

Obviously, this friend writes.

Some people become writers because early on they felt the impact of a well-told story, or saw the way a story could move an audience.

I became a writer because I love to tell stories.

One time, when my grandson was about a year old, he was having a hard time settling down. His parents were exhausted, and I had developed a pretty good method of getting him calm and, eventually, asleep. This usually involved a lot of holding and bouncing and songs that I would make up on the spot. On this particular winter night in New Jersey, I got him asleep and quietly told his parents goodnight and headed out the door to my car so I could go to my hotel room.

By the time I had backed the car out of the apartment complex's parking lot, and headed toward the street, I saw my daughter-in-law on the sidewalk trotting toward me. I figured I had forgotten something.

"He's awake again," she said, with a bit of panic. "Want to take another run at him?"

I could hear him wailing well before I got to the door. He didn't want me to pick him up from his crib, so I got my face as close to him as I could and started telling him a story about a rabbit that kept sneaking into the apartment and making a mess, and how other people tried to find him but he was always smarter than the people and could escape. I used the softest voice I could muster, and just made it up as I went along. My grandson had a stuffed rabbit in his crib, and soon stopped crying and stared at me as I drew out this tale. It will not win any Caldecott awards, but the story involved how the rabbit got into the little boy's crib and wanted to be held and hugged, but didn't want anyone other than my grandson to see him. My grandson took in the entire story, laid down, hugged his rabbit, and went to sleep.

Other than stories that I make up under special circumstances—like sleep-deprived babies—I don't do much in the area of fiction. But I am in awe of those who do.

Some of the writers I have interviewed became writers because it was in their DNA. Their parents were storytellers. Or they had a great teacher who encouraged it. Or they read something. Or experienced something. Or they wanted to impress someone, or distinguish themselves from other groups.

As you'll see below, Garrison Keillor wanted to write because a teacher gave him a copy of the *New Yorker*. Amor Towles and Billy Collins wanted to write because of the wordplay—the way the words sounded together. Alice Walker just knew she was a writer from the beginning. Robin Jones Gunn wanted to write because she saw what the young girls in her youth group were reading, and she thought they deserved better.

There are billions of people on this planet, which means there are billions of ways one can become a writer. But as you'll see with these interviews, they all start with a reason, an inkling, an itch, a desire, to string some words together. You have your own reasons. Maybe you'll see some similarities with your own awakening below.

Amor Towles

AT: I decided I want to be a writer in first grade because . . .

DN: [interrupts] Wait, wait, wait. You decided you wanted to be a writer in first grade?

AT: Yes. I'm going to tell you the story. But, yes. Yes.

What happened is my first grade teacher Mrs. Gum was friends with a rather well-known regional poet named David McCord. He came to our class, and he read his poetry from different books. And then he signed books and gave them to us at the end of class. I thought everything about it was great. I loved hearing his poetry, I loved the wordplay, the rhyming schemes, the surprising endings of the poems. I loved hearing him read them as an audience member. I loved the effect it was having on us as a group of young kids. I loved having the book to bring home. I thought that was really cool. And so I began writing poetry like him, trying to match what he was doing, and that was just the beginning.

From there, you keep reading, and so I would read something and then I would explore in writing some version of something that I had fallen in love with. Ray Bradbury was a hero of mine when I was probably ten, eleven. And then you discover Agatha Christie and Ian Fleming's *James Bond*, and I would read a whole bunch of them and go down that road. But then you're seventeen or eighteen, and then suddenly you're being introduced to literature—novels that have the capacity to touch us in all these incredible ways to be meaningful 300 years after they were written in another country. It's a crazy thing when you think about it—and to be stimulating at the same time. When you experience novels like that as a young student, that's where you start to say, "Now I get what this can be. This thing I've always liked—writing—it can be this." Then you're really in it.

Chitra Divakaruni

DN: Did you come to the United States from India with the idea of, "I am a writer, and I'm going to become trained as a writer?"

CD: No, no. In fact, even nowadays, sometimes I ask myself, "I'm a writer? me?!" There's a sense of amazement, truly in my life, when I think of that. I kind of slipped into being a writer, just through doing it and doing it, and persevering and trusting in it. I began by writing very bad poetry; very sentimental poetry, which I have since destroyed!

Joseph Wambaugh

DN: Where did your knack for storytelling come from?

JW: I have three grandparents from Ireland, so that probably helps. And people talk a lot, drink a lot. I grew up in the years before television, so I had an advantage that a lot of writers today don't have because they had to get their entertainment as children watching TV. I had to go to the library and check out books and listen to the radio, listen to people. So I probably developed an ear.

DN: So you came from a family of storytellers?

JW: No. A family of liars.

Peter Matthiessen

PM: I went to boarding school and was raised in a very sheltered way. When I was thirteen, though, I volunteered at school. They were sponsoring a charity boys camp for really very, very poor kids from New Haven, from the slums there. They asked for counselors, and I volunteered with a friend of mine. These kids came in on a bus, and they were rough kids. They were tough, too. But mainly, they broke your heart. The camp laid out a big spread for them—all kinds of hot dogs and hamburgers and corn-on-the-cob. And these kids didn't eat it—they attacked it! I mean, they really went for it. And all the time, I noticed they're all doing this: [looking over his shoulders]. I think it was maybe the first meal they ever had where there wasn't an uncle or bigger brother or somebody taking that food away from them. And they just stuffed themselves! Poor little guys. And they were all sick all night long. It really kind of woke me up. I began to realize that I lived a very sheltered life. My parents were very, very nice people and very fair and very generous about everything, but they lived a sheltered life. And I started, at that age, thirteen, splitting away. Even when I was in school, I started to get in trouble and protested certain things. So when I started writing, that's what I started writing about—that kind of thing.

Alice Walker

DN: So much of what you write about gets into what a lot of people might call "forbidden topics" such as rape, abuse, female genital mutilation, all kinds of injustice, racism, exploitation, and it seems like this is a calling for you to get into these kinds of taboo topics. Is that a conscious thing, where you say, "what secrets can I expose next?"

AW: No, no. I was born to do this. I was prepared out of my own suffering to do it and do it well. There's a line in one of Zora Neal Hurston's novels where she says, "I've been in sorrow's kitchen, and I've licked out all the pots." When you've been in sorrow's kitchen and you've licked out all the pots, if you don't expire from that, you gain the real feeling that you know what's there in those pots. And you can help other people survive licking them.

DN: You also write about quilting, where it sounds like you're describing writing.

AW: I'm making art. Quilting is art. For most of us who grew up in small communities where people didn't have any other way to make art, quilting was a high craft. Mother was very good at it. I remember as a small child coming into the room where the neighborhood women had the quilt hanging on a frame, and they would be sitting around it, talking. There was such a feeling of safety for the little children because it was clear that the older people were talking about them—I mean not in a bad way at all—this is where they had the opportunity to discuss the common children in the community. So it was very functional. Quilting was also how you used up your old clothing, so it was very economical. And also chicken feed came in beautiful sacks at this time, and they used those, and nothing was wasted. In fact, I was trying to explain to someone that when I was growing up, there was no such thing as litter. It was just totally a foreign thought, that there would be litter.

DN: You went through a personality change when you were little. When you got shot in the eye with a BB gun by your brother, told by your brothers not to tell the truth about it, you were denied a ride to the hospital by a white driver, and you got substandard medical care—that drove you inward. You lost confidence and self-worth, and you felt like you were an outcast. Would you have become a writer had that not have happened?

AW: Well, with my life something else would have happened.

But I see your point, and who knows? I often think about it; the little girl or little boy to whom nothing ever mars anything about them, can grow up to not get very much deeper than their facade. They don't have to. I mean, they think they don't have to. But I enjoy living life at such a much deeper level than the facade, that I would just be bored I think. I need to feel that the depths that I have are plumbed, I want to go there; I don't want to miss it. The life that we have, to me, is just so incredibly mysterious. It's just a wonder, truly a wonder. To miss any opportunity to just dive in and learn more about it, I don't want to miss that. That's part of what writing is. It's going into those deeper levels, and going under those deeper layers of whatever this is that we have in life. I love it. I love this.

Luis Alberto Urrea

LU: The quarterback got all the attention, but I stole his girlfriend. You know what I mean? Poetry! And you could sum up my entire early writing career as "Any female name here." There's a poem: "Oh, Colette, I am so drunk on your smile. Colette." That's what I did. I didn't know I was practicing. It's what I had. They were words, and it came from loving to read. We had a very loquacious family—the Urreas—they are masters of B.S.

I don't know if you have these characters in your family that talk and tell stories. We have this aunt, Tia Leti, called her "La FLACA." She was blind in one eye from diabetes, and she wore cat glasses with glitter in them, and was always smoking, and she would tell us these crazy stories. I remember one Christmas, in the house in Tijuana, they had a kerosene heater. And they would turn the lights off, and this stinkin' heater had etched flames in the glass, and it would cast this ghastly, sort of orange-green light, and Tia Leti, "La FLACA", told us this Christmas story which I've never forgotten. Imagine her with the twisted up eye and the cigarette, and she's lit from beneath—it's Christmas! And just to set the scene—our grandmother, Mama Lupita—she was sort of a lapsed Catholic and seemed to think that if she burned incense, that would hook her up with Jesus. So she burned incense. And so there were these gray cones of ash, and I stupidly—because if you asked Tia Leti anything you're an idiot—and I said, "Hey Tia Leti, what's all those gray cones?" And she says, "They're the souls of dead men!"

And she said, "Oye, if you touch those, you're going to unleash the spirit in the house." I was like, "yeah!" [scared]. And so this Christmas story, and this may be where my writing came from, she says, "you know, your abuelo Juan Urrea was riding a horse in Culiacan, and it was late at night, and he was passing the cemetery, and *alli* stopped *parada una muchacha muy bonita*, beautiful girl. And he said, "No, it's not right. You shouldn't be out here all by yourself." And he got off the horse, and he said, "*Oiga, senorita*, I will take you on my *caballo*," you know? She tells this whole story and we're listening, and my dad was too. And she said, "They got on the horse, and he began riding, "*Hijo, que suerte tengo*"—you know, good looking girl. And he's riding and he decided to do a *piropo*, when you say something dashing—so he turned to the young woman to say something like "I did not know lilies bloom at Christmas."

And she says to us, "*Y voltea*, she's a skull with no flesh on it, was going to bite his throat and drink his blood!" And then—this was the thing that I love—she says, "Feliz Navidad, cabrones" [smoking cigarette hand motion].

I was like, "yeah" [does hair standing up motion to head and whistles insinuating fear]. Wow, what a hero! And in that atmosphere she starts telling me about "The Hummingbird's Daughter." So I'm thinking "Yeah, right! Sure!" I didn't know it was a real story. But that urge towards the story, I think our family instilled it in me.

Joyce Carol Oates

DN: I love that you were inspired as a little girl by reading *Alice in Wonderland.* You were about nine years old at the time?

JCO: I was about eight or nine years old. I lived on a farm in upstate New York, and I think the Alice in the Alice book is the very antithesis of a little girl from upstate New York, a snowbell. I was given this book by my grandmother whom I loved so much. And she really changed my life by giving me books basically for every birthday and Christmas. This was a nice illustrated book that really imprinted itself very deeply in my memory.

DN: The Alice character was so different from you. But her character encouraged you to be bolder, to question authority, and to look at life as a possibility for adventure, correct?

JCO: Yes, I think so. There may be a different tradition in American children's literature than in English children's literature. Or it may simply have been that Lewis Carroll was writing a book for adults and it's not really a book for children. But the little girl in the Alice books is extremely inquisitive, she doesn't really take no for an answer, she is adventuresome. She has this sort of boldness that real little girls of about eight or nine would not have. So I think that made a strong impression on me. It seemed to me a world—a possible world that I had never had any experience with, being from this farm and knowing very little about the world.

Garrison Keillor

GK: When I was young, I was writing poetry but I was writing it for the wrong reason. I was writing it to make myself appear more mysterious than I really am. And so I was writing deliberately obscure, surrealistic poetry, which now as I read it all these years later, makes no sense to me at all. I can't remember what I had in mind except that I was showing off, which is not a bad thing. I don't mean to put it down at all. There's an element of exhibitionism in all of this, no doubt about it.

I decided to become a writer when I was in eighth grade in Anoka, Minnesota, in a little town on the Mississippi River. And an English teacher, I remember nothing more about him than that his name was Frayne Anderson, and that one day I walked into class and he handed me a copy of the New Yorker magazine and said, "I thought this might interest you." I have moved, since I was fourteen years old, at least thirty-five times and I have carried this magazine with me, which is a totem.

My family read Reader's Digest. They read gospel magazines. They read National Geographic. We were not a New Yorker family. But what was inside was A. J. Liebling, the great writer writing about boxing, writing about food, writing about France, writing about journalism. John Cheever was in there. And S. J. Perlman, the humorist, as well as advertisements for very fancy things that no one in my family would know anything about or aspire to. But the writing, the writing, is what interested me. It was so cool and it was so precise at the same time. And it was very elegant writing. and I thought, this is what I want to do. I want to write and be published in a terrific magazine like this.

It was an aspiration that was so ridiculously extravagant that I never told anybody. But I saved that copy of the magazine. How do you get there? Well, you get there by persistence and by good luck. That's what you need. Those two. Talent? Meh! But persistence and good luck. Persistence, every day, every day, you sit down and you do your work, which is not so different from a carpenter or a dentist or anything else. It requires attention and focus. And it requires that you survive disappointment and you learn to be self-critical. And you come back the next day and you do it again.

And then good luck, of course, you have to be prepared to be lucky, but it helps if there are kind people who see you and offer gifts. Owls flying through a dark wood and they lead you to a tree and you look under it and there are golden shekels. That sort of thing.

Billy Collins

DN: You grew up with your mom reciting verses, poems, during your childhood, right?

BC: She didn't really recite, because it wasn't a terribly literary family. I was the first one to go to college. She grew up in rural Canada in Ontario; she was born in 1901, and lived to be ninety-seven, so she just about covered the twentieth century. When she grew up, memorization was a very legitimate way to present poetry. Unfortunately, that's kind of been lost, but she just knew a lot of poems. So it wouldn't be, like, the poetry hour where she'd get up on the table and recite, but almost any occasion, she would have some lines, often from Shakespeare, if it were cold, if some friend of hers seemed ungrateful. Poetry was sort of threaded into her talk, and that way, even as a child, I recognized them when she started speaking that way. It was a different kind of talk. Or it wasn't talk, it was something different, something *better* than talk. I could hear it modulate. I don't even know if I knew it was poetry, but I just knew that she would talk funny now and again. She'd come up with these images that would not be part of her normal speech.

DN: Do you assume that that had some kind of marking on you of how you started thinking, maybe in cadences or rhythms or images?

BC: I don't know! It's hard to say. I mean, a lot of this constructing, how you became what you are, is very much an act of fiction, you know? You kind of make it up as you go along. Seamus Heaney mentioned something that I think was just as formative for me, and that is, as an altar boy in Catholic school, memorizing the Latin responses to mass, and I didn't know what I was saying, except I knew *dominus* and a few other words in Latin. But basically I was just memorizing syllables. Like "su-shi-pi-a-dom-i-nus-a . . ." like that. I would echo that. It was an interesting exposure to nonsense, in a way. It was pure sound, without the meaning.

And that certainly is a component in poetry, just that you go by the ear, you write by the ear. I have a poem in which I mention going to camp in the Adirondacks, and a couple of times people came up to me after, and said, "I went to camp in the Adirondacks! What camp did you go to?" And I said, "well, actually I went to camp in the Catskills, but *Adirondacks* sounds better than *Catskills*." I mean, Adirondacks almost sounds Italian. [Italian delivery, gesture] *Adirondacks!*

DN: Which, you kind of have to gesture when you do that.

BC: Yeah! But Catskills is like [flatly] "bleh-bleh." It's a spondee. And there's lots of instances in Shakespeare particularly where sound triumphs over sense.

Jane Smiley

JS: When I was in junior high and high school we had to read a play every year. We started out with the comedies and we ended up with King Lear—we ended up with the tragedies. I love different authors. I loved all the forms. When I was in graduate school, I loved the old Icelandic sagas. That was my first true experience of the epic form. I really love comedies, and I really like tragedies, so I studied medieval literature too. And I like romances.

So it never occurred to me to stick to one form. I went on a Fullbright to Iceland, and when I came home I knew that I wanted to write *The Greenlanders*, and I knew that was going to be the epic. But I also knew that I had to practice in order to write that kind of a book.

DN: You had to work your way up to it?

JS: Well, I had to practice plotting, I had to practice getting it organized, and so I decided then that I was going to write in every form, but I knew that I had to prepare. And so the first few books were trying to figure out what to do. So in *Barn Blind,* I took material that I knew pretty well and I fiddled with that to see if I could make a novel of it. And then in *At Paradise Gate,* I took some family material, fiddled with that, tried to make a novel of that, I decided, nah, I didn't want to write about my family. Although they were receptive! They weren't upset about it, or anything. And then I knew that I wanted to do *The Greenlanders* and it was going to be really long, so I decided that I would better write a murder mystery, because that would teach me how to construct a plot, and so I wrote *Duplicate Keys*. I call those the practice novels. I had a lot of fun, and the great thing about doing practice novels in my day was that, yes, they got published, but no, they weren't any big sensations. So I could try stuff out, and then publication and a couple of reviews constituted a little pat on the head. And so I could keep going and there was nothing saying to me "oh this is so fabulous! You've got to keep writing!" No, there wasn't that. But there was also sufficient success so that I could keep going and enjoy it. And that was my biggest piece of luck I think.

Lysley Tenorio

LT: I wasn't a wiz kid or a literary Doogie Howser. I've always liked to read and I was good at writing essays in high school, but when I was in college I didn't have a strong sense of direction.

I ended up taking a short story class with an Indian American writer named Bharati Mukherjee and I decided to look at her books. I figured if I was going to be studying with her, I would see what she had written. She wrote a collection of stories called "The Middleman and Other

Stories," and it was the first time I had seen contemporary immigrant life portrayed in that way. It was just very unsentimental and very sharp and I especially admired how she was willing to write from the points of view of people who were completely different from herself.

DN: They weren't all from Indian heritage?

LT: Some of them were, but I remember there were some Filipino characters, Trinidadian characters, she wrote from the point of view of a Vietnam vet and that kind of daring was something that I wanted to try and take on. I had no sense if I was good at it or not, and frankly those first stories I wrote were quite terrible.

DN: You called them "Immigrant of the Week"?

LT: "Immigrant Tragedies of the Week." Like those Lifetime movies of the week where there's always some immigrant family with a dark secret revealed at the end. Quite formulaic and quite cheesy. That was the early stuff.

But I realized that was the only class I was losing sleep over. You take a creative writing class, you do the work and put in your effort, you get a good grade. So I wasn't worried about the grade. I was worried about the quality of work. I remember lying in bed trying to fall asleep and at two in the morning I would think, "Whoa, that is a really terrible paragraph on page eight," and I'd be mortified if anyone were to read that, so I would get out of bed and just retype it. I thought if this is something I'm losing sleep over, it must be something I care about. And again, I didn't know if I was any good at it or not, but because I cared about it so much, I knew that I had to make it an integral part of my life. I didn't know how I would do that at the time, but I knew that I had to.

Carlos Ruiz Zafon

DN: There's a character early on, in *The Shadows*, where a customer in the bookstore says, "Few things leave a deeper mark on a reader than the first book that finds its way into his heart." What was that first book for you?

CZ: I've talked to many readers about that first thing they read that changed their lives, because it opens their minds to the world of language, literature, ideas, etc. In my case, it was the world of language, the world of books. I don't have one specific book that I remember. As a very young child, I was fascinated by languages, and especially by words, by books, by storytelling. It was very interesting how stories were built and engineered, and how you could kind of reverse-engineer these things. We grew up with a mixture of movies, TV, and books. To me, it was all these codes, all these languages, all these things, images, sounds, words that you could use to communicate to create something. I was fascinated by that. So I wanted to find out how they do this, how it works, how the engine of this thing works, because I want to do this for life. I believed the greatest gig in the world would be to be able to create these things that I found so wonderful, and that have impressed me so much.

DN: You were influenced by Dickens. I mean, when you talk about reverse engineering a story and trying to figure out how they do that, could you have picked a simpler author than Dickens?

CZ: Dickens came later, as I grew older and became more pretentious. I started with comic books and movies and things like that, and then adventure stories and whatever I could find. I think like most readers, you start reading what is around you. When you're a child, you don't have the money to buy books, and you cannot go to a place to get them. So when I was very young, I was just trying to read whatever was available at home, and there weren't that many things because nobody in my family was a reader. My father would buy these kinds of books that were fashionable in Spain at the time, that were competitors of the complete works of the classics. So you would find this humongous thing: T*he Complete Works of Thomas Mann* printed in this thin kind of paper that is transparent and print that is designed to ruin your eyesight from childhood, which is why, to this day, I wear glasses.

I remember reading William Somerset Maugham, Thomas Mann, Dickens, Jakob Wassermann, and authors that now have been kind of forgotten. At the same time, my father would buy a novel by Harold

Robbins. I remember seeing this book by Harold Robbins, which I was very impressed with because it had this very beautiful lady in a bikini, wearing some kind of Kalashnikov rifle. And I thought, "This has to be dynamite."

DN: Yeah, "What a great writer he must be!"

CZ: "What a great writer! He thought of this stuff. Why didn't I think of this?!"

I would read anything I could, and eventually at some point, I started saving money, doing things to get some coins and buy the books I was interested in. There was a bookstore around the corner, so I would buy books from them, or get books from the library, from bookstores, or I had a friend at school whose family owned a big bookstore in Barcelona, so I would get special treatment from his parents.

DN: You once said that Stephen King was your first English professor.

CZ: I've always been very fond of Stephen King, and he's a terrific storyteller.

DN: But you would read him in English?

CZ: I learned English reading Stephen King. I remember there were many times when I was a child growing up in the '70s in Barcelona, where many of the things that interested me were not available to me, or they would be available on these newsstands that sold magazines and newspapers for tourists, and all of them were in English. I would try to pick things in there to read and see if I could figure out the grammar, the words, and everything. I had always liked, as a child, spooky stories and things like that. A lot of Stephen King books appealed to me and I said, "Well, this could be interesting. This could be fun, and maybe I can try to learn from it." So I started reading Stephen King novels, and at the beginning, I didn't understand anything. I just got a terrible headache after five pages. It's like going into ancient Egypt without the Rosetta Stone and trying to translate all that stuff. After a while you go crazy.

Eventually I started finding the cracks in there, and so I started reading them, and then I made a habit of that. They became very dear to me, so I made this thing of reading everything he had written and tried to read it in English. It was especially very useful because Stephen King is very clever in the way he uses idioms, and the way he constructs dialogues to characterize. So you learn a lot about expressions and how people talk—how people *really* talk. Reading these books was very interesting, and the stories are always very entertaining, and very well told.

Robin Jones Gunn

RG: When I was growing up, I got in trouble for telling stories. They called it lying. They'd say, "Stop embellishing and get to the point." They felt like this imagination I had that was so full, was really something that needed to be squelched. But then after I was married, and we had children, and I'd gone to a writer's conference that my husband pushed me out the door to go to, I thought, "I could write a few articles" and I did, and they were published. And then, "I could write some children's books"—because we have two small children—and then I did, and it just kept growing from there.

DN: What were you lying about?

RG: Well, it was more of the story getting bigger than it really was. "My lunchbox didn't make it home from school . . ." There was a really interesting reason that I could come up with why it didn't . . .

DN: Right . . . "The gates had come open in the zoo . . ."

RG: And a kangaroo got out . . .

DN: Yeah, okay, so it wasn't that you were really lying.

RG: No, no. It was just more like this wild imagination embellishing was something that should not be nurtured. Later I just sensed that I wasn't qualified to be a writer. An author was someone who was accomplished and had a doctorate, or, I don't know what I thought, but—

DN: Just not you.

RG: Yeah, just to be a simple storyteller was not a strong enough reason to pursue a career in writing.

DN: And the inciting incident was you were on a retreat with the kids that you taught at Sunday school and found them all reading books in a tent instead of being out there playing in the water or at the beach.

RG: Yep.

DN: And what were they reading?

RG: This was at San Clemente state beach for a summer trip. My husband was the youth pastor, and the girls had brought with them, from the public library, a stack of romance novels. They were thirteen years old, and they were reading very evocative stories that had a lot more description than they should be made aware of at thirteen years old. So I crawled in the tent where they were and read some of the books with them, and said, "Does your mother know this is what you're reading?" And, "I don't want you to read these books. I think there's other things you can read." They challenged me to find the kinds of books they wanted: love stories, and books that would have more appeal to young audiences. And I had a hard time finding the kinds of books they wanted.

DN: I love what you did, though, because you went to a bookstore.

RG: Yes.

DN: And you started going shelf by shelf saying, "Where are some books that would appeal to these young ladies?" And you found some books for them? And what was their reaction?

RG: I gave them to them. They read them, they read them twice, they read them three times, and they gave them back and said, "Give us some more." But there weren't any more. So then they challenged me and said, "Why don't *you* write books for us?" I was timid and terrified. "Oh! I couldn't do that! . . . All those words!" I just write children's books, like seven words on a page that's about my speed.

DN: Or, "I submit a poem here, or a devotional there, a short story there." You still weren't seeing this as something you should be doing?

RG: No, not particularly. Maybe the only hint that I had was that I had a devotional that was published and they asked how I wanted my name to appear, and I wrote Robin Gunn because I had been married about five years already. My parents were at the house and my daddy saw that. My daddy, who was the son of a Kentucky coal miner, was kind of proud. He said, "You put Jones in there. You've been a Jones a lot longer than you've been a Gunn." So okay, Robin Jones Gunn is now my pen name. And that's maybe where I felt like, "Maybe there's something there."

DN: Feels like a writer.

RG: It kind of has a flow.

DN: So you started writing these kinds of stories. But what's so cool about this is the kids were your built-in focus group.

RG: Right. Those girls knew what they wanted, and so when they challenged me to write, and I started writing, and I read it to them, and they told me what they didn't like, over and over and over.

DN: They knew what they wanted? What did they want?

RG: They wanted a love story, and they wanted the main character to be a girl that was just like them: average, a little shy—not anything noticeable. But then they wanted good things to happen to her, so I had aunt Marty, with all the money, take Christie shopping and give her a makeover, and, you know, the fantasy kind of things that they hoped would happen to them so they would fit in better in their school.

Don Winslow

DN: You've lived in Rhode Island, Nebraska, Africa, New York, San Diego. You've been a private investigator. You intended to go into the foreign service but ended up leading photographic safaris in Kenya. You led hiking expeditions in China. You directed Shakespeare productions in England. So, of course you end up writing about drugs and cartels. I mean, it's a direct line, right?

DW: Yeah, I don't know what you're curious about there.

Listen, I wanted to be a writer since I was a kid. And nobody stamps your papers for that. If you go to medical school, you're a doctor. If you go to law school, you're a lawyer. There is no equivalent for a writer. I knew I was going to have to make a living doing something else because it was a long time before the world agreed that I was a writer. And so I wanted to do interesting things, fun things. So I sought out those jobs that would let me chase leopards around with a camera, be on the streets of New York or wherever it happened to be.

DN: But you also grew up around storytellers. Your father, a military guy, you said he was quite a storyteller.

DW: The best. Just the best raconteur. He'd get together with his Navy buddies, he was chief petty officer, and he'd get together with his old buddies around the dining room table at the house that we lived in half the year. And I'd get under the table . . .

DN: He knew this?

DW: Oh, yeah. He pretended he didn't know that I was pulling one over on him. And they'd tell stories. Of course, as the years went by the stories got better. And I would sit there, literally at the feet of these great storytellers, hearing about bar-room brawls in Hong Kong, things in Singapore or Africa, and think, boy wouldn't it be great to be a storyteller?

DN: So the combination of that and your mom in the library, it's sort of your destiny.

DW: I think so. Funny you should say that, because there are two kids in our family, both of whom became professional novelists. My sister Kristine Rolofson wrote forty-three romance novels. Very successful at it. So, you have these two kids growing up in this tiny town who both become novelists.

DN: You were also motivated, as I've read, by wanting to get out of the town you were in. I think the quote was "my ticket out of the fish factory was to write stories."

DW: My old man used to drive me to within 500 yards of the fish factory and you could smell it from 500 yards away. And he would say "if you don't buckle down and study," because I was a terrible student, "if you don't buckle down and study, you're going to spend your life shoveling fish guts in there." And he was right.

Writing was always the goal. I thought I was going to be a journalist.

DN: Nothing wrong with that.

DW: Nothing wrong with that. In fact I went to the University of Nebraska because they had a really good journalism program. I learned to write simple, declarative sentences under a guy named Jim Neal. He stood up in front of the freshman class, basic reporting, and said, "my goal is to flunk a third of you out by next month." And he did. So, back to the fish factory for you, Winslow! It was the days of typewriters. And he would walk around and look at what you were writing and rip it out of the roller, crumple it up and throw it at you and walk away.

DN: Is he still lurking somewhere in you, as you're writing, thinking, Oh Jim Neal would tear that sentence up?

DW: Every once in a while, yeah. I've never been asked that question, but you're absolutely right. Every once in a while I might have an adverb in there that just is doing nothing but hanging out.

DN: The way they do . . .

DW: The way they do. So sometimes I'll be looking for those "lys" at the end of words, and be thinking, you know, Neal would rip this one right up.

Nnedi Okorafor

DN: You only considered writing when you couldn't do what you really wanted to do, which was play tennis and study bugs, right?

NO: Yes, that's a very good way to put it.

DN: So, while you were recovering from some really bad surgery, you started thinking, "I've got stories running around in my head." But it was that forced stillness that brought it out?

NO: Yeah, yeah, the sitting in a hospital bed, paralyzed, will do that to you, you know? I had to save myself because in that moment where I had been this great athlete—it was not only my identity, it was my way of being. Athletics and the feeling of motion, I had a love for it that was so, so deep and profound.

DN: You were a pretty ferocious tennis player.

NO: Yeah, yeah. I was.

DN: And then that gets taken away.

NO: Not just taken away. It was taken away suddenly and it was taken away fast and immediately. Like one minute, you walk into the hospital for scoliosis surgery, and you're told there's a one percent chance of paralysis, but you don't really believe that's gonna happen—I mean come on. And then nine hours later, wake up paralyzed. Like, literally half your body feels like it's just gone, you know? So when that happened, it was in the first few days where it was such a shock. It was such a shock to my system, to everything where I could have easily just lost my mind. Lost it, let it go, and never returned, and had good reason to lose my mind. Instead, I chose to save myself. And the way I saved myself was those stories. I remember picking up the pen, and I remember the first story that was in my head was of a woman who could fly. And you know, when you can fly, you don't have to walk, and I just started writing it. It wasn't like I was trying to escape myself; it was like going in.

DN: You were engaging.

NO: Yeah, yeah. And once I did that, it saved me. So it wasn't like, "okay I can't do this, let me do this." It was something far more profound.

Anthony Doerr

DN: Let's talk about your first book. It was a nine-pager called *Molluscs*—you wrote it when you were a little kid. Did you have a focus group help you with that title?

AD: That's amazing! Never gotten this question before. It was a school project, was super excited because Mom had a blank book—Mom sewed a bunch of stuff—and she made a purple cloth cover for it and even put some cotton underneath it so it's puffy. As a kid, you're like, "Puffy books. Pretty cool—"

DN: Those are awesome.

AD: And she was like, "Yes, you can have it, but make sure you do a draft or two before you start filling the pages with your book about molluscs," which, of course, was very popular. But my most clear memory of my first lesson in failing at graphic design was I sit down very carefully to write the "M" for molluscs, and I put it right in the center of the puffy purple. And then I'm like, here comes the "O," and the *two* "L's," which sometimes you forget about. And then I'm like, okay, I'm turning the book, like the "USCS" is all down. My huge effort filled about two-and-a-half pages of the forty-page blank book. So it probably left readers a little unsatisfied.

DN: I think they were unsatisfied just looking at the cover, probably. Not with the—

AD: That's wrong; molluscs are so interesting! Let's get into it.

DN: Well, they're kind of meandering down the page. That's actually probably how they do it.

AD: Yes. I didn't realize this at the time, but it was mimicking the motion of a clam's foot. It is called multi-layered.

We only got to go on one vacation a year. My mom was a school teacher. We lived in Ohio, and I was obsessed with the ocean—I don't know why. But she had two weeks off, so she would pile me and my brothers in this old Suburban and drive us to Florida to a place called Sanibel Island. It was like paradise. Mom was a science teacher—she let us keep all kinds of creatures—probably illegal. And we would bring them back in milk jugs, like crabs and octopi and stuff that would die, and bring them all the way back. So you leave, and it's snowing, and she's in a white-knuckle panic all the way home, and then we try to keep them alive in aquariums in the kitchen. And there was something so powerful and profound about that, like wrenching the creature out of its habitat, and you're putting it next to the wood stove while snow is falling down, and you're like, "Hm, that's a lionfish that my brother got stung by." I don't know; it was very powerful stuff in my childhood about me and shells.

DN: I think it comes through in your writing, that kind of fascination and wonder about those lives.

AD: Yeah, the umwelt of shells—of snails and mollusks—is so different than ours. The way they see and experience the world is just a reminder that ours is just one way of experiencing the world. Every time you study any creature, they're experiencing the world in different ways. Bees can see patterns and ultraviolet and flowers that we can't see. Snakes can see heat in ways we can't see. The metaphor that we probably got together in biology of the animal kingdom always kind of implies there's a hierarchy. So we're at the top, and evolution is all "finished with us." And then you get older, and you're like, "It doesn't seem like evolution finished my back."

So learning, I think from Mom, to appreciate that the life of every creature is just as valuable, and just as interesting, and just as worthy of curiosity as our own, and that 99.9 percent of species have gone extinct, and humans, why in the world do we think we're going to be some exception? Those things teach you a kind of humility, a really wonderful humility. Experiencing wonder in your life every day teaches you this beautiful humility and transcendence. And that doesn't have to be something magic. I think maybe the pandemic taught so many of us you don't have to go to Positano to experience wonder, necessarily; you can just stand out there and check out the ice plant between visiting Dean's classes.

Anchee Min

DN: You went to an English as a second language class, right?

AM: Yeah. And the writing classes. They say you have to write. I said, what do I got to write? I don't have a life in America. I tried to copy American classmates. I didn't have a life. So the teacher says, oh, Anchee Min, you're such a lousy writer. But you have wonderful material. So I say, who do you think is a good writer that I should be studying? And he turned around and he gave me his book.

I went home . . . studied . . . What I'm gonna say, you're probably different. Don't take it personally, okay?

DN: Maybe.

AM: Well, I studied. And I said, well, I can do that, too. If he gave me Virginia Woolf's book. If he gave me Hemingway's or anybody that's . . . I probably would not have the guts.

DN: But you read his book and thought, "I can do that."

AM: Yeah. So that's what I did.

DN: So you collected your stories from that class, and that's what became *Red Azalea*?

AM: Yeah. So this is my plot, my thinking. My goal was to improve my English. I have very difficult English grammar. In Chinese, you don't have to say "I am drinking," or "I drink" or "drank" or "drunk." You know, those kind of things. My most difficulty was "have been," "has been," "had been." I could never get that. So I figured, if I asked people how, would you teach me about "have beens"? And these people wouldn't know where to begin. So I had to have a draft so I can carry with me, I stand by the elevator at the school. So, who—our school, you know, in Chicago, it's like a eight floor. Twelve floor. I say, which floor you go? If this person say eighth, or eleven, or ten, that be great. I get in the elevator, I say, *now see*, can you, is this "I was there tomorrow"? Is that correct? And the answer is no, "I will be there tomorrow" not "I was there tomorrow." So this is how I got *Red Azalea*.

N. Scott Momaday

DN: You knew you wanted to be a writer at age eight. You told your mom that you wanted to be a writer. How did she react to that?

NSM: I think she said, "Good."

DN: Because she was a writer?

NSM: She was a writer herself, so I think she was pleased that I was thinking in those terms. But it's clear to me now, Dean, that you know more about my life than I do, so maybe I should be interviewing you.

DN: Yes, I'll tell you when your answers are correct. You have a character in one of your books who hears his grandmother's stories and this is how you describe it: "When she told me those old stories, something strange, and good and powerful was going on. I was a child and that old woman was asking me to come directly into the presence of her mind and spirit. She was taking hold of my imagination, giving me to share in the great fortune of her wonder and delight. It was a timeless, timeless thing. Nothing of her old age or my childhood came between us." You had those experiences with your grandmother, didn't you? When she would tell you stories? And also with your father?

NSM: Yeah. But primarily my father. He was steeped in the oral tradition of the Kiowas and he told me stories when I was first able to understand them. They made a great impression on me, and gave me the sense of the power of beauty in language.

3

Subject Matter
Where Do Ideas Come From?

I'm so grateful I had such a horrific childhood, because I have so much material now to draw from.

AMY TAN

Every kind of writing instruction includes something along the lines of "Write what you know." That doesn't always work for fiction writers. Did Ray Bradbury have personal experience with colonizing Mars when he wrote *The Martian Chronicles*, or did Nnedi Okorafor have personal experience with time travel and shape-shifting when she wrote *Who Fears Death?*, or had Anthony Doerr experienced space travel when he wrote *Cloud Cuckoo Land*?

Probably not.

But did they know something about ambition, the drive for adventure, love, fear, taking risks? Of course. So they actually ARE writing about what they know. In many cases fiction writers are drawing from their deep caverns of memory.

While the writers below describe story ideas and where they come from, it's worthwhile to plumb your own mind and heart to see what *you* could write about.

Families are ripe with possible inspiration for ideas. The writer Roxana Robinson said that stories about families are a well we can return to over and over. "As a subject, the family is inexhaustible," she wrote in an essay.

"All this beauty and fury makes the family a rich literary source. Much of our greatest fiction comes from conflicts within it: look at 'Oedipus Rex,' 'King Lear,' 'Anna Karenina,' 'The Sound and the Fury,' 'To the Lighthouse,' the Rabbit quartet. These works reveal us to ourselves, and it seems to me that this is who we are: we're people driven, damaged and tortured; we're people elated, sustained and nourished, all by the powerful, devastating, inescapable bonds within the family."

Ultimately, she said, she writes about trouble.

> With each story—and by story I mean anything I write—I am trying simply to work something out for myself. . .. I write about the things that disturb me, the things that won't let me alone, the things that are eating slowly into my brain at 3 in the morning, the things that unbalance my world. Sometimes these are things I've said or done; sometimes they're things I've heard about or seen. Sometimes they're only sentences, sometimes scenes, sometimes complete narratives. I carry these things around inside my head until I'm compelled to write them down to get rid of them. I sit down and begin. (https://archive.nytimes.com/www.nytimes.com/library/books/071700robinson-writing.html)

No one's life experience is exactly like yours. You could start by making a list of the components of what makes you uniquely you. Do you have siblings? Was your home happy? Dysfunctional? Did you excel at anything (sports, music, cup stacking)? What have you achieved? What do you *wish* you had achieved? Have you ever been afraid—*really afraid*? Have you lost something that you treasured? Did you find something you never expected to find?

Some things give you a lump in the throat. That's what Robert Frost said when he was asked how he chose what poems to write. Certain things—the sight of a bird in the snow, the twitch of a horse's neck, a child reaching up to take your hand, a starry sky, an unexpected act of kindness (or hostility)—perhaps they startle you momentarily. Why? That's why you write about them. You want to explore why they reach you the way they do.

Where else do writers get their ideas?

The first time we had Garrison Keillor come to our campus, I picked him up at the airport, and he was friendly enough. We have some mutual friends—I grew up in Minneapolis—so we small-talked a little about Minnesota in the car. On his radio program A Prairie Home Companion, he has this persona of being a shy, awkward guy, and to a certain degree it's an accurate portrayal of himself. He wasn't rude at all—he's an introvert. So conversation at first was a little slow. His performance was going to be in the evening, well after the sun went down, so I asked him if he wanted to see the campus before I took him to his hotel. He nodded and said, "Sure." We drove for a little while in silence, and he asked, "So what is a Nazarene?" Our university is associated with a church denomination called the Church of the Nazarene, so I gave him a brief history of how it is an offshoot of the Methodist Church, patterned in its theology after John Wesley. I was aware of his own Christian upbringing, and I told him how the Nazarenes differed from the Brethren Church, and since Minnesota has millions of Lutherans, I pointed out the distinctions from them as well.

He seemed mildly interested. We pulled onto campus and walked around a little. I gave him a brief history of the school—how it started in Pasadena more than 100 years ago and moved to this location on the ocean in San Diego in 1973. I told him about how the campus used to be inhabited by the Theosophical Society, that the Society attempted to create a utopian community with orphans through beauty and the arts, that the Theosophists believed in reincarnation, that the Navy took over the area, and then it became the site of a university, where some of the Society's buildings are preserved.

Throughout my tour of the campus, he didn't say a word. He didn't ask a question. If people on campus recognized him and came over to say hello, he was very charming and seemed happy to see them. When it was just the two of us walking around, stopping occasionally so I could point out something I thought was significant, he was silent. I didn't know if this was his true introverted self, or if he was tired from his flight, or if he was bored, or what. I just couldn't read him.

After a little while he said, "I should get to the hotel."

So I took him to the hotel and said I'd be back in a few hours to pick him up for the evening show.

When I got to the hotel he was waiting outside for me. In the car he hummed to himself a little. Again, pretty much silence. I pointed out the line of cars waiting to get on campus for his event. "You're creating quite the traffic jam," I said. No response. To be clear, it wasn't as if he were angry or sulking. I just got the sense that he wasn't a small-talker. If there was something that needed to be said, he'd say it. So far, nothing needed to be said.

We got backstage and waited for the auditorium to fill. A few dignitaries stopped by to say hello. They usually said similar things about the radio program, about Minnesota. No doubt they were conversations he has hundreds of times a week. It seemed that everyone who had ever moved out of Minnesota had to tell him their story. He was gracious, but not loquacious. Then, about five minutes before the program began, he reached in his jacket pocket, took out a paper napkin, jotted a few notes on it, and put it back in his pocket.

At the appointed time I went onstage, introduced Keillor to the packed house, and I went to my seat in the front row. He strode out to the whistling and stomping and cheering of his loyal fans. As his two-hour performance of telling one huge convoluted story began to unfold, I couldn't believe what I was hearing. He told the story of a group of Nazarenes who moved down to San Diego from Pasadena, having to contend with this utopian community that the Theosophical Society was trying to develop, and how the Navy got involved, and on and on. He wove in every detail I had told him just a few hours before. At one point in the story he walked to the edge of the stage and looked down directly at me and raised his massive eyebrows. It was as if to say, "You thought I wasn't paying attention on your little tour!"

Later, people came up to me and said, "Wow—he must have a whole staff of researchers who prepared him with all that history so he could tell that story!" I just shook my head and said, "You have no idea."

This is what writers do. We pay attention to EVERYTHING. What people say, what we observe and experience, what we wonder about, snippets of dialogue we overhear—it's all potential material. The whole world is material from which writers get their ideas.

What ideas have been circulating, recirculating, lingering in you?

All of the writers below write about something that was growing inside of them. You can do the same.

Anthony Doerr

DN: So many of your themes deal with these enormous issues. It could be building of a dam that floods a community. It could be infertility. It could be apartheid, Alzheimer's, environmental disaster, war. Do you start with the big issue that you want to dig into, as in, "I want to tell the world a story about apartheid?" Or do you just create a character and follow her around for a while and see what trouble she gets into?

AD: I think you oscillate between the two. But I really want to maybe disabuse beginning writers. It will get really itchy when you say you start with big ideas because often then you stay up in the big idea world. You have students come to you, and they're like, "Well, I just want to write about love, so that's why I included no details in the story. I just wanted it to just be about love. And that's why I didn't want to describe the town they live in because I wanted it to be any town." And you're like, "Well, if you actually describe the town, the reader would have something to see in the town and might enjoy reading it."

The great irony of fiction writing is that the path to the universal is through the individual. The tunnel to the universe is through the little pieces of glitter that are shattered in the pavement down below Dean's office in the Point Loma faculty parking lot. That's how you tunnel toward these universal things Flaubert is fumbling after. So you can't lose yourself too often in the big ideas, but you also can't get so focused in the minutiae of your characters' lives that you forget that you're trying to tell something that other people can relate to.

Regarding *All the Light We Cannot See,* the idea came to me in 2004. I was at Princeton for a year. I'm on the train to go to New York City to see my publisher's art for a cover for *About Grace,* my second book.

There's a guy in the seat in front of me, the train is going fifty miles an hour, and he's talking on his 2004 cell about the movie *The Matrix*—super important conversation. And as we go into the city, you start going underground, steel and concrete are above the train, and his call drops. And the guy got, in my opinion, unreasonably angry about the call dropping. It occurred to me what he's doing, what we're all doing every time we're like, "Let's see if somebody liked my photo of my pie," is a total miracle.

It's an utter absolute stunning miracle. We're sending little packets of light from a radio that's way smaller than a deck of cards, and we're sending them at the speed of light to radio towers positioned around San Diego, and they respond to other towers all the way to your buddy in Madrid, who's like, "Cool pie, Brenda." *Bloop.* And then that's coming back to you at the speed of light, and you're like, "Why isn't this working?" It's astonishing; it's like the gods can do that stuff. I don't usually get titles early, but I carry a little notebook, and that day I wrote *All the Light We Cannot See*. I just was like, I want to somehow explore how we use invisible light to send messages.

I thought, "All I have is this germ of a girl who was trapped, using a radio to send a story to a boy who was also trapped, and he needed this story to somehow survive." So I knew I wanted to remind ourselves of the wizardry and the magic of electromagnetic communication. That's I guess a big idea, but then immediately when I start writing that next day, start trying to piece out ideas. By the time that comes out in 2014, we're just beginning to start to see the negative effects. And then the pandemic hits, and you see that the vaccine will give you eight arms and turn you into a cockroach, and you're like, "That's what I was writing about, and that's what was going on in 1938 to begin to lay the groundwork to exterminate millions of human beings."

DN: You got all of that out of a guy losing his call?

AD: The whole world's super interesting; you just have to get out there. But I hope that's motivational for people who are getting started writing. There's not some muse who tiptoes down from her angel garden and is like, "Here's your book, Steve." The book comes to you in these moments that you steal between your kids' swimming lessons and then the night that you're out there under the stars and you're like, "Look at this place," and then you're like, "I've got to fold the laundry." You're always moving between the sublime and the mundane.

DN: In *Cloud Cuckoo Land*, one of the aspects of that book is the importance of preserving a story. This has its genesis in your grandmother living with you.

AD: Good backgrounding, Dean! It's probably something to unpack with a therapist, but I don't mind. When I was fifteen or sixteen, my grandma came to live with us. I was, of course, self-centered and not thinking about what my mom was going through. My grandma had been diagnosed with Alzheimer's, but I had never even heard the word before. In those days, it wasn't a word everybody knew. I graduated high school in '91, so it was probably like '88, and my brothers were already off to college. It was just me in the house, and I watched this disease dismantle her cognitive capacities in this really visceral way.

She could still beat me at gin rummy but didn't know my name. Or she would remember lyrics to Christmas carols, but she'd totally forget where she was. It was so emotional for my mom, but, of course, I was too self-centered to really understand. My dad would come home from work and deal with this. She had sundowner's, so she would get upset in the evenings. I think it infected me with the sense of how fragile memory is. Everything that is yourself depends on you remembering your past. And when holes start getting chewed in that, your self starts to disintegrate.

I think there's a lot of anxiety in me about that. And I think it's astonishing that culture survives the ravages of time. But, erasure is also important. If you go to Gettysburg or if you go to some of the World War I battlefields to see the way the land has healed, this is so important; otherwise, the human race couldn't go on. So this tension between erasure and memory has always been present, I think, in all my work.

Cloud Cuckoo Land was probably my most explicit way of dealing with it. It's about a manuscript that survives over centuries.

It's my middle-age book, because *All the Light* my kids were zero to ten when I worked on it, and the kids were ten to seventeen when I worked on *Cloud Cuckoo Land.* And I realized the most important thing about being a parent is the decentering it causes you. You get moved out of the center of your own needs and your own experiences, and you start thinking about yourself as a link in a continuous chain of human culture. I was linking this idea of environmental stewardship with book stewardship and cultural stewardship, and the way libraries and librarians and teachers have preserved texts and stories over time. It's somehow linked to the same stewardship that I think we need to be thinking about in terms of the quilt of species we all share the earth with.

DN: When I read *Cloud Cuckoo Land*, I was part way through it, and I'm just thinking, "Dude, I'm trusting you; I have no idea where this is going." I don't know if I'm in a Ken Kesey novel or I'm in some sort of time warp when I'm reading this, but there was something about it that made me trust you. Then as you start pulling those threads together, of course, that's the great pay off. Were you nervous at all that you were going to lose some people or that you were just going to confuse people?

AD: Of course. Confusing is a little sadder of a word for me.

DN: All right, I'm sorry.

AD: No, I'm just kidding. During the seven years I wrote this book, science continually discovered unimaginable linkages between things that you just didn't think were connected. Probably the easiest example that may be from, say, the work of Richard Powers. A lot of the work that's been done on forests in the past ten years has upended the metaphor of forests that we grew up with. It was a very capitalist metaphor that trees compete with one another for light and nutrients. That was like, "The best of—the McDonald's of—trees get the biggest," and that's wrong.

It's the forest is all totally cooperative and often will divert nutrients to its weakest members. They will send messages and alerts through the mycelium fungus underneath the ground, and it often kind of functions as a superorganism. It really inverts this metaphor. Another one is, say, of course, climate and fires, which affect all of you in California. If you think about, say, the Gulf Stream and the Atlantic, is a stream of water up the coast of the Atlantic. It's 100 times more powerful than the Amazon River. It's slowing down rather suddenly, really suddenly; it's frighteningly suddenly, and it keeps temperature stable in places as distant as London, and Miami, and Tampa Bay. What we're learning—we think the reason it's slowing down is that this huge amount of freshwater is pouring off the Greenland ice sheet. They're disrupting ocean density, and they're disrupting these big conveyor belts that are moving through the ocean. It's all connected to warming up the air. It's somehow running our air conditioners and running our aircraft carriers. It's running these big industrial systems, which is warming up the air, is connecting to the movement of water in the Atlantic, which is changing temperatures in places as disparate as London and Tampa Bay. Things that you don't necessarily think of as connected we're learning are deeply connected.

I wanted to somehow suggest at the beginning of *Cloud Cuckoo Land* that these things that you think are totally disconnected, if you trust me, I'm going to try to show you these little filaments that connect all of us through time. If a book like this can remind you, "Oh, if I just trust, then maybe I'm going to remember I'm connected to my ancestors and the kids in my future that I'll never get to meet." Maybe that'll help you think through some of those stewardship ideas in your daily life.

Amor Towles

DN: In your book *Table For Two*, the second short story is the one that drew me the most. It's a story about a frustrated writer. You write he had "a fear so dark and disturbing that it could barely be acknowledged: the fear that he had no story to tell."

AT: Right.

DN: This is a story about a guy who wants to write, and he moves to New York because that's what people—that's what you did.

AT: Yeah, that's true.

DN: And he moves to New York, but his greatest inconveniences in his life had been "mowing lawns, raking leaves, shoveling snow. He'd never been an alcoholic or been divorced. What could he possibly write about?"

AT: Yes. And I think what the narrator of that story says is his parents weren't even willing to get divorced or be alcoholics for his benefit.

DN: Yeah. Help the guy out!

AT: Give him something to write about.

DN: Exactly. But this is actually leading up to a question. I'm continuing here. It says, "he dreamed of fame, but he had nothing to say." Has that ever been a problem for you? I mean, you've aspired to be a writer most of your life; you were writing when you were a little kid. But did you ever get to a point where you just thought, "I don't have anything to say now?"

AT: No.

DN: I didn't think so.

AT: The character in this story is about twenty-five years old. I think that's a very natural thing for many young writers to be grappling with, which is, "What has happened in my life that is worth covering? What do I know about the world, and do I have something that is important to say?"

For the most part, I've tried to keep my focus on telling a story without worrying about what it might mean to others. Some people really write towards having a message. For me, when someone says, "what is your book about?" If I could say to them what my book was about in a few sentences, that book would be a failure for sure. Let's use the example of the novel for a second. For me, I often will think of the novel as a machine for meaning, that the goal of a finely made novel is that you have to picture that a novel is a composition of thousands of elements of craft. So, within it are conversations, and settings, and personalities, and backgrounds, and memories, and philosophical observations, and debates, and the poetry of the language, and metaphors, and similes, and allusions, and allegories. That's all packed in there. And in a finely written novel, this wide array of elements feels very diverse, but yet it feels like it's all there, belongs there. But what it allows for is that many different readers from different walks of life—men, women, old, young, rich, poor, different religions, whatever—can come to a well-written narrative, enjoy it in a similar fashion, but they could each walk away with a very different impression of what it means to them. Because it's the way that they're assembling the various elements in their mind and the connections that they're drawing, the emotions that have been stirred up for them and partly because of their own memories and their own observations, their own relationships that become a filter for that.

The end result is that they may have very different understandings of what this book could mean. That's the big ambition for me, someone having grown up reading literature, is to create something that could achieve that goal. The enemy of that is by starting out and saying, "What's this book going to be about?" Or what's the major theme? What is it going to mean? I really don't do that. What I do instead is I focus on what is the story that has come to me. What events happen? Who are the people? What occurs? And then to try to write it as best as I possibly can and just assume that later on someone else is going to figure out what it means. Because I don't know.

DN: That's the reader's job, I suppose.

AT: That's the reader's job.

Nick Hornby

DN: Many of your books deal with themes of masculinity, marriage, marital disillusionment, moral and emotional confusion, and difficult relationships. After reading almost all of your novels, I have one question for you: is anyone in England happily married?

NH: [laughs] If they are and they've got a successful job, what is there to write about?

DN: Well, there you go.

NH: Especially if something or some part of what you do is attempting to be funny. I don't want to read a novel about a CEO who has a beautiful wife that he loves, and they've been married for thirty years, and there's no problems with their kids. That's not even a paragraph. So, you're always writing about people at their point of crisis. The whole thing about fiction is you're choosing a defining moment in a character's life, which is actually one reason why I don't really like novels where it's the same detective every time. You think, "Really? This isn't as exciting as the thing you did four years ago." And I guess whatever you call my kind of fiction, but non-genre fiction, there isn't anything else to say about those people other than that they lived this moment of crisis in the pages of my novel.

But you're right: no one is happily married in England either.

DN: That was kind of a roundabout way to get to the answer.

NH: Yeah, it's the weather.

DN: A fundamental truth about really any kind of story is that only trouble is interesting.

NH: Exactly.

Joseph Wambaugh

JW: Police procedurals generally tell how a cop acts on the job, and I was more interested in how the job acts on the cop, on the cop's head. So from the very beginning that was my interest and that's what I wrote about and that's what made my stuff different. Some of my police stories have virtually no action whatsoever. Nothing much happening except what's happening inside the head of the man or woman who's doing the job.

There are a lot of people who write books about their first encounter with a girl or a boy, and that gets pretty boring. I mean, really.

DN: You've got some pretty exciting first girl and boy experiences in your books, though.

JW: It's a little different because the girl and boy in my stuff are kind of clinging to each other because they're being attacked from all sides. And they get confused that they don't even know who their friends are or who their enemies are. That's what I found interesting about being young cops, that pretty soon you start to distrust everyone. You think everyone is a liar and you think everyone is no good and you're not even sure about your own partner after a while. That's when the premature cynicism takes over and that's why there's such a high instance of police suicide and divorce and alcoholism and drug abuse and so forth. That's all I was ever interested in with the stories I wrote—how that happens to young people who were not that way when they started out and what makes them that way.

Anne Lamott

DN: Years ago, when I first started reading what you write, it seemed like you were one of the few people who would talk openly about grief and loss. You gave such profound language to it and you made it so personal, which of course, made it so universal. But now, doesn't it seem like everybody is writing about grief these days? It's like its own genre now.

AL: Grief is like the "it girl." But it will pass. People will lose interest in it.

DN: But you were one of the early ones.

AL: My first book was about the loss of my father to brain cancer when I was twenty-five, and the book came out when I was twenty-six. I've been writing about it for a long time because I actually think that the reason people and countries and families are so troubled and scared and screwed up is because we were never allowed to do grief. You were not supposed to cry, or if you needed to cry, because there had been a devastating loss, there was a grid, and if it was a spouse, you could grieve for a year. That was the system. If it was a brother or sister, you could have, I think four months, and if it was a best friend, three months. If it was a pet, a week and a half. But it was all laid out.

It turned out little by little, people were discovering and I was writing about the fact that grief is a Lazy Susan, and it spins until it starts to spin so slowly that it's very quietly in the background. But some days the Lazy Susan lands on numb. You might actually have a really great phase of numb. Then the Lazy Susan spins again and you're in the almost hysterical and stunned that you could ever feel this much devastation and like a burn victim that you have no protective covering. Then the Lazy Susan spins and you feel this depth of soul connection, umbilical connection to the person who passed, and really to much more of life because you're not hiding from so much anymore. So, yeah, I notice grief is just having its day.

DN: It is, which I think is wonderful. We're actually giving voice to it and permission. But one of the things I appreciate about you is that you were doing this a long time ago.

AL: Well, thank you. When my dad got sick, I was twenty-three, it was 1977. I did what you do when you have a crisis. If you're a writer and a reader, you go to the library or you go to Warwick's, you go to a bookstore and you find books that are about what you're going through and there was nothing on cancer and death because it was still considered unseemly. You weren't even supposed to say the word cancer because there was so much superstition, people might catch it. So, in Hard Laughter, I wrote a lot about our family, announcing it all the time, so we could deal with it in a way that was more authentic and that wasn't so guarded and girded. My dad and our really close friend, Susan, who had cancer at the same time, we would all sit outside the bakery in this tiny seaside town, and my dad would say, "Well, Susan, how is your cancer today?" But really loudly. Then Susan would say, "Well, my cancer is progressing. How is yours Ken?"

DN: I'm sure people loved hearing that. In your novel Hard Laughter, the main characters are tied together by fear and emptiness and loss and pain, and yet, I'm curious as to how you make these characters also so buoyant and fellowshipping with one another, and have even some hope about them during these painful lives they lead. How do you do that?

AL: Oh, God, I don't know. It sounds so wonderful to be able to do that. But I think that what you've just described sounds to me like most of the people I'm close to. They *are* people who have had a lot of pain and who have survived a lot and who are aware of a lot of darkness pressing in all around them as they go through their lives, and yet who are nurtured and enlivened by simple human love. Those that are not people of faith, and especially in the earlier books, when I was still a secular writer and—

DN: Wait—what does that mean?

AL: Well, I mean, the first three books I wrote, I was drunk, and I believed in God in a kind of ecumenical, let's-not-get-too-specific here-and-lose-our-minds kind of way. And then the next four books, from All New People and on, I was sober and a converted Christian. So there's always characters in the two novels since I got sober and converted, although I converted drunk, and that's another story, but there are characters who are people of the Christian faith.

But in the first three books, there are people who I just think have really ordinary human lives, which to me, means there's a lot of loneliness, there's a lot of disappointment, there's a lot of hope that certain things might pan out and fill up those holes that are inside. I think usually people are trying very, very hard to stuff themselves full of achievement, or reward, or finances, or romances, or whatever "-ances," and that just gets bigger and bigger the more you step into them.

But these are all books about people that are in community, because that's all I know; that's what's kept me alive, was the love of really great people. So probably, if you had to pick a theme, what you just described is a theme I write about: how people stay alive, how people survive, how people don't. It's like the last paragraph of *Bird By Bird* where it talks about being on that kind of rickety ship in a really bad storm at sea that if your heart is open, and you're trying to be a person of love and connection, then you get everybody singing and you transform it into something that's much much less chilling and hopeless.

I was teaching a couple years ago and I was meeting Sam's babysitter at this place where I was teaching and Sam said, "Are your students going to be famous?" And I said, "No, probably not. In fact, most of them won't get published." He said, "why do they write?" I said, "good question." And I said, "They write because they're living these very intense human lives and they're trying to make sense of it. They're trying to be undefeated by things that are very confusing and disappointing for them sometimes and they just want to understand life; they want to understand who they are, and why it matters that they live really fully." And he said, "Well,"—you know, he's forty pounds at the time—"I understand life." Isn't that wonderful? And I said, "What do you understand?" He said, "Pretty good, some problems." And I thought, "well that about says it!"

DN: Was writing *Crooked Little Heart* a way to grieve for you?

AL: I wrote a piece on grief when my friend died. And curiously, I went to Club Med. I'm like the world's worst traveler.

DN: Hold it—you went Club Med to grieve?

AL: I went to Club Med. I didn't know I was going to Club Med to grieve! I thought I was going to Club Med to get my mind off of it. And I got to Club Med and I could not stay one step ahead of it anymore. And I started to cry. It was scary because I could see that I wasn't going to be able to stop crying. And at Club Med, I mean, *a single tear*, it's like, well, "you're ruining this for all of us. There's 1,200 people here and you're ruining it for all of us, Mrs. Unhappy Face. You know, go to your room, you grieve in private."

You grieve in private and you put a nice face on and when you've cried for a bit, you splash cold water on your face, and you reapply some makeup and you go back out there and you become a flight attendant. And I went to Club Med and I started crying, and I couldn't stop and I came home. I didn't go around just sobbing all the time, but I had stopped pretending. I'd never cried about my dad's death. I've *sobbed* about my dad's death. I was a drunk, you know? I also cried about the dog we had that died when I was twelve. I'd go to bars, "don't get her started on the dog or her dad."

And I'd cry, and I'd cry, and I'd cry, but I didn't cry sober, and I didn't cry holding space for myself to connect with these *huge* amputations that happened to me. When I was young, at twenty-three, the world came to an end. By twenty-four, I was tending to my father as if he was an infant. I was too young to do that. My younger brother was nineteen. He was too young to do that. When I was thirty-seven, I did it with my best friend for two years, and I had to stop pretending that it hadn't just about killed me. So I wanted to write a book that said, in effect, these people found their way home by insisting on the right to feel what they felt and to know what they know: that it really hurts to be alive, to be human.

DN: If it hurts so much, doesn't writing about it hurt even more?

AL: No. It is often is like cleaning debris off of a lot. It helps me find out what it is I actually think about and what I actually know. It helps me capsulize some of it. It helps me find people that can act out the drama of humankind, you know, which is about birth, and it's about death, and it's about romance, and it's about relationships, and it's about children. I am an incredibly happy person. I may be getting so happy that I may have crossed over into some form of mental illness.

Chitra Divakaruni

CD: One of the things I like to show in my stories or like to explore in my stories is how life takes a very different course often from what we expect, and how life is full of surprises, and how the consolations and triumphs in life come from very unexpected directions.

DN: I'm thinking specifically about a character in *Sister of My Heart* who goes to her wedding with tremendous expectation, tremendous hope, and something happens at the wedding where you can just tell *right there,* that this marriage is not going to be what she thought it was going to be on her wedding day. And yet, by the end of the novel, we still have something to cling to.

CD: That is exactly what happens to her. I think that just goes to show, again, as human beings, we hold on to particular ideas, maybe even time-tested, or stereotypical notions of happiness. And we discover that happiness is something quite different.

DN: What would some of those stereotypical notions be?

CD: Well, in the case of *Sister of My Heart*, one of them, of course, is the idea of romance and marriage, which in the context of traditional Indian society, that's supposed to occur together. Both main characters in *Sister of My Heart* find that it's not that simple.

DN: There are other themes in your writing about people with certain expectations—coming to America, for instance—and those expectations change dramatically, similar to the expectations of what a marriage would be. Was that a purposeful idea of yours? Or is it just one of these reflections of what is part of the human experience?

CD: This was certainly a theme I wanted to consciously explore. I've said this before, in talking to you, that it seems like each age has its own myths and legends, and in the twentieth century, America is one of the last myths and legends that still exist.

DN: What does that mean?

CD: I think what that means is that, for many people all over the world who are planning to come to America, they view this as the *golden land*: the land where once you get here, everything will be all right—in fact, better than "all right"—everything will be perfect, everything you ever wanted, and you have an opportunity to get it. And so many people continue to come to America with this dream, and then find out that just like every other place, America has its problems. It has its good points, and then it has its negatives.

DN: There are some dark pieces to many of the things that you've written. Your writing always has some kind of theme about independence, and loyalty, and families, and tradition. There's also a lot of reference to domestic violence, and to crime, and to economic disparity, and abortion, and divorce. I'm wondering if your time working with the South Asian women in the Bay Area had an impact on introducing those kinds of dark pieces to your writing, or would that have happened anyway? In other words, has your real-world experience had an effect on what you write about?

CD: Yes, definitely. The numerous years I've been spending now working not only on the South Asian women's hotline, but also in mainstream shelters, has really made me sensitive to those issues, particularly issues of women's abuse. Also, the work I've done in general with my community has made me aware of the problems that immigrants face: problems dealing with racism, and inequality, and just being made to feel perhaps unwelcome in America. And so these issues become very important in my writing.

DN: Were you sensitive to those issues *before* you worked in these shelters, and in these groups?

CD: I was aware of them. I became aware of them, actually, pretty early, in my experience here. The second day that I was in America, something happened in my life, which later became a story in *Arranged Marriage*, called *Silver Pavements, Golden Roofs*, where I was out on a street, walking in my Indian clothes, and a group of teenagers came up and shouted names and called me "nigger" and told me to go home and threw slush at me. It was a very frightening and a very traumatic experience. So I was certainly aware of that, and it became something that made me suddenly realize that life in America was going to be very different from life in India, which had a number of challenges, but where my skin color had never been an issue.

DN: Which goes to the theme of expectations and having to alter those expectations.

CD: Right. But also the other side of that, what I found in America is that there have been wonderful things that I never expected in people who have been very kind, and very open, especially other ethnic groups with whom I felt so much at home, and friendships that I've been able to have, which I really wouldn't have had in India.

DN: Anybody who has tried to write and have small children in the house knows that can be a challenge. I read in a column where you said you realized you couldn't write about your children, but you *could* write about being a mother. Why one and not the other?

CD: Well, even writing about being a mother is difficult for me. But it's a more introspective and internal thing. When I try to write about my children, my emotions get in the way, and I don't see them clearly and objectively. However, having children has really helped me write about fictional characters who are parents and children, because I understand that relationship, the dynamics, the tension of that relationship, much better. When I write about my own children, I turn into mush.

DN: I believe you said it sounded like Hallmark cards.

CD: Bad ones.

DN: Is it because you're too close?

CD: I'm too close to them.

DN: So you can be too close to an experience?

CD: Oh, yes! In general, it takes me many years of internally processing an experience before i can start writing about it. My whole writing career started more than ten years after I moved over here. So I had to let that experience of immigration process itself for a number of years before I could start writing. I'm working on exploring another part of the immigrant experience. I think a number of these stories are going to focus on parent-child relationships. First of all, the parents that we leave behind in our home countries, when we emigrate to America. What happens to them? Their loneliness, their isolation when they're back home, but also when they come to join their loved ones here and discover that perhaps they don't fit into this lifestyle, and that they cannot really communicate anymore with their children, or their grandchildren. The other side of that is, of course, us as parents, bringing up our children in America, the second generation, children who are far more American than we will ever be. How do we connect to them? How do we pass on things to them? What do we pass on to them?

Ray Bradbury

DN: You told the *New York Times* years ago that "my business is to present the future."

RB: Prevent.

DN: Prevent! But a number of things from your books that you wrote about years later have actually happened. Here's just a partial list: the

Sony Walkman. I read about that in something you wrote forty years ago.

RB: That's in Fahrenheit 451.

DN: Lawns that grow to only a certain height and then they stop growing. I read about that in one of your books. Mechanical dogs. That was in Fahrenheit 451.

RB: Right.

DN: Interactive television, virtual reality technology.

RB: That's right.

DN: Space travel. Even references to "Who wants to be a millionaire?" in some of your books.

RB: Yeah, that's right.

DN: You said that you write to prevent the future and yet some of the things that you wrote about have in fact come true.

RB: Well, people weren't listening, were they?

DN: Can you see into the future?

RB: No. If you pay attention to what's going on in front of you, it's very easy to predict what's going to happen because human character doesn't change that much. The best thing I predicted and hoped for was space travel of course. Landing on the moon, and we've gotta continue. We've been doing things with the space shuttle the last fifteen years which is a bore. That's not where we belong, 200 miles above earth. We belong on the moon. We belong on Mars, goddamn it.

People always ask, "Do you write about dreams?" I say no. I write about a semi-dream state. Every morning, I just love that moment of waking up with an idea floating in my head. It's not a dream and it's not completely awake.

You might experiment with this. Maybe it won't work for some of you, but it's been working for me for years. Another good time is the shower. The water hits you and you have total relaxation and your brain's loose inside your skull and you can think anything you want to. Or sometimes taking an afternoon nap, you're not completely asleep and not completely awake. These are all good states for discovering stories that might be of some help to you.

Peter Matthiessen

DN: It seems that over the thirty or so books you've written, to me your best gift in writing is your ability to observe. You have some very, very keen observation skills, and those observations have this underlying concern for habitats, or species, or groups of people, who cannot defend themselves and cannot speak for themselves. Is that a conscious thing, or just something that became a theme in your work?

PM: It started pretty early. I've always been interested in how we've treated our Native People—American Indian people—which isn't very well by and large. And I discovered that there's an American Indian character in virtually all my early books, and in my nonfiction, too, so it was obviously something that was in my head. I wasn't thinking about it; I wasn't even particularly well-read on it, but it seemed to be there. It went right along with worrying about the whole natural world, natural North America, the new world, that all the first people who came here talked about—this great paradise on earth. We were not treating it well.

This is my way of protesting something that I find very, very painful.

Jon Foreman of Switchfoot (Interviewed by Karl Martin)

JF: I think the best ideas I've ever had were somebody else's. I mean, timeless, transcendent truth is not something I'm going to come up with. Those are the best songs—the times when you simply put something that's timeless in a frame and allow it to speak to somebody new.

One of the better metaphors about songwriting I've come up with is it's like an oyster with a grain of sand in it, and you wrestle with it. And sometimes, you come out with a pearl, and you can get rid of it, and you feel like you've gotten through it. But usually for me, I write about the same things every time. It's just the same irritant. The trick is for me to try and not write the same song because I think the same irritants exist in my life that existed when I was twenty-one.

Two of our singles center around the theme of entropy, and the idea of social entropy, and the idea that if gravity is the force that keeps bodies with mass attracted to each other, and keeps things—keeps us—here, glued on the planet, why is it that the social equivalent does not exist? Those are the types of things that you're kind of wrestling with in your head. You see in physics this kind of parallel universe. And you say, "Well, let's write a song about that." And maybe that will have a certain light to bear upon our social situation.

Amy Tan

DN: You said that there are things that make you either psychotic or a fiction writer. Is that what writing does, stave off psychosis?

AT: Perhaps I was exaggerating a little. I think that what I went through was something that caused me to ask a lot of questions in life and what I was trying to write about in that piece there was this dichotomy that I had between faith that my father had and faith that my mother had, and my trying to find something that worked for me. So as a writer, I think I got my origins from that period of mass confusion when so many terrible things happened. I needed to know what the right questions were, first of all, to ask before I could come up with the answers. I think it also happens to people who become troubled. They become mentally ill or psychotic. You begin to get overwhelmed by the questions or the circumstances in your life and you don't know how to deal with them either internally or externally with whatever resources you have.

Fiction is certainly a way of meditating on those, of coming up with the questions and also coming up with one set of answers via the form of a story.

DN: You still probably have the same questions now that you had when you were trying to sort out faith and fate.

AT: I do. And I think I'll always have them. They're the basic questions that I had when I was six years old. The question, how do things happen, why do things happen, how do I make things happen. What is my role in the universe?

I'm so grateful I had such a horrific childhood, because I have so much material now to draw from.

Garrison Keillor

GK: Childhood is very attractive to write about. It's also a place in your life where the memories stay clear for so long. I mean, whole big swatches of my late middle age I can't remember very well, but I can remember, I have very clear distinct memories, sometimes spotty, of when I was 4 and 5 and 6 years old. So it's a natural territory for a writer to deal with. It's a time when you are essentially powerless and you did not have the defenses that you will carefully build up for yourself later in life. You really are completely dependent on these strange people around you. You are so susceptible to cruelty and to meanness. One more reason to be grateful for growing up in evangelical culture and evangelical family, in which you know God himself is telling your parents to be careful. Be gentle. Be loving.

Chris Hillman (Interviewed by Karl Martin)

KM: You have said there is a difference between narrative songwriting and emotional songwriting. There's the songwriting that strives to tell a story and there's the songwriting that's a cathartic experience for the songwriter. The balance of those two seems to be very important.

CH: You could hear somebody utter a four-word phrase and it'll catch you—some stranger on the street or even a friend. Write it down. That can start the song process. Where it goes from there, sometimes it's beyond your control. You're really sort of guided through that. It could end up being something down here inside of you and it becomes cathartic, a catharsis where you get out something that is sitting inside of you.

Other times it can turn into some sort of narrative and a storyline. I had a song called "Desert Rose," which the band was named after—and I wrote that back in the early eighties. My daughter was about three. And at the time, we were going through some economic problems in this country, mostly in the northeast. A lot of people were leaving their families and going down to Houston to find work. And I wrote this song, "I Love My Sweet Desert Rose." My daughter's middle name is Rose, and so here's the song idea. The chorus was, "There ain't no money in our hometown and the mills have all shut down. They say there's work but it's always the next town." So there's this guy he says there's no work here, so go on to the next town. But he's left his home, he's left his daughter and his kids behind and it's eating him up. So there was a sort of story but there was an emotional bent to it.

Billy Collins

DN: It seems like you write about real stuff that all of us see—the sky, boats on a river, a barking dog, eating a piece of fish, listening to jazz. This is all stuff that we do too, and when we do it, it's just dull and routine. But when you talk about it, it seems really profound. Are all of your moments profound moments? Are you just that guy?

BC: I have a special gift, it's true. But not all of them are special. For instance, there are no moments *here* talking to you. Maybe later! If you're an artist or a writer, one takes on a kind of exploitive view of reality. Because you're always looking for potential material. You're looking for something to write about. And because there are only a few subjects in poetry, four or five, you know. Willa Cather, the fiction writer, said, "there are only four or five human stories." And she said, and this is a direct quote, "but we keep telling them as desperately as if we had never heard them before." Someone said that all science fiction is one of two stories—we go *there,* or they come *here.*

So, as a poet, if there are these four or five rooms of emotional content, one is just looking for metaphor ingresses. You're just looking for metaphoric ways in. So aging would be one of the five rooms. When I read in the *Tribune* that I was the same age as Cheerios, that seemed like a ripe opportunity to enter the world of aging. Because one of the themes of poetry is that we're not getting any younger.

DN: You've talked about poets being the kind of people who look out of a window and fiction writers looking in a window. Can you explain that?

BC: Well, I think if you're writing fiction or plays, you have to be extremely interested in other people. And if you're writing poetry, it's not necessary. You have to be interested in yourself. So, if you picture this architecturally, fiction writers are so curious about the private, not just domestic but sexual and psychological lives of others, that they can be pictured peering into the windows of strangers, or of other people. I would picture the poet as looking out his or her window at the world, and saying, "this is the way I see the world." Like, "I went out in the world and saw daffodils." There's no one else in this poem besides Wordsworth. I have very few people in my poems except me. The dog is there occasionally. In love poems, there's another person there, but usually there's nobody else. My parents are in my poems sometimes. My parents were never in my poems until after they were dead. Now I can write about them for some reason or another.

The fewer people you have in your poems, the more alone you are with the reader. I want to be completely alone with the reader in the poems. I mean, I'm happy to get up and read poems, and perform them or whatever. But I'm writing in silence for a person who's got a book in her hand or his hand. And I want to be alone with that person; I don't want to talk about mom and dad and my uncle. I actually don't even want to talk about anything about myself. I don't want to talk autobiographically. There's all these books and you wouldn't know much about me. You would know about this persona, who's not me, but a definite improvement over me. He's not burdened with the job, or family problems, or those kinds of things. He's more of a spectatorial figure. He's just looking at something out of no where. But he doesn't bring a knapsack full of autobiographical baggage with him and unload it on the reader. Because he assumes that the reader does not want that to be unloaded.

Lysley Tenorio

LT: Funny, sad, and beautiful are things I aspire to. Those are things I aspire for in the work. I like funny. If I have to sit with a set of characters for a particular plot for X number of hours a day, I want to at least be entertained. So if I can give myself a set of circumstances that on the surface seem funny, I'll at least be entertained. For example I have this story of these guys that beat up The Beatles in the Philippines. And it's a true story, The Beatles really did get beat up in the Philippines.

But I don't want to write fiction for the sake of telling a joke. That's not my job. My job is to try to illuminate various possible truths in a given narrative, so I want to find the polar opposite of that which is sadness and melancholy. I like the challenge of trying to take something that seems funny on the surface but maybe quietly sad or even quietly tragic. If you can relay that in language that is hopefully beautiful as well, you can take a moment from a zany situation and identify a real moment of beauty or even grace.

DN: You said in an interview, "To me, life is always complex, in life, in fiction as in life, no one is a pure winner, no one is a pure loser, no one is purely happy, no one is purely sad. That's what I am striving to render on the page."

LT: Okay. I think maybe I was drinking during that interview, I don't know. There's this sense of what I'm writing might be called literary fiction.

DN: How is literary fiction different from fiction?

LT: Literary fiction, in my understanding, really is a category. Here's work by someone like Toni Morrison that is complex—and I'm not comparing myself to Toni Morrison—but here's work by Toni Morrison that is complex and layered, and it's concerned with layers and with language and is meant to be emotionally as well as intellectually substantial. On other shelves you have the spy thriller that's just for fun, where you just want to get immersed, and won't necessarily be in an academic study as an artistic artifact.

DN: It won't be anthologized

LT: It won't be anthologized. I am pursuing what one might call the literary fiction route, but I'm not even comfortable with that term. I sometimes feel like I'm in a community that tries to separate highbrow from lowbrow. When I grew up I liked what might be called lowbrow things.

DN: That's okay, I mean you're acting like you're ashamed of it. We want to celebrate and receive your confession.

LT: No, no, I repent. So a show like "Buffy the Vampire Slayer" is very entertaining, but it's also smartly written. What I like about "Buffy the Vampire Slayer" or even comic books for that matter—when they're well done, they transcend their own subject matter. So much of the show "Buffy the Vampire Slayer" worked with the idea of monsters and vampires on a metaphorical level. If you read interviews with Joss Whedon who created Buffy, his whole take was that high school is Hell so I'm going to actually manifest demons and Hell to show that high school really is a troubling thing. So it's a little tongue in cheek, but if you get invested in the narrative enough, it can actually become quite moving.

I feel like my relationship to that kind of material helps me with my work so that when I'm writing a story about the making of a really bad monster movie, it might be easy enough to laugh at that, and I kind of laugh at them too, but as I said before, my real job is to find the seriousness in it, to give these people, these individuals who might have what we might find as silly goals, to give them humanity and to give them dignity. So I need to find what is serious underneath the whimsical.

DN: You really like the musical group The Carpenters.

LT: Right. The Carpenters were like this cheesy band, but if you know Karen Carpenter's story, she had a very tragic life. She died of anorexia. That's what really got the idea of anorexia into the national conversation—that was a real problem with young women. So when you listen to what might seem like these cheesy, overly joyful songs, Karen Carpenter's voice and the tenor of her voice really relays a kind of ache. And that's a really interesting juxtaposition, because here's this kind of bouncy, happy music that you can just bop your head along to, but if you really stop and listen to her voice—where it's not just *what* she's singing or what she sang but it's *how* she sang it. It's that voice she's using to express these lyrics that gives it a sense of irony, of a multi-layered-ness.

There's one song in particular and it's called "Top of the World," and it's this very bouncy song. But there's this one line—"tomorrow will be just the same for you and me"—a very cheesy A-B rhyme scheme. But it's the way she sings the word "same." Like if you really stop and listen, when she sings the word "same," I detect this very quiet desperation and sadness. It's almost like a plea, and I'm not saying she meant that consciously but she just possesses this kind of quality to her voice. I like the fact that on the surface you have something that seems maybe shallowly joyful but underneath is this layer, this life of sadness.

DN: There's a real melancholy to her voice.

LT: I'm trying to do that with some of what I'm writing about.

If you can't figure out what you want to write about, ask yourself what you are obsessed with. I think one of the obsessions I had growing up, not even just as a writer but as a human being, is what home means. Where are you your truest self? I always imagine that's where home should be, and I think part of that might come from the fact that my parents referred to the Philippines and to America as home.

Destin Daniel Cretton (Interviewed by Karl Martin)

KM: The film "Short Term Twelve" gives viewers a glimpse into a day at a home for troubled adolescents and the counselors who work with them. The genesis of this story comes from your own work in a similar home. What was the process of adapting personal experience into a screenplay?

DDC: It's a wonderful process to go through as just a personal learning experience, and as a way to analyze and work through things that you experienced. I didn't start writing the short film screenplay until about three years after I had worked there. I worked there for two years and then I went to film school and it was my thesis project at film school. I think that distance was important for me. To be able to see it not just as my experience but to be able to see it as something that I was now a bit outside of and I could create into something that other people could relate to. It started from just going through my journals I had written at that time and some of the stories that I had written initially just to process—there was no thought in my mind of turning it into a film. But some of those things that I read just really hit me. So a lot of it was just putting that straight into the screenplay, and then combined it with interviews I did with other people at other facilities who worked in similar situations.

Joyce Carol Oates

DN: There are so many themes in your writing that I kept picking up on in your short stories, your essays, or your novels. There's racism, there's alienation, there's poverty, sex, feminism, serial killers, family disintegration, criminality, greed, fame, and celebrity.

JCO: I'm sure you've left something out. Rollerskating.

DN: Rollerskating wasn't a theme.

JCO: It is in upstate New York. It was a part of my childhood.

DN: Right, right, but all of the stories you write seem to have these underlying things of that list that I just gave you.

JCO: Oh, I really write about people. I write about human beings, people who react to one another. Some of these issues are sort of peripheral. But most writers write about people, not about sexism, or sex, or violence.

You can't exactly write about violence. You have to write about people. There's not violence in every sentence, but they're doing other things, and there's a little story. They undergo some transformations and maybe they come out stronger than they were before. I think most writers are interested in telling stories about human beings. And the themes that people see in the work sometimes are surprising to the writers.

DN: What has surprised you about what people have found in what you've done?

JCO: Well, Faulkner, for instance, said he writes about the truths of the human heart, and probably that's what most writers would say. And if you're Faulkner, then you're also writing about the American South, you're writing about the defeat of the Confederacy, you're writing about racism, so forth, because that's part of your story of your life. But basically it's about the human dilemma. That we yearn for so much that we can't really realize . . . that we love people and we want to protect and save them, but we have to relinquish them. Eventually we lose everything, and eventually we die ourselves. And this great mystery is so profound that it's a story that people keep telling over and over and over again in different ways because it's the human story.

DN: You mentioned Faulkner—a couple of your books really felt like Faulkner. You were getting inside the head and motive and backstory and point of view from all of the different characters in a story. Usually a story comes from a particular point of view—there's a narrator—but you're telling the same story from all of these different perspectives.

JCO: I'm very interested in human personality and different voices. So for me, it's an exciting idea to take one episode, you know, and then there are different people who witness it from their different perspectives and they see it somewhat differently though it's the same thing. And they have different voices—to me that's just very exciting to hear different people speaking. I try to really bury my own narrative voice sort of in the background so allowing the characters to speak.

DN: In the book, *The Faith of a Writer*, you have two sentences that sum up why we do what we do. The first sentence was: "The writer's first thought is: 'I have to tell.' And the second thought is: 'How do I tell it.'"

JCO: That's right. How do we do it, that's the challenge. I have written a good deal about race situations. Sometimes from the point of view of a white person. Sometimes from the point of view of a Black person. I grew up fascinated by this division in the United States. But since Ferguson, Missouri, it's become such a conscious thing in the culture now, which is really wonderful. But I think there are many many many *many* white people, the great majority of white people, are not racist at *all.* But the racism is almost like a toxic clot of invisibility, and we don't know there's racism going on—it's hurting fellow Americans, but it doesn't hurt us, so we don't see it.

Now we know a lot more about police brutality and so forth. I have to say I really didn't know much—I didn't know much about this when I was growing up. Sure it was going on, of course, but we didn't really know much.

DN: So, walk us through your thinking in one of your books, and I'm thinking in particular the one that just came out, *The Sacrifice*. And apply this "I have to tell and how do I tell it" kind of thing. I assume that somewhere along the line the Tawana Brawley story from the '80s was still percolating in your head after it occurred, and you're still wanting to write about racism at some point. I mean your book *Them* being that precursor to the race riots in Detroit. So at what point were you thinking with *that* book, "that's a story I have to tell?"

JCO: I had always wanted to write a novel from the point of view of a Black family. I lived in Detroit at the time of the riot in 1967. That was a long time ago. There's always a little ripple of terror when you mention it—people say "What? I didn't quite hear that." But it was July in 1967 and my husband at that time and I were in a house, only about two blocks away from looting and burning and there were sirens and gunshots. We sort of huddled in this house in Detroit in a residential neighborhood. It was very shocking, and it was like being in a war zone. And as time went on, after that—I remember the emotions very well—I really wanted to write about that experience, like what led up to it? And what caused it to erupt that night down on 12th Street in the inner city of Detroit? Why was it that night, what was going on? So I wrote a novel called *Them*, which is about white people. But at the time there wasn't really much known.

As the decades have gone by, there have been many many books about what is called civic disorder in the United States, which usually means some sort of riot that might be attributed to race and police brutality. These civil, civic disturbances all around the country have been written about, and so I was able to do research, and know a lot more about the city I was living in. This time I wanted to write about a Black family. Therefore, the Tawana Brawley case seemed a very appropriate plot to connect with that theme because it was a tabloid phenomenon, which many people today have probably forgotten. But it was an event, it was almost like a *non* event, because it was a hoax. It didn't happen, but it got into the media, and then one thing led to another and all these articles and tabloids and *New York Times* and so forth, it just became like a huge snowball and it got enormous, and yet there was nothing actually to it.

So I wanted to write about that phenomenon, of the how the media could take something and trump it up and exaggerate it even though probably some of the people in the media might have known, might have guessed that it wasn't authentic. So part of writing the novel was to deal with the media.

Regarding Family Secrets

Many families have secrets, things that are not exactly discussed openly among children. So children aren't aware of something that happened right at the periphery of your vision. I was well aware of that, but I didn't really know specifically that my mother's father had been murdered, I didn't know that till I was quite an adult. But I probably had a sense of there being something not quite right. And my mother had then been given away because she was from a large family of nine children. She was just a baby; she wasn't even one year old. Consequently, because my grandfather had been killed, she was given away to a childless couple. So the whole trajectory of that family was broken by the death of the father, and then my mother was put in a different home. And so she had a new story. Basically, she had a new life. She was their only child, whereas with the other, she would have been one of *nine* children. So, she had like a different identity. And my brother and I, of course, were born to my mother in that new identity.

Many crimes and acts of violence are enacted among our ancestors or our older relatives. They may not tell you about it. You may not know about it. But some great disappointment, or your mother was viciously treated by her first lover or something, so she married somebody else. There are all these stories that probably you'll never know, but they're kind of all at the boil. I think I have been influenced by many of these things. And I love to write about that. I love to write about how something that seems like a crime in one generation, as it works out, it wasn't that bad. The consequences were not going to be ultimately that bad for the younger people. It actually turned out to be like a happy story. Because my mother was given away from a very poor family to a family not so poor, then we were born. I went to college, and I became a professor. I don't think probably if my mother had stayed in that other family, very, very poor, huge family, I don't think it would've been the same story. Of course I wouldn't have been born, so it's irrelevant.

But if you trace these family stories and junctures in your life that seem like a bad event, if you look back at it from another point of view, maybe it was good? You know, that things turned out, *therefore*, and then this happened, and this happened, and *then* this happened, and it actually turns out to be pretty good. It's like what's called grace, that sort of working in some invisible way, we don't really know what name we're to give it. But it's not necessarily a negative thing. It may seem that way superficially.

So I actually write about that quite a bit. Sometimes I even use—well, I don't use the word "grace," but I'm thinking about that. The mysterious workings of some sort of fate, even though the superficial, like you mentioned all those things like violence and all that, those are like the superficial things. But, I'm really writing about the truths of the human heart that are deeper. So, the violence in a play like *Hamlet,* particularly in *Macbeth,* there's a lot of violence, and there's a fair amount of violence in *Othello,* and *King Lear* also. The acts of violence are more or less on the surface, but the deeper changes in personality are beneath the surface, and that's why that's a work of art. I mean, *King Lear's* a great work of art not because of the things on the top, but because of the deeper and compelling transformations of Lear.

DN: Let's talk about boxing for a second. You became an expert in boxing—writing about it. And two of your observations about boxing have stayed with me. One is that "boxing is primarily about being and not giving hurt." About being and not giving hurt. That sounded to me like, just, living. Right? That's a lot like just trying to get through your existence, isn't it? So it was a great parallel there.

JCO: I wrote a lot about boxing; I've said many different things about boxing. And my feelings about it have probably evolved in different ways. It's very complex. I never thought of boxing as a sport. I thought of boxing as almost like theater, theater of cruelty and cultural drama of some kind, almost like tragedy—Greek tragedy.

Carlos Ruiz Zafon

CZ: My book *The Shadow of the Wind* tries to be many things. There's the issue of the past, there is the issue of moral consequence, and the consequence of actions and how our actions have consequences not just for ourselves, but for the people around us through time. It is a story about fathers and sons, how the sins of the father get passed upon the son, and the grandson's, and different generations, and how everything we do, our every single action, has a moral consequence. This is one of the themes that the book wants to explore.

DN: In this book and in *The Cemetery of Forgotten Books,* memory is crucial to these characters and to a country.

CZ: Not just to a country, I think to the human identity. I think we are what we remember. The less we remember, the less we are. When I was starting working on this novel, I was very concerned about that, maybe because I was living in LA, and LA is a city in which you see the past being erased every single day. There's kind of an industry of destruction of memory. My novel was coming from a very old city in which you can touch the stones of twenty centuries, when you walk around in twenty minutes, in contrast with California, such a new place. It seems like every night when you go to sleep, there's the brigade that gets out there and starts erasing the past. And next morning, you're driving around, and you say, "Wait a minute. What was here?" It has just disappeared. And nobody remembers, not even you. "What the hell was here? They just tore it down, and I don't know what was here."

I was very interested in this process, and I thought that essentially people, all of us, we are the things we know, the things we remember, and if we don't remember anything, we don't know who we are, we don't know where we're coming from, we don't know where we are going, and we're easy to lead one way or another. This was something that at the time—and I'm talking the late '90s, which was at the time where I started working on this series of four novels, of *The Cemetery of Forgotten Books*—that intrigued me enormously.

So I came up with this visual metaphor for the destruction of memory. It was just *The Cemetery of Forgotten Books*, a part of being a very cool scenery, and a labyrinth of things. It's a metaphor for many things, not just for forgotten books. It is for forgotten identities, for forgotten ideas, for all of those things that make us human, that we are forgetting every day, because we have other more pressing concerns.

It is like science fiction. Science fiction sets stories in the future or in different timelines, but we're actually writing about the present. So when you're writing historical fiction, you're always writing about the present and you're writing for your contemporaries.

Nikki Giovanni

DN: You have said that you can write things now that your mother is gone.

NG: Mmhmm.

DN: Like what? Why couldn't you write it when she was alive?

NG: My mommy died, and the first thing I did I legally changed my name. Because I'm Yolande Cornelia Giovanni Jr. by birth. And I would never have changed it when mommy was here. But when she left, I changed it to Nikki so that I am officially Nikki Giovanni. So that was the one thing that I did.

And I've gotten to rethink my father, because my father had issues. He was married to her, he wasn't married to me, and I needed to put it aside, because it was none of my business. And now that he's gone, I need to rethink the things I saw. I learned to say it onstage, that if you asked me what I was doing at 11 o'clock on any Saturday night, I was listening to my father hit my mother. And that's something I just had to put in the back of my mind, because there was nothing I could do about it. And now that she's sitting in heaven, I can sit there and say, ". . . and that disturbed me." So now I can begin to explore, because I'm a writer. I can begin to explore what did he get out of it? And why would that happen? I don't pick on men, but you have to wonder, how did that happen?

Robin Jones Gunn

RG: When a story taps into that echo, as you've called it, we feel the camaraderie and we want to be friends with that main character. We want to journey with them. We get to see what they're really thinking and feeling, and we say, "I feel that way, too. But I'm not going to tell anybody."

DN: That's one of the great things about fiction is that people can read it and say, "I so identify with this character" but they don't have to tell anybody; they feel like they have told somebody because they've seen it in her in a story. Is this a conscious thing with you where you say, "When I write a book, I want to give a positive view about relationships and values and love?" Are you starting out with a premise of "I want something positive for my audience to read"?

RG: Absolutely, absolutely. I want love to triumph and I want the characters to see who they are and grow through that, and also to have hope. Every story I write, I want it to have hope, because we need that as humans; we need to feel that it's going to be all right, or "I can get through this."

When I wrote the second *Christy Miller* book, the publisher asked for me to do it a lot quicker than the first one. I think it took two years for the first one, but I think they gave me six months to write the second one. I was working, working, working, and I had it all figured out: Christy's parents are gonna get a divorce, and her brother's going to end up in the hospital. Christy is going to develop an eating disorder, and I was researching everything on bulimia I could find. I wrote about three-fourths of the story, and my editor wanted to see it to see how far I was coming along. I sent it to her and then I also showed it to some of the girls in the youth group that had wanted to read it. One of the girls picked up the pages and just threw it at me and she said, "I have to live this stuff! I don't want to read it too! Christy's parents can't get divorced, her brother can't be in the hospital. She has to make it through high school without throwing up and trying to make herself lose weight!"

DN: Wow.

RG: "Like, let all that happen to her friends, but Christy, she's my role model." And I went, "Okay, okay, now I know if we're going to be able to continue a series Christy has to be experiencing all these teen issues but in terms of those around her and how she responds, and reacts, and enters in or doesn't, but we can't destroy Christie after the first book; we loved her you can't do that to her."

DN: They got so attached to her. You would think you would want to read something that was similar to what you're going through, because then you get that "me too" kind of feeling. But these girls were saying, "Yeah, but not that close."

RG: Because at the core, it *was* a romance. Christy and Todd—we want a happy ending. Don't take us so far down that we don't think we're ever going to get back home. We want to ride along with her with her ups and downs, but we want to feel hope for all the things we're going through that this is gonna be okay.

Chris Bohjalian

CB: I knew in 2010, when I decided to embark once again on this material about the Armenian genocide, that no one is going to read a novel about 1.5 million dead in the desert. So I thought about the kinds of books that I love to read. I've always loved big, sweeping, epic love stories set in the midst of war, such as Michael Ondaatje's, *The English Patient*, a love story set in the Second World War in North Africa and Italy, or *Atonement* by Ian McEwan, a big sweeping epic love story set against the heroic retreat from Dunkirk. I also wasn't writing *The Sandcastle Girls for* my Armenian, or the Assyrian, or the Greek communities because we know the story. It was our families who either were slaughtered or against all odds managed to survive.

I was writing *The Sandcastle Girls* for my readers in Indianapolis, or Jacksonville, or Houston who couldn't find Aleppo on a map. Further stacking the deck to ensure Americans read the novel, I thought, let's make one of the lovers an American girl. Mount Holyoke, a Women's College in Massachusetts, had an Armenian and English-speaking seminary in what is today Eastern Turkey, but is the historic Armenian heartland. So, I decided to make one of the lovers an American girl, Mount Holyoke class of 1915, who ventures to Aleppo with her father to bring aid to the Armenians there, but instead finds the innermost ring of Dante's Inferno.

Nnedi Okorafor

DN: So much of African literature is rooted in the past, but you write about Africa, Nigeria in particular, and you connect that past to the future. Why the different approach?

NO: First of all, why not? I think in every part of the world people should be imagining what the future there would be like. That's necessary. But for me, it really started with the trips I took back to Nigeria with my family when I was younger. Those were pivotal. First, there was the American experience I was having, where we were one of the first Black families to move into the neighborhood in South Holland, Illinois, a south suburb of Chicago. It was extremely racist, so we were dealing with that.

Our parents came from Nigeria in 1969 for school and they ended up staying. They viewed the United States as a place where there was racism and all of these problems, but it was also a place of opportunity. They started taking us back to Nigeria during the holidays. And those trips, especially early on, were pivotal to my sense of self, my identity, my worldview, all of that. We went from dealing with a very racist environment, and then going to another part of the world that was all Black and there was no racism. But there was something called tribalism. You have family there, and you're part of there, but you're also part of this in the United States It was a lot.

As I grew older, I started understanding and noticing the politics and the political situations and the complexity of those dynamics. And I realized there was also technology. It was that technology that started making me think about what would the future be like here? Because the technology started showing up in these really organic ways, in the most, at least to my eye, the most peculiar places and unexpected places. Places where there previously was barely any technology, like the villages of southeastern Nigeria where there would be homes, but there would be no running water or electricity. We're talking very rural parts, like my father and my mother's ancestral land. And cell phones started showing up in these places before there was running water.

It just leapfrogged over those structural things. You had these cell phones that were bringing all this information. Also, there would be one house that would get cable, and the two networks they got were MTV and BET.

DN: They didn't get TMZ too?

NO: They didn't get anything but those two channels. The way cell phones just became part of the world was really fascinating to me. That's where I started thinking, "Okay, what is this place gonna be like in the future? What are the possibilities?" The possibilities I started thinking about were really interesting, and that's what made me start writing it.

DN: You've got racial and gender equality running through most of your work; political violence is in a lot of it. The destruction of the environment, genocide, corruption, and then you also have these really strong themes of friendship, and ancient wisdom, risk-taking, all with really really really strong female characters. So, are you just absorbing what you're seeing around you?

NO: I think a large part of it is absorbing. It's not that I think "I wanna write one book that has genocide, female genital mutilation, child soldiers, deals with patriarchy,"—I didn't sit down to write all that in one book. But when I started writing, it all came forth. It all came forth.

I'm very sensitive to the stories of the people around me. I'm always listening and taking it in. So when you sit down to write, you dig from within and you dig from those places of energy that shine or burn brightly. So that's where all of that comes from. It's not that I have an agenda. I don't. Not a conscious agenda. There are certainly things I'd like to see change, but when I'm writing, it's not something I think of specifically. It just comes forth.

DN: One of the things that I think also comes forth in everything of yours that I've read, whether it's a short story, or a comic, or a novel, is the fundamental issue of identity. Almost all of your main characters are different from everybody else in some way. It might be skin color, might be their hair, it might be special gifts, but there's always some kind of a dimension of outcast and different and not fitting in. Would you agree that that's running through there also?

NO: Yes and no. The yes part is that the issue of identity is something that is always central to me. Especially being Nigerian American. But I'm also aware and interested. I could have easily said, "I don't have any interest in going back to Nigeria, I don't have any interest in that part of my culture." But I've always been interested, like deeply interested and aware of the dialogue around being American and being Nigerian and how those come into conflict and how those work together sometimes. I've always been aware of that, and I've always grappled with it.

DN: Based on what you just described, you didn't fit in.

NO: It's like you fit in, but you don't fit in. For example, being Black in the United States, I fit into the African American community. But at the same time, I don't have the same history. So I've dealt with the racism, I've dealt with the worst of it—or some, not the worst, but you know what I mean.

DN: No, actually I don't. I'm a white guy, so no.

NO: But you still know what I mean.

DN: I've read about it.

NO: I'm kind of that outside inside thing. Of belonging, but not belonging. The same goes with being Nigerian, where I am outside and inside. So there are those issues of identity. And it's not just in terms of being Nigerian American. I was an athlete, but when I wasn't on the tennis court or on the track, I was in the library. That's the conflict between being a jock and a nerd. Those are the stereotypes, and I was both of those.

DN: You can't be both, though!

NO: Exactly. Well, you're not supposed to be both. But I was definitely both, like strongly both. I was female athlete of the year in Illinois. At the same time, I was all about books. I consumed books like candy. When I wrote "Binti,"—Binti means "girl" in Arabic—so in my head I'm writing about an average girl who has an extraordinary adventure. But when you read it, you see that she's a mathematical genius, and she goes on to do all these amazing things. This is her story. So there's the idea of her just being an average girl, and then her being extraordinary. I'm on both sides with that.

DN: The female characters in your books are a violent bunch. They like to fight, they like violence, they're drawn to chaos. Why can't your characters just get along?

NO: I have to admit, I think a lot of that comes from me. There's a reason why I was an athlete. But it's not that I like violence. It's not that.

DN: Your characters do.

NO: My characters do, but a lot of times they are exhibiting things that either I'm thinking about or I wish I could do. So I don't quite know—I haven't figured out exactly why or where, but there definitely is a part of me—I mean I'm wearing a Godzilla t-shirt. I love Godzilla.

DN: A lot of people wear Ghandi, but no not you. We're going Godzilla.

NO: Godzilla comes out of the water and just destroys everything, and sometimes there's no reason. I like that. I like Kaiju. That's part of why I was attracted to apocalyptic fiction, just seeing everything destroyed is something—this sounds really bad—that is very, very prevalent in me. There is rage in me, there is that angry Black woman in me, and you can call it a stereotype or whatever, but there is a lot to be enraged about. A lot. And I put a lot of that in my fiction. I channel a lot of that into my stories.

The books *Who Fears Death* and *The Book of Phoenix* came when I was in dark places for completely different reasons. *Who Fears Death* was inspired by the passing of my father. The way that it happened with him was disturbing. He was a cardiovascular surgeon, one of the chiefs of surgery in Chicago. And he passed from congestive heart failure and Parkinsons. Parkinsons makes your hands shake. So what is one of the prized possessions of a surgeon when they do open-heart surgery? Steady hands. I watched this for five years. When he passed, I was angry as all hell. I was angry. So when I wrote "Who Fears Death," it was inspired by just how I felt during his wake keeping. The very first scene was drawing off something I felt and dealt with. When I wrote it, I had no idea where it was going. I just started writing this story, this character. I didn't know who she was. As I wrote it, these other narratives kind of spun into the hurricane. That was the story.

Those narratives tend to be dominated by women, strong African women dealing with patriarchy. Those are narratives I've been hearing all my life. I never thought, "Okay, this is a story of a strong African woman dealing with patriarchy." It wasn't like that. It was very much I was just gathering these stories, I would listen to my female relatives, my mother and my aunts and cousins, and I would listen and I would watch, and these narratives were just there. So when I sat down to write *Who Fears Death*, all of those came forth. I didn't hold back anything. I was like I'm just writing this thing, I'm not going to worry about how this sounds, I'm going to revel in the pain, I'm going to write truth. So that was where all that came from. It was all very much not planned. But it was drawing off of things that were around me.

DN: Wasn't it also informed by what was happening in the Sudan at the time?

NO: Yes. As I was writing it I came across a narrative of a woman who was in the Sudan. She was a Black Christian woman who was talking about how the Janjaweed—the men on horses—had attacked her, and then the women in her village. One of the things I always look for in these narratives are the women's voices, the specific women's voices. Not someone telling what she said, but her speaking. This was in the *Washington Post*. I contacted the journalist to thank her because it's rare that we get their actual voices. I know why some of them don't want to speak, but this was clear. It was brutal and disturbing and detailed. I remember taking that story and putting it right into "Who Fears Death," and that's why that particular scene reads like that, because that scene is not just fiction at all.

DN: It was clearly about rape being used as a weapon.

NO: Yes, yes. The news story I was reading called it "weaponized rape." It blew my mind because this is genetic warfare that they are enacting. Whether they're conscious of it or not, they're trying to basically plant their own genetics in these women—because these were Arab men doing this to Black African women. And in that culture, if a woman has a child, that child is the man's, so by doing that, they are breaking the bloodline. That's really deep. That's some serious evil. I remember being absolutely shocked by that, and I knew it would have to go in the book.

DN: The inspiration for Binti, where she sneaks out of the house at night, doesn't tell her parents, so she can go to college on a different planet . . .

NO: Yes, with aliens.

DN: You snuck out of your own house to take a teaching job in Buffalo, New York. Are you saying Buffalo is like going to another planet?

NO: One of the faculty at Buffalo asked me that exact question: "We're not the aliens, are we?" I mean, not so much. But in the context of coming from a very insular Nigerian American family in Chicago where none of us leaves, this idea of leaving is like breaking up the family. And yeah, Buffalo, in some ways, is like another planet in the winter, I will say that.

DN: Didn't your daughter give you the idea for this book?

NO: She gave me the plot. There was a major plot point where I was stuck, and my daughter—she's fifteen—and she's always around me. Some writers have to go hide in the log cabin to go write and leave their family and everything. That doesn't work for me. I write with my daughter there, from when she was a baby to now. So I'd be writing and I got to a point in the story where I was a little bit stuck, where I'm like, "okay, I don't know what happens next." My daughter always knows the summaries of all of my stories as I'm writing them because I tell her and she's always interested. And so I'm like, "I'm stuck in this part, what should happen next?" And she gave me a major plot point and it worked. She's awesome.

DN: A lot of the things that I brought up have been about rage and evil, but there's this beautiful scene in "Akata Warrior" where the friends reach out to touch the points of their knives to one another and the Sunny character can suddenly see them and herself completely and feel love. Are you drawing from something where you just felt completely loved?

NO: I wouldn't say drawing specifically from something, but that was an important moment for me. Because she had her own insecurities and she was seeing herself through the eyes of someone who really admired her and really saw her as a necessary friend who loves her. I think everyone should feel that moment. For this character to have that, it was almost like she was being fortified for what was to come. Like, whatever comes at her, she now had this shield against anything, any negative thing to come at her, because she was able to see herself through the eyes of someone who loves her. That's a powerful thing.

DN: She had the shield of community, of being loved by others. It was a beautiful moment. It wasn't all just fighting. Although I'd like to bring up one thing about fighting. I'm back to "Who Fears Death" regarding the strong women characters. Here's this great quote: "Like those disgusting men outside the tavern, they hadn't heard me until they feared me." That sounds like something in the present culture.

NO: There's a lot of that in "Who Fears Death." With issues of patriarchy in the Nigerian community, I listen and sometimes participate and sometimes fight. There are things that you'll hear, not just things that are said, but also those things that are unsaid; there is societal pressure where you won't be heard unless you do something profound—be it something violent or something that's greatly admired. Women who want to be heard sometimes must resort to the extreme to be heard. There are several lines like that in "Who Fears Death" where I'll come at things from the side, but every so often just go right for it. Almost like a snake. Rattlesnakes will go to the side and then they'll strike and then move back. In "Who Fears Death" I do that a lot. It just felt like the right way to write that book. There are some things where I had to just strike, and that was definitely one of those lines—there were several in there.

DN: But I wasn't even looking at it from a Nigerian context. I was looking at it as a present context in the United States, where I thought you were saying, "If women are going to be heard in this culture, we have to be afraid." People like me have to be afraid of you.

NO: There has to be that element. Things are specific, but are also universal. So, where I'm talking about patriarchy in Nigeria, that can be applied worldwide, easily, easily. It sounds dark, but it is what it is.

Christian Wiman

DN: You tell a story in an essay about confronting your father. He strikes you. And then you strike him. Very shortly after that, in this essay, you have moved away and started writing poetry, "to get as far away from all of that as you can." Was that one of the motivations for writing poetry—to not be a part of that whole West Texas thing you were involved in?

CW: Oh, definitely. Poetry seemed to me as far as I could get from the life I grew up in. I had never met anyone who had read poetry. It was never a part of my life and the people that I knew were hard scrabble and rough and it just wouldn't have existed in that context at all. Initially, I thought I was going into poetry for that reason. I'll go into the furthest thing I can find. But then it turned out that the kind of intensity I had discovered in poetry, matched up pretty closely with the kind of intensity that I thought I was fleeing. Those two things were fused in a way. Partly it was a form of energy. The form of the art had a kind of crackling energy to it that I recognize from the emotional dynamics of my childhood. But then the subject matter just started coming into my poems and I wrote poems about a lot of those people that I'd grown up with.

DN: You have said that sometimes you don't even feel like you write poems, it's like poems happen to you.

CW: Sometimes that's true and I can point to those very poems. It's definitely not true of all of them. Some of them I work on for a long time. I've carried poems and not been able to finish them for a decade, so those I feel like I have more hand in. But some of the others do feel like they just happen, like those are the gifts. Those are the ones you can't even be proud of, really. It's like something that happened to you and there they are.

DN: Let's talk about memoir. You're not a fan, as I recall.

CW: I think I did write something critical at one point.

DN: Let me tell you what you said. You were actually quoting Blake when he said, "imagination had a higher plane than memory." Blake wasn't big on memoir either. But why are we so drawn to memoir? That's one of the biggest genres there is, bigger than poetry!

CW: Thanks <laughing>

DN: So what's your problem?

CW: You know, I don't know. I wrote that when I was young.

DN: You want to know what else you said about it?

CW: No, no, no.

DN: You called it a symptom of failing cultural imagination.

CW: I'm not sure I disagree. It does seem to me that it probably is a symptom of cultural failure, of cultural lack of imagination that we need to attach these things to real life. We can't handle a work of art. We don't respond to a work of art in the same way. I don't read memoir much. Almost never. I don't think of my books as memoirs. They get marketed that way because it sells them, but I just don't see how my book is a memoir. It has some elements but not much.

DN: But memoir is big.

CW: I know, believe me. I've had pressure put on me to write a straightforward memoir.

Alice Walker

AW: I was in Kenya when I was a teenager trying to help build a school out of stalks. I overheard some of the people talking about the women having their bath—this was a euphemism for female circumcision, cutting away everything. It took me twenty years after understanding what they were talking about to actually get my courage together—and my finances and my housing—to write *Possessing the Secret of Joy*. During that 20 years, millions of children were harmed by this practice. I felt that I could help make a child's life free of that fear, and free of the consequences. Because the consequences—many people think, you know, they call it circumcision and it's nothing like that—you could be sick for the rest of your life. Incontinent for a while. Just terrible things you don't even want to hear about.

To be able to contribute to the ending of this practice, that was joyful.

DN: So you started with "I want to really change it" when you began writing that book?

AW: Definitely.

DN: You said back in the '80s, "the Black woman writer is not taken as seriously as the Black male writer." Do you still think that's true?

AW: Well, I don't remember saying that, but it probably was true.

DN: You said it back in the '80s. I just want to know if you still feel that way.

AW: I don't think about that much anymore. The novel that recently just completely blew me out of the water was *The Water Dancer* (by Ta-Nehisi Coates). What I love about it is Black male writers have "caught up," not to be making them mad by saying it this way. But Black women writers have had to be both women and men in writing. We have had to create men and women as real human beings. And a lot of Black male writing, because of misogyny, it was impossible for the writers to actually see women, to really see us as we have had to see them.

So I think now we're more the same. When I was reading *The Water Dancer* I was so delighted because those male and female characters are fully seen and felt. It's just lovely.

Katie Manning

DN: You write a lot about bodies, the human body. Women's bodies, your body. I saw this really interesting parallel in your chapbook, "*28,605 Nights*," where you have a line about your grandmother: "Your body of work is other people's bodies," which I thought was amazing. And in your book, "*Tasty Other*," you have all of these different ways of measuring the baby growing inside of you, inside your own body of work. You're measuring your grandmother's body, but you're also measuring this baby's body and your own body. Is this a conscious thing, that you're always aware of bodies?

KM: I didn't necessarily set out to be a body poet, but I did have a professor in my master's program say, "We can never experience poetry outside of our bodies." When we're writing poetry, we really need to be speaking to other people's bodies. So we need the sensory language that's going to communicate and allow other people to feel what we're talking about. I started writing poetry when I was very young, and initially it was about playing with language. But as I developed and started caring more about the content of my poems, I have been really drawn to women's lives and experiences, and I don't think you can write about women's lives and experiences without writing about real, embodied experiences. We have some messy lives that we experience through our bodies. I've never connected those two poems before, so thank you for that.

DN: In your "Gospel of The Bleeding Woman," you have this person, but we only know her in scripture because of her body, and what her body is doing, and then what she is being drawn toward—Jesus passing by. She's not named, and because of the tradition she was viewed as this marginalized, unclean person. You honor her and you give her a name. How did you come to that?

KM: I always was just fascinated by the bleeding woman, who appears in three of the gospel accounts. I was a Bible quizzer when I was young—

DN: Oh, there it is. That answers everything.

KM: Yes, I was a strange young person who studied scripture very closely and then competed over knowledge of scripture. So I was aware of some very minor characters who had these side stories, and she especially fascinated me. Part of it is that it's not her story. She interrupts Jesus during someone else's story. She is this character who doesn't have a name, she's been bleeding for twelve years, and if that doesn't fascinate you, I don't know what will. What would her life have been like, why is she bleeding for twelve years? So I did a lot of research that was scholarly and some that was not so scholarly, and I mixed it all together and let my imagination run wild. I did go through Aramaic baby names as if I were, you know, choosing a name for a child, and looked at the meanings of the names. I put in a whole lot of time and heart into that, and I love her.

DN: When I use an essay written by Phillip Lopate called "Portrait of My Body," in some of my classes, he gets really specific and personal, and it's interesting how students react to it. Some of them are just turned off and grossed out by the specifics. But what surprises me is how many students, I would say particularly female students, look at that and say oh you can write about something that vulnerable? You can write about something that intimate? It isn't just voyeurism or narcissism, it's an excuse, empowering, for them to take the risks that Phillip Lopate did in his. Have you seen that with audiences, with students, in response to your work, where the reader says, "Oh if she's going to take those kinds of risks, talking about her body, I can maybe open some doors, some chambers that I've kept closed for a long time?"

KM: I have. I'm thinking of a poet who I just watched reading a couple days ago, and in the Q and A afterwards she was talking about her book, which she was writing about motherhood, and someone asked her about poets who had influenced her, and she talked about my book "*Tasty Other*" giving her permission to write about motherhood and the mothering body. When I teach Lucille Clifton's work, she has many poems that talk about the body, but especially I love using the poem "Homage to My Hips." I've had students connect with that poem in so many ways, the way that she talks about these hips are big hips, they need space to move around. I've had students choose that poem for their recitation in my class or choose it for their creative response, where they talk about other parts of their own bodies. I had a male student talk about being overweight when he was a child and how he responded to that poem so personally. When we write honestly or vulnerably in our own poems, it gives others permission to be honest and vulnerable about their own experiences.

Margarita Pintado

DN: I was drawn to your poem "The Contortionist" for a couple of reasons. It describes a girl you saw at a circus who could contort her body in all these strange ways to entertain the audience. But then at the end of that poem that say you also contort yourself. You turn it inward. This could be a general statement about contortions that all of us—particularly women—go through to entertain and be accepted by audiences. Were you thinking of the parallel at the time, or did it dawn on you while you're describing her, hey wait a second, all of us do this?

MP: That part came after. My husband and I were very deprived from art when we were living in Arkansas, in Arkadelphia, where there wasn't much to do. A circus came, and it felt like the fifties. When I saw that woman, I mean she was from a country I've never been in, and she was very tiny, and she was doing this spectacle in this small town where most men were older and white and they were in the first rows—the way they were looking at her was, it was just shocking to me.

But at the same time I looked at my husband and he was so moved by the artistic expression. Because we were so—we were living in a desert, let's put it that way—and when this woman was contorting herself, that was art. And I could see how my husband and I were processing everything, like this is wrong, this is beautiful, what is this, where are we? All of these things were going through our minds. Once at home I start thinking about what I saw and wondering why I'm feeling the way I'm feeling, I couldn't help but identify with her and think that I'm also in this spotlight in this strange place and I'm not from here and I have to do all these kinds of things to adapt or seem like I'm from there.

DN: Another one of your poems, "Still Life," you describe fruit but—

MP: A tiny anecdote: I published that poem first in an online journal where people can comment. And I loved that poem because people hated it. I got the nastiest comments about that poem, and the director of the journal loved the poem so much he intervened in the comments and said it was a valid, solid poem. So go ahead.

DN: Well, A: It's kind of cool that a poem can generate that kind of passion, and B: It's even cooler than an editor is stepping in and saying "nope, this is good stuff." So let me ask you something about it. On the one hand you're describing fruit. But it's so much more than that. Can you describe what else is going on in that poem?

MP: Again, this is a poem that I wrote in Arkadelphia, where we didn't have many things to do. So Walmart became a very important place for us because it was the only place that was like four minutes away. If we wanted to go to another supermarket, we had to drive. We discovered Walmart was kind of a social scene, with people hanging out in the parking lot. I was at home and I saw the fruit we had just purchased that day sitting in the fruit basket, and I was thinking how the fruit looks so sad under a certain kind of light. It was like five o'clock, and it was looking sad. And I was thinking that we don't eat as much fruit as we should, so we always end up throwing the fruit away. I was trying to make a funny point about this couple who's kind of bored and we didn't have children yet, we go to Walmart and we just stared at the fruit for hours and the vegetables and we make a very conscious decision of the kind of fruit that looks beautiful, but that's it. We don't want to eat the fruit; it's just sort of a way to stay alive. So it's kind of a sad poem, but I wasn't sad when I was writing it. That's what I want to point out—I thought it was hilarious, but it didn't come across as funny.

DN: You name all of these different emotions of terror, tears, compassion, all occurring at distinct times of the day as you're looking at this fruit, which you could broaden that out to those are stages that we all go through in our lives as well. Maybe I read way too much into that poem.

MP: No, you're right. Because I'm blaming the fruit. It's like I'm super angry at what the fruit reveals about ourselves. Because the fruit is dying before our eyes and we don't eat it.

DN: Maybe this is confessing too much, but I'll tell you what else I thought was going on in there. I thought you were describing a miscarriage.

MP: Wow.

DN: I reflected on that poem for a while, and then I looked at the title again, "Still Life."

MP: Well, wow, Dean. Well, I'm going to say something I've never said, but I had a miscarriage around that time.

DN: I'm so sorry.

MP: It wasn't that dramatic because by the time I found out I was pregnant it was already miscarried. But that was present obviously.

DN: In one of your prose poems you ask What is an event? When you land on "This is an event," that means you're going to write about it, correct?

MP: I was staring out the window and I saw a guy who was cleaning his motorcycle. I'm looking at this man who I don't know and now I'm going to invent or create a whole story for him. That's an event.

DN: You were really disturbed by a particular poet who said, "If you want to be a poet, you gotta live in the city." You gotta live in New York, you gotta live in Boston, maybe Los Angeles. But then you turned to Rilke in "Letters To a Young Poet." What was Rilke's advice about moving to the city?

MP: Rilke would say no no no you gotta move back to your childhood because that's where all your poetry is. That's Rilke's view. And of course I don't only write about my childhood, but boy, there's a lot there, and you never stop being a child. I find in my poems these kind of dual perspectives, or this fight between the grown-up and the child, and the things that the child must let go in order to become an adult.

DN: Rilke also says, "to the creator, there is no poverty and no indifferent place." You took that to mean "turn your attention tighter." You were able to personalize that and say I don't have to move out of Arkadelphia, I don't have to move to this city, this is not an indifferent place, right?

MP: Exactly. I can't say I always was a poet, but I've had always been drawn to poetry and to words. I never grew up in a city. I think the whole thing about the city is about becoming a professional and a success, which has nothing to do with poetry and the value of poetry.

DN: Is everything an event? Is everything worth writing about? A cute thing one of your kids says, or watching a guy clean his motorcycle, or whatever? I'll give you an example. I'm here in New Jersey, where it's been snowing for two straight days. And a couple mornings ago, I'm walking across the parking lot to my kid's apartment, and I hear the most beautiful song coming from a tree. I stopped until I saw this cardinal sitting at the top of a tree, framed by a pale blue sky. I think there's a poem in there. Is that an event?

MP: I was on the beach and I saw an open watermelon. It's red, it looked like blood, and birds were fighting to grab pieces of it. I wondered, is this an event? Or is every bird a separate event? Is the fruit the event? Is the fighting the event? You know, what is the event? It has to be in the interaction between the poet and the thing that's being observed. I hear birds singing all the time, and sometimes I am just absolutely annoyed by them.

DN: That's an event, too!

MP: But we're not so contemplative all the time, trying to turn everything into poetry.

N. Scott Momaday

DN: You have said that all stories come from one cell, one story and the original story. What is that story?

NSM: It can be any number of things. The important point is that there is one story, but there are many stories in one. Tracing down, trying to find out what the first original story is impossible.

DN: But that's the attempt of writing, right, to drill into it?

NSM: That's right. I wrote somewhere that the story has to do with a man who goes out on a pilgrimage and comes back to his home a hero and his wife has been faithful or unfaithful, and his son has become important in the story. It's a story of pilgrimage, I think. That's repeated again and again in my culture anyway. So makes for good storytelling.

DN: You've also said that the original story and all stories come out of this root of God's pursuit of man. You've said that in the past, too, which struck me as different because I would have thought it was the other way around. It would be man's pursuit of God. What does that mean, God's pursuit of man?

NSM: I think I heard that in something that was said by an actor. At one time he was talking about having purchased a painting by a French painter, and he was proud to have this new painting in his possession. The title of the painting was *God's Pursuit of Man*. Now, yeah, that makes sense. We are all pursued by God.

DN: So are these creative urges always addressing that?

NSM: Largely, yes. I think that's a dominant theme in literature. And probably in painting and other forms of art.

DN: When you mentioned the pilgrim's journey, I was thinking of Joseph Campbell and his discussion of myth and the Hero's journey and pilgrimage. But you connect ancient myths differently from how he described them. You are connecting to the Kiowa people and Native American people. Do you ever think of myth in the way Joseph Campbell did, where it's the hero?

NSM: Certainly I know Joseph Campbell and I have a high regard for him. And I'm very much interested in myth. I like to quote Borges, who said that myth is at the beginning of literature and also at the end. That's a good thing to keep in mind as you're writing or painting.

DN: But you're always drawn to the myths of where the Kiowa people came from. Is that true?

NSM: It's very important in my mind and in my work. The origin myth of the Kiowa as it that they came into the world through a hollow log. I like thinking of that image. And I've always wondered what was on the other side of the log. I don't know. No one does. But it's fun to speculate.

DN: You've also written plays and a screenplay. The screenplay was about the Carlisle School, the Indian school, and I'm still stunned by the statement that the mission of the school was, kill the Indian, save the man. In what universe is that kind of a statement okay? That was the goal of the school, right?

NSM: It was the goal of the man who founded the school. That was his purpose. He meant well.

DN: Really?

NSM: He wanted to bring the Indian into the modern world and to make him a part of the modern age. But it's a terrible statement. Kill the Indian to save the child. You're right about that. I mean, it's unthinkable really.

DN: Let's take away all of your cultural heritage, let's take away all of your ancestry, let's take away any memory you have of where you came from . . .

NSM: That is basically what Carlisle was about. Yes. Shave the heads of the kids, put them in uniforms and forbid them to speak their own language. It is a terrible thing. The scars are very deep and great. A lot of people were destroyed by the experience of the boarding school. Some benefited from it. We don't know why or how, but that happens. But many, many, many did not survive that experience. Cemeteries at the schools are there and poignant.

4

The Voices Outside Your Head

Where Did You Receive Encouragement?

The teacher gave my work to Langston Hughes and
he immediately published it.
ALICE WALKER

In my graduate school program in journalism, the university brought in visiting writers, usually for just a semester. They were usually working on book projects, so the prospect of coming to the middle of Missouri with its few distractions, and teaching one small group in a seminar class, in exchange for a stipend, housing, and many hours of solitude, was attractive.

A writer named Bil Gilbert was coming to town to work on a long piece for Sports Illustrated. Students could submit work to him to see which twelve of us would be admitted into his seminar, and we all wanted in. I don't remember what writing sample I submitted, but I thought it was pretty good. Submissions by the other students were better, though, and I didn't get in. I was devastated.

I made an appointment to see the director of the school overseeing that seminar, and made my case. I said something along the line of "This kind of seminar is the reason I came to this school, and not [I filled in the names of some of this school's rivals]" and on and on. My mom has always said that when I feel passionately about something, my eyes become red-rimmed, as if I'm about to cry. I believe I had that going on in my plea to get into this seminar.

Somehow, my name got added to the list. It was one of the best classes I've ever taken. It challenged us not just as journalists, but as writers and thinkers.

For the final project I turned in a story about watching a man die. He was in the barber chair next to me, and somehow he just snapped forward out of the chair as if he had been yanked by a bungee cord. He died face down amid the hair trimmings, still with the apron around his neck.

I felt self-conscious writing it in first-person, so I did it in third-person, describing me watching the man die. I took some risks and didn't know what my new guru would say, since I was clearly stepping out of my usual lane. I wanted to please him, but I also wanted to write about something that threw me in significant existential ways, and I didn't want to just be a reporter about it.

Bil typed a reply that I still have, decades later. Here is some of it: "For the first time you have something substantive and original to work with. In this is the kernel of something quite good and worth whitling, pruning, thinking and feeling. You have gone over the edge beyond newspaper journalism or features and are giving writing a try—good. I feel maybe I have harassed you to the point of wildness, which is my aim."

When I read that note, my eyes got red-rimmed. A professional writer saw something in me.

Wildness. Over the edge.

I was on my way.

Amor Towles

DN: You were taught by one of the greats, Peter Matthiessen, when you were at Yale—he was here as part of the Writer's Symposium in 2005. I can't imagine being under the influence of that guy in your writing. He changed your trajectory, didn't he?

AT: Yeah, he did. I was at Yale, and he came to spend a semester on campus to teach a writing seminar. I applied; I got in. You were invited to submit stories every week, which I did. And at the end of the third week, as the class was breaking up, he said, "Hey, listen, can you stick around for a minute?" So, everybody left, and I stayed, and he said, "Listen, Amor. I don't know who you are, I don't know what you want, I don't know why you're here. But on the basis of the three stories I've read, I think that you may be gifted at this, and so I'm going to take my time with you very seriously, and I hope that you're going to take your time with me very seriously too."

That was a very important moment for me in my life, as you might imagine, because when you're a teenager, as an artist, whatever your field, you have these two sides of you. On the one hand, you're like, "I think I can really do this thing that I love," whether it's your music or whatever it is. But in writing, I felt "I think I can do this." I would compare myself to my peers who are writing. But then I compare myself to books that I admired. I'd be like, "Yeah, there's something about this. I think I can do this." So, that's half of you. And the other half of you is like, "You're out of your mind, Amor. Why would you think that you can do this?" There's no proof of that. And your mother can't give it to you. Mom gave me lots of things, but she's saying, "Oh, this is such a beautiful story." It doesn't matter that she thinks that.

This is the point where you first have an outside person who is talented in your craft, whom you admire, who singles you out to give this message, and it has changed my life. Well, then what happens? There's a Part 2 to this story. So, I kept working with Peter, and he became my mentor and a friend. But when I was twenty-five and I had moved to New York City to write novels, I was living in an illegal sublet with a friend. I was a little frustrated and claustrophobic and bored and broke. And so, I joined a friend of mine who had started an investment firm. It was just the two of us at first, and twenty years later, we were still working side by side. For the first ten years, I did not write fiction as we were building the firm. And I would see Peter; we'd have lunch or dinner, maybe twice a year. And he was very upset and rightfully so because he really felt like, "I gave you this time."

DN: And once you're out, do you ever really get back into it?

AT: Yeah. And he would say, "How's your book coming?" And he could tell by my response that I wasn't making progress, and it just broke his heart. So, finally, after a couple of years of this, maybe five years of this, at the end of dinner, he says, "Amor, I want to tell you something." And maybe he's approaching seventy at this point. He says, "Amor, I've now seen multiple generations come and go through the arts, starting with my own. And what I can tell you is that in the course of seeing those generations that there's something about working on Wall Street that it's interesting enough. The people are interesting enough, it's challenging enough, it pays well enough. My experience now is that when an artist goes to Wall Street, they never come back. And so, I think that you should consider your life as a writer over."

DN: Oh, my.

AT: Yeah. And so, that was the end of dinner. I was like, "No dessert for me, thanks."

DN: Did you take that seriously?

AT: He was right. On that day, I was not writing. Here's an odd thing about—at least for me, but I think this is true for many artists—is that I love it. I love it more than anything in the world, with the exception of my wife and children. And that, as it turned out, wasn't enough. Loving it wasn't enough to get me to do it every day. What ended up really turning me back on, flipping the switch, was dread. It was the dread of waking up at the age of sixty or whatever and having failed to fulfill the promise of this talent, which Peter had observed, and to some degree letting him down, being able to look back. So, I then began writing on the weekends, and I spent seven years writing a novel I didn't like and set that aside. But I learned a lot from that experience. And then I wrote *Rules of Civility*, and that became a bestseller, and I retired from the firm. And God bless, Peter was still alive at the time because it would have been very sad for me if he had not lived to witness that I did come around and ultimately fulfill his confidence in me.

DN: So, when you were writing *Rules of Civility* were you thinking that you were writing this for Peter?

AT: No, and that's an interesting side note. I was really doing it for myself because it's what I really wanted to do. But one funny thing is that Peter gave me these gifts, so he recognized my talent. He lit the fire under me when I was drifting away from my purpose as a writer. Then, he gave me a third gift. The third gift was that I finished *Rules of Civility*, and I called him up and I said, "Hey, listen." He knew I had written this seven-year book and it failed. "I started taking another crack at it. It's a totally different book; I think it's great. I'd love to hear your take." He said, "Great, send it to me." Sends it back to me. He's like, "Amor, it's not for me. I don't really get it. I don't know why you're writing a book set in 1938. And I don't like your heroine. I think she's too sassy, and she kind of bugs me, and I'm sorry." He really panned the book for me. As I say, this was the third gift because it was very upsetting receiving the letter. But then you retreat from it, and I would go back and look at the book and say, "You know what? I think he's wrong. I think it's really a good book." And then you got an agent, it ended up being sold at auction, and you start to gain, and it all worked out. Then he sent me a beautiful note saying, "Dear Amor, this is my eating crow letter."

DN: Awesome.

AT: And I say that's a really important gift, in which it was an unintentional gift on his part. I mean, it was intentional in that it was honest. But having your mentor not like what you're doing is a very valuable thing to go through. Because at the end of the day, you've got to really carry that water yourself. You have to have faith in yourself, understand your own work, advocate for your own work, know how to edit your own work, and to be confident when the critical moment comes. And so, having his negative response at that moment helped me kind of build that muscle.

Joseph Wambaugh

DN: What was the early encouragement you got from an Atlantic Monthly editor when you sent them a story?

JW: That was a famous editor with the Atlantic Monthly, Edward Weeks. He was the first editor of Ernest Hemingway. That's how old he was. He edited *The New Centurions* and he came to visit me at my little home outside of Los Angeles where my wife and kids and dogs lived. We, of course, had never entertained anyone like that. He came to present my check when the Atlantic Monthly Press and Little Brown bought my manuscript. It was a 4,000-dollar check, the most money I had ever gotten at one time, and he came to our house for lunch. He was this grand old man, and I was extremely impressed. My wife had lunch and we had paper napkins because that's all we ever had, and Edward Weeks talked as he ate. And he talked. And he talked. And he ate. And he talked. And he kept using this paper napkin. The more he talked, the more pieces of napkin got stuck to his face. My wife and I were sitting there looking at each other, and here was this old, famous man with little pieces of paper stuck all over his face.

DN: Was he the one who had initially rejected your story?

JW: No. The Atlantic Monthly rejected my short stories and suggested I try a novel. And this was the novel, *The New Centurions*.

Amy Tan

AT: (Regarding her agent, Sandy Dijkstra) We only have one life to live, and if you devote it to something that you're not passionate about, that becomes your life. [Sandy] gave me a life that I could be passionate about. I could have gone off on another direction and continued fairly content on one level, but this was such a different life. It's everybody's dream to do something that you're absolutely passionate about, where you can just sit in a chair all day in your bathrobe and be passionate about it. There's a lot of bonuses that go with it.

Lysley Tenorio

LT: I was lucky to continue to get support in many ways. After graduate school I did about four years of fellowships and a writing fellowship.

Whenever you get any kind of support, what you're really getting is an investment. If there are individuals or institutions who want to invest in your work, that's a sign they believe in it, that they believe this is worthy of being out there. Because I felt that's what was happening to me, I felt this obligation to keep writing. The only real obligation is to myself of course. I felt like if I had the support, if other people believe in the work, it's worth continuing and it's worth plugging away even though many of those days or months or even years can seem quite thankless with very little payoff. But you keep doing it.

Alice Walker

DN: Teachers played a big role in your development as a writer. There was one in particular at Sarah Lawrence who would, without your knowing it, take some of the writing that you would do for her class and she would submit it to editors. A: that has never occurred to me to do with my students' work; and B: that's just a startling thing. Isn't that how Langston Hughes found out about you?

AW: She sent my work to the *New Yorker*, and they rejected it. I had never read the New Yorker, I didn't know what it was, and then when I did see it I said, "Oh well that's okay, because the print is too small!" The same teacher gave my work to Langston Hughes and he immediately published it in a book called The Best Short Stories by Negro Writers. He and I became friends.

DN: And this was the essay, "To Hell With Dying," correct?

AW: Yes, and there's a story behind that story. I had come north to college and I couldn't afford to go home for the funeral of this old musician that we loved. And so I wrote the story in place of trying to be there.

5

Emerging Path
When Did You First Think You Were a Success?

It's just a thrill to get published.

BILLY COLLINS

Success is a tricky word. Does it translate into dollars? Acclaim? Awards? Maybe.

For most of us in the writing world, we equate success with the first thing we had published. It didn't have to be a big magazine or a publishing company. But it usually had something to do with an editor reading something we'd written, taking note of it, passing it along to other editors, and putting our work in print. It could be a little local paper, an academic press, or something much bigger.

The fact that someone other than our moms read what we wrote and separated it from all of the other possible options, and published our work, is how most of us think about our first success. Everything builds from there. You're in the game. You have just enough incentive to do more.

Some of the writers below tell of their first success as these incredible financial payoffs. But I don't think their first success is when they got a huge contract from a publisher. There were other steps they took before getting there. I think their first success was when the tiny magazine that had thirty readers published their story originally, and then things progressed from there.

Or they showed someone something they had written, and that person didn't laugh or roll their eyes—maybe a parent, maybe a spouse, maybe a teacher. But it was an acknowledgment. It was confirmation. It was a reason to keep going, getting past the fear or embarrassment. It was a means for saying "I can do this."

Joseph Wambaugh

DN: I remember seeing television programs like Hill Street Blues or NYPD Blue, where there was such a human and raw side to police work. But you were before all of that, right?

JW: My first book (*The New Centurions*) came out in January 1971, so that was a long time before those other fellows. I was still a cop at the time, and I took my first manuscript prior to publication to Jack Webb of Dragnet fame, because he was the guru of LAPD. He had heard about me, heard about my book, which was already picked up by the Book of the Month Club as its main selection. He wanted to find out about me and he knew that I was in trouble with the police department for writing this book, particularly without permission. No one had ever written a book, with LAPD permission or no permission, and I was in some trouble, which was reported in the papers. Mr. Webb asked that I bring my manuscript to his office out on Sunset Boulevard, and if he believed in what I wrote, he would intercede with the chief of police and perhaps keep me from getting in serious trouble.

I guess what Jack Webb thought was that the book would be Dragnet approved, and when I took *The New Centurions* to him, they kept it for about two weeks. I phoned them about it and they told me I could come pick it up. When I came to pick it up I didn't get to meet Mr. Webb, but someone came downstairs from his offices and handed over the manuscript. It weighed about ten pounds more than when I took it to him, because every place where there was something objectionable, he had placed a paperclip. There were about a million paper clips. And Mr. Webb never interceded on my behalf with the chief of police, but my job survived anyway because the book was such a huge hit. It became a film with George C. Scott, who was very hot at the time, having come from Patton. There was too much publicity, so the chief had to back off and sort of let me be. I stayed with the police department for three more years. Even though I was still a cop, I kept writing.

Luis Alberto Urrea

LU: I went to Muir College at UCSD. I wasn't really that interested in college, but the parents made me go. And I could not believe that, when you went to college, you could study stuff you liked— I thought, "What is this?!" I started out as a drama major, and I switched over to writing, and it was just like going to heaven for me. I had this mad professor, back in the day, you know, you had these crazy professors—I had a twenty-six-year-old professor who wore love beads, who, during one workshop, climbed up on the table and went to sleep. He's like, "you guys keep talking," and he went to sleep, and I thought that's really cool, you know? He had brought Ursula K. Le Guin, the science fiction writer, into the school. My father was killed the winter of my senior year of college. And I did not know how to process this event, which was terrible for all of us, so I wrote about it. To get into Ursula Le Guin's workshop, you had to audition. She took that story, and put me in the class. Then she accepted it for an anthology. So it was my first sale.

I used to feel like my father sacrificed all that and gave me a life without knowing he was doing it because he started my life. But the other side of that coin is, you think, wow, you know, start out with Ursula Le Guin!

Amy Tan and Her Agent, Sandra Dijkstra

DN: Here's the Amy Tan lore that I read about before I met you tonight. Your first book, Joy Luck Club started as a short story which was published in Seventeen magazine which somehow found its way to you, Sandra. You asked for more stories and then poof, a book, a movie, more books and then the pinnacle of your career, our Writer's Symposium and I'm just thinking, "Wow." Alright now, how much of that is true?

AT: Well, the last part is true. I'm here. The first part is actually even more humble than that. It was a story that appeared in a very small literary magazine called FM5 that's now defunct and it had a circulation of 300. Then it was reprinted in Seventeen. Sandy saw it in Seventeen but had also heard from somebody, Molly Giles, who today is my editor. She thought it was a story that Sandy might be interested in taking a look at. So that part is true.

DN: Sandy, what does that mean, somebody wants you to take a look at a story?

SD: Well, you're going to hear two sides. What I recall is that Molly Giles had just won the Flannery O'Conner award and I was going up to San Francisco. I was a baby agent and I wrote Molly a letter, saying I wonder if you're represented, because I love your stories. And Molly said, "Well I'm represented but I think you should meet an author I'm working with, Amy Tan. Amy was working as a business writer.

Amy and I had a phone conversation before we met and I said well you could write some business books or you could collaborate on some business books and you said, "No that's what I do for a living. For my pleasure, I want to write fiction." I said well then show me, because I hadn't really read anything yet and you sent me three stories.

And when I read those stories, I said, "Oh these are really good. Let's have a meeting." And we set up a meeting at the Clairemont Hotel and I said to Amy, "would you please give me an idea of how these stories would connect or how this might become a collection of stories." And so Amy came armed with an outline.

AT: It was sort of like that except that I remember we agreed to work together and at first I was just saying well I won't have anything for you to sell for probably ten years and I'm a business writer but I don't need an agent for that because I was quite overwhelmed with business writing and it was later when you said, "well I'll be your agent and I'll give you encouragement." And so I said, Oh, that's fine. You said you'd be patient. You'd give me encouragement. Well, every week like a Jewish mother, Sandy called me up and said, have you written another story? And then I had three stories.

SD: That's possible.

AT: And when I had three stories, she said why don't you write an outline of what a whole book of these might look like. So when I had a couple of hours free, I sat down one afternoon and I just sort of off the top of my head, I wrote down all these ideas for stories and I sent it to her and thought that she would just look at it. It was not a formalized thing at all. I spent two hours writing this outline and she, unbeknownst to me, or maybe I wasn't paying attention, went to New York while I was in China for the first time.

When I came back from China she called and said, "Oh thank God you're back. I have three offers." And I said, what are you talking about? She said, "I have three offers for your book." And I said, "what book?" And she said "Joy Luck Club." And I said "Sandy where are you? What have you done?" And I thought, I didn't know this woman. She was a new agent and I thought, did she take something from the Dream of the Red Chamber and just hand it to somebody and say this is what my client wrote? I couldn't believe that publishers would actually make an offer on something that hadn't been written yet. But you know this is the amazing talent of Sandy Dijkstra to get people to believe in the vision.

SD: Well I had a lot of talent in you. Amy you were going to use the title, Wind and Water. And I said well coming from California I will be laughed out of Manhattan if I come in with a book called Wind and Water. I mean that's what they think we are basically. But Amy had this synopsis because I had said to her, what would hold these stories together? And in the synopsis were these four magical words, The Joy Luck Club. And I got goose pimples when I saw those words. I said could we use that as a title? And Amy said that's just the club my parents have, you know they meet on Thursday nights, they play mahjong.

AT: It was like the Girl Scouts of America, I mean it just sounded so prosaic.

SD: It's a stock planning club you know? And I said well I do believe that titles have to be catchy. Authors often say they're not important, and they're really not. We can change them later. But the truth is that the title is the gateway to an author's imagination. It's the first thing the publisher knows about you and it's the thing that the editor running through the halls saying I have this project from an unknown author called The Joy Luck Club. I mean who doesn't want joy luck? Who doesn't want to be a member of that club?

By the way, there's a restaurant in New York which is a derivative called the Soy Luck Club which Amy and I have to try. We'll have to have a little party at The Soy Luck Club.

DN: I'm glad we got this cleared up because, Sandy, I just had this vision of you sitting down somewhere in your home and reading Seventeen magazine like I'm sure you do all the time, seeing this story and saying I've got to have this person in my stable.

SD: No, no. And in fact, my assistant read it, and she didn't actually like it but she said I think you should see this. And when I read it, I said Wow, this is really good.

Here's another thing Amy did, without any advice. All authors are sent an author questionnaire, PR kind of thing to prepare the publisher for how to promote you and the book. Well, Amy wrote a little story about how she came to be a writer, which they put in the PR kit. What she said was that she was exhausted, stressed out as a business writer, and she went to her shrink to ask help. As she was pouring out her heart to the shrink, she looked over there and he had fallen asleep.

DN: That's a sad day. This is a sad, sad story.

SD: And at that point, Amy decided that she had to save her own life and the way to do that was to write fiction. I saw it as a coming out. Those of you who are wanting to find agents and work with agents, the main thing of course is that it all starts with your belief in yourself. But then you need somebody else who believes in you and who has the conviction of the worth of your work.

When Amy came back from China and I got her on the phone, I had just turned down Knopf. Amy said "what?"

AT: Knopf is, for those of you who don't follow the publishing world, one of the more literary houses, and every literary writer would hope to be with a publishing house like Knopf, so to be told that she had turned down Knopf was like saying, "You know I turned down *The New Yorker*." Oh, I turned down Knopf. And I went, "What? Are you crazy?"

SD: They had made an offer which, to me, translated that Amy would be the lowest little author on their big list. So I said to Amy, if you'll trust me, I think I can put together something. I said, how much money do you need to pull the plug on that business writing job? And Amy said $50,000. If I can have $50,000 I can pull the plug. So that was my number and I believe Knopf was offering 15.

AT: That was a decent advance too.

DN: Which any number of beginning writers would have taken.

SD: For three short stories, it was. And when I told them to bring Vintage into the mix, Vintage added five thousand to it.

AT: I don't remember any of the money things.

SD: And I said to Amy, let me just see what I can do. And I remember, for me this was unbelievably strange and exciting because Doubleday had just made a two-book offer for $120,000, the stories and whatever else Amy would write. And I'd never been offered for something that didn't exist.

AT: Two things that didn't exist.

SD: Amy empowered me by saying you make the decision, which scared the hell out of me. She said I trust you, which is terrifying. So I turned down the two-book offer for $120,000 and then we had this offer from the most important literary editor at one of the most commercial houses in New York, Putnam. But her offer was $50,000, and the poor author I was then touring New York with kept saying who is this Amy Tan? Because every office I would show up in and I'd get a phone call for somebody was asking me about Amy's book.

Putnam's offer contained world rights, and I said you can't have the world. Well, Amy has a very beautiful home in San Francisco now that is partially related to the decision to keep world rights. Amy came down the day of the auction and we were in my office which was in my home at the time, and we went to dinner because we couldn't stand it any longer. It was taking so long. There were fourteen houses bidding.

Vintage, which had originally offered $5,000 for paperback rights, offered $1.238 million and got the paperback rights. And her publisher at Putnam called me the next day, the toughest woman in New York, other than me, said, "I will sue you if I hear you're talking to any other publisher about Amy Tan." And then we began negotiations for the next book. Anyway, it was an amazing high-wire act and it all began with conviction and trust.

Chris Hillman (Interviewed by Karl Martin)

KM: Chris, you were playing music for quite some time before you actually started writing songs. How and when did you start writing?

CH: I started writing around 1966, so I had been in The Byrds oh, a year and a half. We started The Byrds in late 1964. I was a player more than a singer or a songwriter. I did a session for Hugh Masekela, the South African trumpet player. He had a hit back in the late sixties, "Grazing in the Grass." And I played bass on a demo session for him with wonderful musicians from Africa. I was totally out of my comfort zone as a musician—it was a different kind of music. But coming home from that session that day, I sat down and wrote a song. Nothing to do with the music I had just been playing all day. It was a country song. It was my first song—"Time Between"—and it just started flowing. It was like the flood gates opened. And I don't know why or how that happened, it just opened up and I started writing songs.

Billy Collins

BC: I was getting published in obscure journals. At that time, I didn't care where I got published. And if you don't care about that, it's quite easy to get published, if you have no standards of publication. But it's just a thrill to get published.

DN: Then you sent some poems, hoping to get published, to a review at the University of Arkansas Press. You said that that editor did you a great service by putting a paperclip around *some* of them.

BC: Yeah. Well, that was Miller Williams, the director of the University of Arkansas Press. And he's a wonderful poet. He has never gotten the acclaim that he really deserves. Lucinda Williams is his daughter, but now he's her father now that she's more famous than he is. And it's also largely forgotten that he was President Clinton's second inaugural poet. Because Clinton, to his credit, when he was governor of Arkansas, he was very supportive not only of the university, but the University of Arkansas Press, which had a poetry list. I hadn't had a book published, a real book, so I sent a manuscript off to him, because a friend of mine Ron Koertge, who's a California poet, had gotten a book published there, and our poems were a little similar in tenor and voice and humor, I guess, so I gave it a try. Miller Williams sent back the poems with a very short note, and he put a paper clip around seventeen out of the fifty or so poems that I sent. The little note said "I put a paperclip around these poems and these are quite good poems. The other poems don't live up to those poems." So he was telling me that some of the poems didn't live up to the standard I had set for myself.

DN: There was something about those seventeen.

BC: Yeah, that he believed in.

DN: What was it? What was different about them?

BC: I think they were a little less tricky. Less joke-y. I mean, I made a lot of offenses just being too clever for my own good, I think. And some of those poems got very short, because they would just shut down with a kind of punchline. And the others had a little more expansiveness to them, and room in them. They were a little less boxy. So that paperclip was really worth an MFA to me, because I then set out to please this man. I didn't meet him until 10 years later. But for the next year or two maybe, I wrote. I threw all the other poems out, and I saw just what he meant. I couldn't quite articulate it, but I spent a year trying to please this guy, and writing poems that were as good as the seventeen. And I did, so he published my book. Because he said, "if you can write a whole bunch of poems like those, I'll publish your book." That's all I needed. *You will?* I'm off to the races.

Lysley Tenorio

DN: You had some early success. I'm absolutely amazed at how you got your first story published in the Atlantic. You just sent it in. You didn't have an agent, you didn't have an editor, you wrote a story and sent it to the Atlantic and for all we know some intern pulled it out of a pile and showed it to an editor and said, "This is pretty good." You realize that's just so annoying to the rest of us?

LT: I was very lucky and maybe I was just very naïve. But it worked. The Atlantic has been publishing fiction for more than a century.

The slush pile is where your submissions end up if you aren't an established writer with an agent. So the slush pile at the Atlantic at that time had reached about 2,000 stories a month. Somehow, someone pulled me from the slush pile and published that story and that was my publication and I foolishly thought, oh well, if it's this easy, I'll just send a story a month to the Atlantic and finish a book in a year. I was completely wrong.

Joyce Carol Oates

DN: When you were in college, you submitted an essay or a story to *Mademoiselle Magazine* . . .

JCO: Short story.

DN: For a writing contest.

JCO: Yes.

DN: And you won.

JCO: I did win it. A few years earlier, though I didn't know this, Sylvia Plath had won. So there was a tradition of strange young women winning this award. I didn't know who she was. At that time she wasn't yet famous.

DN: Did winning a contest like that give you some confirmation that this is something you really want to pursue?

JCO: I don't really know how to answer that. I never really have had great expectations about the future. And maybe that's just my personality. Yesterday, one of the students at Stanford said, what do you expect from us? They're handing their portfolios in in a few weeks. What do you expect? And I suddenly thought . . . I don't really have any expectations at all! I'll see what you do, and I'm probably going to be happy and interested in what you do. But the idea of having expectations is kind of an interesting and ontological issue. You know like, if you have too many expectations, it's somewhat paralyzing and crippling maybe. So I probably have never had very many expectations. I would have thought it was fantastic and incredible that I won this competition, but I wouldn't therefore think that I would win anything else or even be published. I wouldn't necessarily extrapolate for the future.

Carlos Ruiz Zafon

CZ: The book that became *The Shadow of the Wind* was the first time I had written something that was *exactly* what I wanted it to be. When it was published, of course, I was kind of a new author, for many people "Dude, I've been doing this for many years. You weren't even born."

When it came out, I remember everybody in Spain or people in publishing, thought it was the strangest book, the most un-Spanish book ever, and that it was impossible to sell this book in Spain. They said, "Maybe in other countries, but here, it's going to drop like a rock in the ocean." A lot of people in the publishing house loved the novel and said, "We want to publish it" but nobody thought it was going to survive beyond the first week in bookstores. And what happened was interesting, because there was a kind of a word of mouth, between booksellers and writers and journalists, and people starting buying a copy for their best friend or something.

After a few months, the book was doing quite well in Spain, but actually where it became successful first was outside of Spain. The first quarter was Germany, and then, in Western Europe, it became a big success. There, nobody thought it was that strange or anything, and the success was much faster. So when it became kind of a phenomenon outside of Spain, is when a lot of people started paying attention to the book in Spain.

Jane Smiley

DN: You were writing early in your career, but you knew "this isn't the big thing I'm headed toward."

JS: I knew Greenlanders was the big thing I was headed toward, and I didn't know what was going to come after that. But that was sufficient to sort of keep me moving forward for those first, say, ten years.

Anchee Min

DN: When you started submitting your stories that became *Red Azalea*, you first sent them to some literary reviews and some contests to get them published, right?

AM: I first sent them to Sandy Dijkstra, the literary agent in Del Mar. And her agency said we don't take unpublished author. So I said, how will I get it published? They said if you write a magazine. So I look into the magazine competitions. And *Writer's Digest* costs $25 for entry fee. Then I found this magazine called *Mississippi Valley Review*. National Writing—20th National Writing Contest, that cost me only $5. So I went with that. And I got published, and I won.

DN: So they published you. Then did you go back to Sandy Dijkstra and say "Okay, I'm published now, so what's your problem?"

AM: Well, I just sent them again. I don't hear them for a year and a half. And then one day she called. She says her readers were trying to get caught up, and she says, "I'm on my way to New York, and stopping in Chicago. I read the summary that my readers sent, I just wanna maybe call you. So, would you like to meet me?" I said, sure. So I went, meet her, and she says, "Well I got up at 5 o'clock this morning and I read it, I think, I'd like to try your book? Sign." So I signed the contract with her. Then two weeks later, she says "I have five major publishing house auctioning. Which one would you like to go? Random House" or, what was the second—HarperCollins, right? And I said, who?

And then Sandy says, calls again, says, are you sitting down? I say yeah. And then she says, well, foreign rights just sold, and she gave me a number. And that mathematical number doesn't—$1 . . . a hundred thousand dollars doesn't make any difference. I mean, I'm exaggerating. And then she says, well, I think you need to buy a fax. So, I was fixing the toilet! I'd just bought this apartment house that was burned down by the homeless. I got the loan from my brother who was washing dishes in Japan and I bought the house and I was just cleaning and doing the toilets, you know? That was that moment that came.

DN: Now you can actually hire people to do those toilets, can't you?

AM: Yeah. Well, I have my daughter do it.

N. Scott Momaday

DN: Your book House Made of Dawn was such a powerful story of the Native American experience in modern culture. A person comes back from war, doesn't fit in, now there's this dominant culture and he's trying to maintain his identity. That's always been the struggle. But what was it about that novel at that time that you think resonated so well?

NSM: It told a story of a man who loses his traditional identity, and that in itself is a tragedy. But it was widespread during the Second World War, that's the time of the setting, that's the setting of House Made of

Dawn. So many young men of that generation were exposed to a world they had no knowledge of and unfortunately, it was a world at war, so they were deeply damaged in many instances, and they came back to their homeland and they were lost. There was this desperate struggle to recover the traditional world and some did and some didn't. We don't know because the ending is an open ending.

DN: The ending is a little obscure there, you have to finish it yourself as the reader as to what happens.

NSM: Yes, I like that.

DN: When I finished the book, I thought, "I respect that ending."

NSM: Good.

DN: But you didn't even know it was nominated for a Pulitzer?

NSM: No, I didn't.

DN: Until you got the phone call.

NSM: I got a phone call from my editor at Harper and Row. She said, "Scott, are you sitting down?" I said, "Come on friend, I'm busy. What do you want?" She said, "You've won a Pulitzer Prize." I said, "Yeah, friend (*laughter*) sure I have." Then it dawned on me that I really had. It was a wonderful thing; it changed my life in certain ways. Brought me a lot of acclaim and recognition and gave me an incentive to write some more, so I did.

6

Growing, Changing, Improving

How Have You Evolved as a Writer?

I wanted to come off in my writing as being smarter and more experienced than I was.

GARRISON KEILLOR

One of the things I enjoy about interviewing writers is the preparation. I get to read as many books, stories, essays, poems by these writers as I can get my hands on, and I try to read them in order of when they were written. For instance, when I was getting ready to interview Anthony Doerr, I started with his short story volume, *The Shell Collector*. I got a sense of how he crafts a story, how he develops a character, how he uses detail in a specific and intentional way. Then I read his novel *About Grace*, then his nonfiction book *Four Seasons in Rome*, then his collection of different kinds of stories and novellas in *Memory Wall*, before tackling his epic *All the Light We Cannot See*, and then committing to that VERY complicated novel *Cloud Cuckoo Land*.

I take notes when I read these books, and do a small mental chart of how the writing is different from book to book. It is great fun to see how the writer evolves from the early work to the present. Reading Doerr in this manner allowed me to see him grow as a storyteller, watch him take more risks, spin more plates in the air at once, test the reader's trust in him. Reading an early short story, then progressing all the way to his latest book that deals with past, present, and future all at once, is pure joy. It's an education.

But that evolution might not have been pure joy for the writer! Adapting is hard. Growing as a thinker and a writer is hard. Finding that next thing is hard. And worth it.

We all grow and change and adapt. At least we should! I'm better at grandparenting than I was parenting. I've learned a few things, such as what kind of behaviors to let slide and what to address. I feel less inclination to control things, and more freedom to see what happens next. As writers, I hope we do something similar. Instead of laboring over that first draft, fixated on making it airtight, thinking we're being efficient by limiting it to just one draft, maybe we let a few things go that we're not crazy about, maybe we know we'll be able to make it better in the next draft, and in the next draft. We don't sweat the chaotic first attempts—we just get it written.

And then, if we get it published, the things we thought were so awful aren't so awful as we once thought. Maybe, as we do this more, we trust the process more, trust the writing more, trust ourselves more.

The result, I believe, is that we get better at it. We might make some strange decisions early on, but those aren't wasted. Then we learn. Then we try something else. We grow. We improve. We evolve.

Amor Towles

DN: Was it a little weird to be writing about the entertainment industry—I realize it was set in 1938—while the entertainment industry was making a movie out of one of your books? Was that just a little paradoxical for you?

AT: I guess it was a coincidence. It's very pleasant. Many of you know *A Gentleman Moscow* is an eight-hour series starring Ewan McGregor, and it began airing three weeks ago.

You're very lucky to have, obviously, a novel that somebody would say, "We want to make it into a movie." That's really great. I write books for readers. The idea that it's going to be a movie is fun, but I'm principally interested in the readers rather than the viewers. But nonetheless, it's still exciting, and you're lucky to have it happen. I'm friends with Michael Lewis, who wrote *Moneyball* and *The Blind Side* and *The Big Short*. He's had a lot of experience in seeing his work translated into the screen. We were having lunch about a year and a half ago. He asked, "Hey, Amor, how's the *A Gentleman in Moscow* project going?" At that point. I had just received the drafts for the first three episodes, so I told him that. I said, "They've asked me for my feedback, but I think they might just be being polite." There's a pause, and Michael says, "Amor, they are definitely just being polite. And not only do they not want to know what you think, they wish you were dead."

But it didn't turn out to be that bad. I was invited in early stages in a great way. I was involved in interviewing the directors and hiring the directors. I was involved in interviewing the head writer. I was involved in casting Ewan. And in each of those cases, there really was an opportunity for me to talk to them about, "Why do they want to be part of this project? What would they do with the book? What do they think is important?" The team, which really ended up being part of Paramount, said, "Listen, Amor. Have those conversations, and if you don't like the person or you think they're going in the wrong direction, we won't hire them; we'll move on."

There's a scene in one episode where the Count is with his childhood friend Mishka, and it's an emotional scene, and they're talking about something that's gone wrong and reliving it, and it's not exactly what's in the book. And it's irritating me a little bit. They're getting deeper. I'm turning to my wife to express my moderate irritation, and she's crying. She's weeping. I'm like, "Sweetie, that's not in the book. I didn't write that." She goes, "I know, but it's so beautiful." So, yeah. It's not going to be exactly like the book, but sometimes they do a good job. Sometimes, they add an element, which pleases my wife.

Ray Bradbury

DN: You have said in the past that you wrote for ten years and then at some point, you realized you had been doing it all wrong. Then you wrote a story in one hour that made the hair on the back of your neck stand up and then you realized you were doing it right. What happened?

RB: I learned not to look at other writers. I learned to be myself. Up until that time, I was so busy being enamored of other talents and wanting to be them. That's ridiculous. You can't do that. I had a memory of an encounter I had when I was eight years old on the beach back in Illinois on Lake Michigan, and I was on the shore with this little girl. We were building sand castles. She went out in the water and she never came back. That was my first encounter with death. I didn't understand. I kept asking my mother, "Why didn't she come back? Where is she?" They never found her. That memory came back when I was sitting out in the sun with my portable typewriter and quite suddenly, had the memory of that little girl not coming back. So I wrote a short story, to bring her out of the water, thirty years later. When I finished it, tears were pouring down my face. I realized for the first time I had written something true and honest and real and wonderful. From that day on, I began to go into my subconscious, dragging out all these wonderful things. So thank god for that one memory.

Peter Matthiessen

DN: You have said that it wasn't until you were age forty, that you wrote what you really wanted. What does that mean?

PM: It means that I couldn't afford to really stick to my guns and write only what I wanted to write about. I wasn't supporting my family. I had a wife and two little children. I ran a deep-sea fishing boat, and I worked on commercial hauling fishing crews, and a lot of things on the side to make money because I wasn't making enough as a writer. I was getting good reviews, but you can't eat reviews.

DN: The way I interpreted that statement was, maybe it wasn't until you were forty and had some experience and you had kind of developed your own voice that then you were getting to be able to say what you really wanted to say.

PM: My work got a lot better once I wasn't trying to balance everything. I think what kicked me over the line, I'm sorry to say, was a big movie contract for a novel called *At Play In the Fields Of the Lord*. That was a big chunk of money, and I put money aside to educate my kids. Then I felt I was in the clear. I could do whatever I want. I didn't mind living simply. Then things started to happen. I also hooked up with *The New Yorker*. That was good, too. They paid very well. They paid very well.

Amy Tan

AT: This latest book, *The Opposite of Fate*, my agent asked over a number of years, "You have so many of these pieces that you've done, would you ever think about putting them into a book?" I just said no, no but then the time was right. I said I would only want to do something where it really had a shape to it, and I finally felt that I had enough pieces that I could see the shape. They talk about writers finding their groove later after you've written a certain number of books, you begin to see a certain shape of your work. And I could finally do that. Then I thought, yes I am ready to do this, and it is cohesive. It's not just a bunch of disparate pieces. But Sandy, my agent, really had to give the old kick in the wazoo there.

Garrison Keillor

DN: You were an English major in college, correct?

GK: I was. Not the best use of my time, but I was under the delusion that that would be a good thing for a writer. What it does, of course, is instill in you standards that you will never ever be able to meet. But I didn't know that. Good luck is what you need. I sent my stories in to the *New Yorker* one manilla envelope after another. Back in the day we typed them on typewriters . . . typewriters? They're in museums. You had to hit really hard. You typed on white bond paper. And you put it into a manilla envelope with an envelope addressed to yourself and you mailed it off to the *New Yorker* in New York. One day a few years after that, after I graduated from college, some woman in a dark, dank office in New York, reading through piles of stories submitted by English majors, found a story of mine entitled, "Local Family Makes Son Happy." And they bought it. So that's luck. Just need a few of those things to happen and onward you go.

When I was in college I could not, for some reason, deal with my own life to write about it. And so I wrote these strange poems and I wrote short stories or really fables, and I kept going down that road. What I should have done, as I see it when I look back now, is I should have written about what I saw. What I saw first hand, and tried to describe it. I was suffering from very common malady of a writer, which is that I wanted to come off in my writing as being smarter and more experienced than I was. So I couldn't write from the person I truly was. This was a great handicap, and I'm so sorry it took me so long to get over it. I got over it last week, Wednesday, I think. But it's a real handicap. And it's a terrible, terrible temptation.

Billy Collins

DN: You went to graduate school, got a PhD in what you call obscure poetry, and then you said you wrote obscure poems for years after that.

BC: I did. I don't know why, but I wanted desperately to be a poet ever since I was in high school. Maybe I just thought it was a cool thing to do. And also, I loved to read and I loved the solitude of reading, and writing would provide the same time of solitude, only now you were on the *giving* part of it instead of the receiving end. So that was a sort of switch. But what I understood about poetry at that time is that it was quite hard to understand—because I wanted to be a modern poet, a living poet—it was hard to understand, but you could tell that the speaker was miserable. That much you could understand. And not much more.

DN: And this *appealed* to you?

BC: Well, being a poet appealed to me, and I was willing to do anything to be a poet . . . so . . .

DN: There you go.

BC: So I wrote obscure poems, which gave off whiffs of misery. Even though I was relatively happy as a young person, but if that's what it took, I was willing to go all the way. So I committed all those offenses.

DN: You said that you wrote bad poetry until you were in your forties.

BC: Well, no, until my mid-thirties, I guess. They weren't published until I was forty. But I started figuring out something about writing when I was in my mid-thirties or so. Late thirties.

DN: What did you figure out?

BC: I figured out how to write the poems I just read.

DN: Isn't this because part of what you thought about poetry was that if it was incomprehensible, then that must've been a great poem.

BC: Yeah. Or trochee. And so I dared to be *clear*. I mean, being clear is the real risk in poetry. People talk about, "she writes" or "he writes very risky poetry," and I never really bought that word, because you're just sitting there writing, and I don't know what you're risking. But I think if there is a risk, the risk is to be clear. Because then you're out in the open. The reader knows what you're doing, whereas if you use an obscurity as a kind of camouflage, you become kind of unassailable. I mean you can't be pinned down.

Also, I started admitting some of my personality into my poems, which I was repressing. And that personality was someone who is a lot happier than this miserable persona that I had earlier. And it had a sense of humor. I always liked humor, and my father was sort of the humor element of the family, but as we know, humor was something you didn't want to do in poetry, because it was too frivolous, too light. If you wrote poetry that was humorous, you were kind of sent to this ghetto called "light verse," with Ogden Nash. I mean, I loved Ogden Nash, I wrote a very serious essay about Ogden Nash. But that's where you would be put. He was not taken seriously.

Anne Lamott

DN: You have such a distinct voice in your writing. Was there a time in your professional writing life where you started to feel like, "Yeah, this is my voice now. I'm no longer really trying?" Some writers begin by imitating other types of voices or writers first. The reason I'm asking is that I think there are a lot of people who have started writing trying to use an Anne Lamott-type voice. Hopefully they've gotten past that. I confess maybe I've done that once or twice.

AL: That's a good question. Of course you sound pretty much like who you really are from when you were a little child, but you also figure out what you love and you figure out what brings you joy, and playfully incorporate it into conversation. Like, I hate puns. Puns, for me, are not playful, they're just, like, about rage.

DN: I've never heard puns and rage get combined . . ..

AL: It's true.

When I was a child I was bullied a lot, because I looked so different, and I was very sensitive, and very smart. I just got bullied, bullied, bullied, and I learned to use humor to defuse that, and to kind of get revenge and to get people on my side again. So I was always funny, and I think God just made me this way. Then when I started to write more seriously, in my late teens, I felt so insecure about how seriously I take the world, which I do. I have always, from about three years old, just found it kind of heartbreaking to be here for people and children and animals. I was raised in the '50s, and there was a *tremendous* amount of domestic violence and untreated alcoholism. So I always really took things very seriously, and I always had a great open heart, and I grieved and it was not attractive to the people in my family.

This was the Eisenhower '50s, before the women's movement, before gay liberation, so you were not supposed to be having these feelings that were not charming. So I got sent to my room, and I just got shamed into being a more adorable sort of person in the world.

DN: How'd that work out for you?

AL: Well, you know, I also luckily took a lot of drugs and drank. I am *hilarious* with a few too many in a small crowd, but I haven't had a drink or a drug in twenty-seven years. But I do remember, I was very funny until the inevitable crying.

So when I started writing I was trying to be who everyone had always loved me to be.

What I needed was for people to see that, yes, I write about very serious stuff, I write about loss, I write about true things, I write about our true heart experience of being human, but, "No! I'm not depressed. I'm not like a buzzkill. I'm this fine, happy-happening girl!" It took a long time to be able to claim my humor since I didn't want to use it to convince people that I wasn't a loser.

I have always had brilliant friends and editors, and they have helped me find the balance between being a person who has a sense of humor, and being a person who is a little child still who finds it pretty heartbreaking for most people to be here at all.

DN: Do you feel like you've got it now, though? When you write, are you thinking, "Yeah, okay, this is me"?

AL: I don't try to deliberately write in what we would say is my voice, but there's just certain things that I think are funny. Like the word "bitter" is always funny. I like to say, "Well, you seem bitter." It's just very funny. You should do it tomorrow. You should say to people, "I hope I don't seem bitter." And they will just all laugh. They will. I promise. There's a certain delivery I have that, I guess, I have honed.

I love people that will write plainly and not do a lot of pyrotechnical stuff. I don't like wordplay. It makes me very worried.

Lysley Tenorio

LT: I got a 9–5 job for about a year and a half, had a cubicle at an internet company. We were called World Wide Web Inc and I used to have a phone and people would say "Are you the internet?" and I would say "No, I'm not the internet, but this is World Wide Web Inc." I knew

I didn't want to do that for the rest of my life. Then I found out you can go to graduate school for writing. A two-year program sounded like writing camp. I never did summer camp as a kid but I thought two years just to write your fiction sounds like a lot of fun to me. I remember I even told myself to apply just this year and if you never get in you never have to try again, you can say at least you tried. I'm not at all saying that you need to go to graduate school to be a writer, obviously you don't, but for me I needed that kind of structure and environment. So I applied to some schools and got into a couple and then ended up going to the University of Oregon in Eugene for two years. I never lived outside of California, so to find myself not in California was quite an experience.

DN: And just be writing.

LT: You took your more academic courses, but it was really about the writing. I was writing constantly. I was such a little speed demon back then; I was a lot younger. I remember there were nights I could push out a twenty-page story in one night or two nights and stay up all night doing it. I don't have the stamina for that anymore.

Joyce Carol Oates

DN: When you were in high school, you wrote a bunch of novels that you then threw away. What was so bad about them? Or what were you so self-conscious about?

JCO: I was probably sort of unconsciously doing apprentice work, like playing scales on a piano or doing piano lessons and practicing. I just remember being very influenced by Scott Fitzgerald. Very influenced by Hemingway and Faulkner, those are the three great influences when I was in high school. The Hemingway-*influenced* stories got published in a high school literary magazine. Sometimes when I give readings or visit a college, somebody will have brought these little magazines and say, "Oh, Miss Oates, will you sign this?" I really want to buy them all up and hide them.

DN: Why? Were they just awful?

JCO: I don't really know what you mean by awful. It's a relative term. Many people are self-conscious and wince about work that they've done when they were younger. It may not really be that bad; it's just you don't want look at it.

Carlos Ruiz Zafon

DN: When you were thirteen years old, you wrote a 600-page, science fiction novel.

CZ: Best book ever written? Unfortunately not published.

DN: When are we going to get to see this? Or are you like the character in your own *The Shadow of the Wind* book where he goes and destroys his old work?

CZ: When I was thirteen years old, I was convinced I was the greatest writer in the world. I already figured this thing out. "I'm the best. Let's go out there and have the world find out about this joyous event." So I wrote this monstrous novel, which was some kind of Gothic monstrosity, and mixed some Sherlock Holmes with these automats, and monsters. . . . It was just something *unspeakable*. Imagine how naive I was at the time, convinced of my own talents, that I sent it to a number of publishing houses in Barcelona. Quite a few of them responded very confused. I remember having conversations with editors that told me they found the book extremely disturbing and said, "You cannot print that!"

There was a very interesting experience in which there was a very nice literary editor in Barcelona, Fernando Pereira who I didn't know at the time, but he had been a close friend of Julio Cortaza and his publisher for many years, and his personal editor. He called me into his office, because I think he was extremely intrigued: "Who was this kid?" He devoted an entire afternoon of his time. He cleared his agenda and said, "Please sit down. I read your book, and it's very interesting." He was very kind to me. He told me the things I needed to hear, but that, of course, you never want to hear. He said, "Don't worry, you'll get published, you'll be a writer. But why are you in such a hurry? You're 13 years old." And I said, "I'm in a hurry? I'm already late! I am an old man." And he told me, "I'm gonna do you a favor, and I'm not gonna publish this novel, because you have to write more things. You have a lifetime ahead of you, you have to grow into whatever it is that you will be, and the writer you will be."

I remember telling him, "You're making a huge mistake. This could be one of the biggest books ever!" And he said, "Well, you know, I'll take that chance, and I'll pass on that."

DN: He did you a great favor!

CZ: He did me a great favor. I wanted to hear, "Yes! Your book is the best thing ever! I'm going to publish it and we're going to burn our marketing budget on your book." He didn't tell me this, then he devoted hours of his time to telling me I shouldn't be in a hurry, I should write more, I should explore, and I should continue working, and then, "Don't worry, you will be a writer."

DN: So fast forward to when *The Shadow of the Wind* comes out. At first it didn't do all that and then it but then it caught on.

CZ: When *The Shadow of the Wind* came out, I had been a working writer for quite a few years, but I had been publishing books for young adults. I had been quite successful in that field. But of course, I was kind of an unknown author for adults. For many years before *Harry Potter,* the young adult genre was a ghetto. There was a huge wall of Berlin in there and you didn't cross it.

I got stuck there. I was writing for young adults because I had found success there, not because I thought it was my natural genre. I thought for many years, I was kind of faking it, and that at some point, the police would knock on my door and say, "You're faking it. You're not a real young adult author. Why are you publishing these spooky books that give nightmares to kids?" And then the mothers go back to school say, "Oh, my God, have you seen what my kid is reading?"

I was doing well there and I was a working writer, and I was so concerned because you look around when you become a working writer and you see how hard it is just to survive as a writer and you feel like everybody's hanging from a rope over the abyss. And you look down and there's all these flames of hell. And you go like, "Oh, my God," and you're talking to the guy next to you, and he just drops there. And then you go, "I'm next. I'm next."

So if you find some success—I was very conservative—and I said, "You know what, I'm not jumping from the train." At the same time I started working as a screenwriter, and I thought I was going crazy because I was older and I realized, I've been a working writer and making a living but I've always been writing what other people want me to write and it's not what I want to do. So I need to, before I go completely crazy—I was thirty-two or thirty-three years old—so I needed to give myself a chance to do what I've always wanted to do at least once, and maybe allow myself to fail. Then I won't be able to say, "Well, you never tried."

I was working on a screenplay for a producer, and I asked the producer to fire me. I said, "You know, you're gonna fire me sooner or later. Fire me now. Pay me now, or fire me." He said, "Okay, go work on your art book, whatever. Let me know when you're done." He paid me off, and he freed me to do my crazy thing. My publisher of young adult books asked what I was working on. I said, "Well, I'm working on a new novel, but it's not going to be for you." "Well, what do we have to do to have it?" "It's not going to be for you." "We'll create a different imprint just for it." "No, it's not going to be for you." So I just started working on that, and that book became *The Shadow of the Wind*. It was the first time I had written something that was *exactly* what I wanted it to be. When it was published, of course, I was kind of a new author, for many people. "Dude, I've been doing this for many years. You weren't even born."

Nikki Giovanni

DN: Do you think that the deaths that have occurred around you in recent years and your own loss of a lung, do you write differently out of that?

It's a pretty sobering thing to live through what you've lived through in the last few years. Are you writing a little more seriously, maybe?

NG: I've always been serious. I'm not an unserious person. I think I've grown, and I think if anything I'm probably less serious. I find humor in things I used to not. I lost Mommy and my sister and my aunt and my dog, just in an incredibly short period of time.

DN: Within six months.

NG: You had things to do, and so I did them. I had not learned to cry, so I've been learning to cry now. And it's been the most interesting thing because now, little things are happening and it'll be like, "oh no!" I was reading a poem about quilts. It's sad poem. It caught me up. I think I'm not holding myself in. Like Black Americans, to some degree, I have been on a stage. I've learned to let some of the hurt go. I don't know what it does for my writing. I'm a relatively serious writer, and I think I'm relatively intelligent, but I've let some of the emotion out. I'm not holding it in the same way. But you hold things in your twenties in a way that you don't in your seventies. You say to yourself, "if I don't let it out in my seventies, when am I planning to let it out?" I'm learning to cry, and that's what the new book is called. I'm learning to cry.

Jane Smiley

DN: You wrote a very moving essay where you show that your mother had aspirations to be a writer, but your father told her that writing was for second-rate minds?

JS: His ideal piece of written work was the Army Field Manual.

DN: "Nothing could measure up to that," is what he said.

JS: Because it was very organized. He didn't see the novel or literature as a thing that was organized or precise. And that probably fits in with his mental issues. He had PTSD or was bipolar or schizophrenic. He could maybe—*maybe*—find himself getting lost in emotions when he's reading a novel. You can't get lost in emotions when he's reading the Army Field Manual. He went to West Point, he didn't do very well in the army, but he aspired to do well in the army.

DN: You have an interesting perspective where you said that his absence and your mother's distraction freed you from being raised with a lot of preconceptions. Then you write: "Sometimes from the outside my work and my life looked daring, but I'm not a daring person." As a writer, you're pretty daring.

JS: Well, but why not? You're sitting in your office, you're playing around with your materials, you have things going through your mind, and you want to try this, and you want to try that, and it's so much fun to play around with it, and so you just try it, and the sense of pleasure in creating whatever it is, gets in the way of worrying—"oh my god, what's happening"—and you know, some of the books appear daring from the outside, like *Ten Days in the Hills* . . .

DN: Completely different kind of novel of yours.

JS: Yes. After 9/11, I decided I was going to read some books from a long time ago to get my mind away from 9/11. So the first one I read was The Tale of Genji, which was 1000 years old. I figured, "What could be farther away from 9/11 than this?" Except that it was all about the ephemerality of existence. And I thought "Oh dear, OK, I'll try something else." So then I picked up the Decameron, which I'd heard of but never read, by Giovanni Boccaccio. My goodness, it's set in the Black Death! And this is around the time that those envelopes were going around with anthrax. There was a lot of anxiety about that. And here are these ten people outside of Florence in the middle of the Black Death, trying to distract themselves from what's happening all around them. I thought, "that's really fascinating." I loved the exuberance of the stories, and I loved that Boccaccio had taken a lot of the stories from the Hitopadesha which was actually Indian rather than European.

So I was casting around for the next one and I had never heard of this one before. It was the Heptameron by Marguerite of Navarre. I didn't even know who Marguerite of Navarre was. I've heard of her brother Francois I, and so I started reading the Heptameron and I was absolutely captivated because she had decided—she and her friends were stuck in Coterie and the Pyrenees in a spa, and they couldn't get out because of floods—so she decided she was going to re-write the Decameron, which was then 200 years old, now.

So she rewrote it and she said, "my two favorite rules for telling a bunch of stories." The first rule was every story had to be true. And the second rule was, every story had to be about whether a young woman could know true love and retain her virtue. They collected seventy-three stories. Some were funny and some were scary and some were interesting, and they talked about the stories once they were finished telling them, much more than they had in Boccaccio. That was because the Reformation and then the counter reformation had come along. They had learned to investigate their own ideas and thoughts and feelings a little more. At the end of the Heptameron, they decided "no, a woman cannot know true love and virtue at the same time." Then about a hundred years later, one of the next books I read—

DN: This is all post-9/11 reading.

JS: Yes. One of the next books I read was *The Princess of Cleves* by Madame de Lafayette. It's still a book they read in French schools. And the great thing about that is that she knew about the Heptameron. And she thought she would solve the riddle. She got the woman to know true love but still retain her virtue. But in a very characteristic way, a very seventeenth-century way.

But as soon as I read all those books, I thought the novel is really interesting as a historical form, as a form where it asked the reader to look within, where it says to the reader, "you have an inner life, and the more that you read about other people's inner lives, then the bigger your inner life gets." So finally, when you get to a book like *Orlando* by Virginia Woolf, which goes back and forth over the years, and goes between male and female, and that character has a huge inner life, and there's nothing that ever stops her from paying attention to her own inner life or his own inner life and enjoying it.

And that, to me, is what the novel is for. It's for cultivating a child's inner life so that when the child is sitting there, minding her manners, she's looking at the family saying, "God, this is *ridiculous.*" She's keeping her face straight, but thinking, "these people are *crazy!*" And I'm going to write a book about it!

DN: But did reading all of those really deep and historical works help you in some way get through the trauma of 9/11?

JS: Well, it inspired me. How did we get through the trauma of 9/11? For a lot of writers, the thing that they were working on when 9/11 happened suddenly looked tiny and worthless. For me, to go and read all those other books and to understand the events that those authors have lived through, it put 9/11 into perspective. Am I going to say to Giovanni Boccaccio, "well, 9/11 is more important than the Black Death?" No. Reading how all of those other authors had processed the worlds that they lived in and the trauma that they lived through was very helpful to me. I get more excited and interested the more that I read them. I didn't set out to write *13 Ways*. But I just started reading those books and I just had to do it because it was so interesting.

Christian Wiman

CW: I want my poems to be read a hundred years from now. I'm aiming for that. I work really hard to make them last. A poet that I've loved recently is Yehuda Amichai, the great Israeli poet. He says "not like a cyprus but like the grass." He doesn't want to be this iconic thing towering over people. That's a memorial. He wants to be like the grass, so it's everywhere, it's available, it's in people's lives. I aspire to that as well.

DN: You said once that writing poetry is trying to address some sort of an absence. Isn't that really what all art does?

CW: It's a good question. For the longest time I thought that art arose out of some sort of destitution. Dickinson calls it "sumptuous destitution." I thought it was always trying to fill some lack. If you didn't have the lack, why would you make the art? If everything is just right in your life, there's the old expression "light writes white." If everything is great, if your life is all light, well then you've got a blank page: it's white. Light writes white. There's no inspiration. There's gotta be some friction, some tension, something's gotta be wrong in order for you to get some ink on the page. I don't really believe that anymore.

I think Nietzsche had it right when he said that he judged all work based on whether it arose out of hunger or super abundance. One or the other. And he had contempt for the ones that came out of hunger. He was only interested in the ones that came out of super abundance. I think a couple things about that. The line is too strong, too stark. Those things, hunger and super abundance, can be linked and fused with each other. Part of my maturation as a writer and just as a person, has been learning to recognize moments of joy. Of super abundance, of excess, and those have definitely led to art.

DN: But in story, which is more my area than poetry, it seems like only conflict is interesting. So if everything is going great, I'm probably not in the mood to write about it.

CW: I'm not sure. More and more I feel and I respond to poems that manage to help me to recognize joy. I did a whole anthology of poems about joy. It is true that on this side of the grave, in this side of Eden, there is no unalloyed joy.

DN: You have said that some poems you created, and some you channeled.

CW: Oh yeah. I've been writing poetry since I was eighteen, nineteen, and younger than that if you count what I did when I was seven years old. It is as much a mystery to me now, if not more, than it's ever been. I don't understand where the poems come from; I can do nothing to make them come. I seem powerless to make them come. And powerless to determine their quality. In one sense it's an exalting feeling. It's wonderful to have that in your life. On another—it's frustrating to spend your life learning this thing and still feel so baffled by it.

DN: One of your poems, called *The Ice Storm* you have these lines ``And who would guess that as the years find their final focus you're bothered less by the dark that lies ahead of you, than the dark lies that lies behind?" It's just such a beautiful way of looking at uncertainty.

CW: The future doesn't matter in that instance. It's not the dark that lies ahead of you that you're scared of, it's the dark that lies behind the chances that you've neglected in the past. It's the life that you haven't lived. That poem—*The Ice Storm*—is about a couple, a man and a woman spending a single day together, a long-married couple, and it alternates with their voices. I knew them intimately. It's a sad poem. The person speaking that poem is realizing that there's a lot of unlived life behind her that she fears worse than the death ahead.

DN: Do you live with that kind of regret?

CW: No, no. I don't. No, I'm happy with my life. I've gone all in with poetry. If I hadn't gone all in with poetry I think I'd be in real, real trouble, but I really went all in, I really did it. So I don't regret that.

Alice Walker

DN: It seems like you're fearless. Are you?

AW: Seems like I'm furious?

DN: No, I'll try to enunciate better. Fearless. No, you do not look furious to me right now. You're such a gentle soul, where it's all about love. And yet, when you write, you swing a pretty big hammer.

AW: I'm free.

DN: What do you mean?

AW: It means that I take responsibility for my life, for myself, for being here. I feel that the least I can do on this incredible planet—wherever it is we are in space—the least I can do is to be my full being and express what it is that I am. And what I see then, I have a right to address it.

DN: So that freedom gives you a sense of "I can write about whatever I want"?

AW: Exactly.

DN: One of your poems is about wanting to take you own life. There's a line: "writing poems is my way of celebrating with the world that I have not committed suicide the evening before."

AW: Oh yeah. But I didn't take my own life. I can only be grateful that I had this experience of being very near to ending this phase of whatever this is, this existence in this realm, and I managed to stay around for forty or fifty more years, which is remarkable! I always say to people who are suicidal, wait until morning. Don't do it now, when you feel like you have to, because who knows what the gift is that is trying to be given to you, in terms of understanding, and growing, and being compassionate to yourself and other people.

DN: You also battled Lyme disease. You said that opened up your inner self, "as if my illness had pushed open an inner door that my usual consciousness was willing to ignore." That's the key to great writing, right? Where you get to those interior rooms that we've been avoiding for so long?

AW: I think of it as healing. I think that whatever the writing is, it's an expression of the healing. In other words, what I'm able to offer to a reader is in some ways like the medicine that I already had, so I know it works.

DN: But can't we do that kind of healing, or get to that really amazing artistic expression without having to go through all that crap?

AW: No.

DN: You were pretty quick with that answer.

AW: Some people like to be kind of a lightweight.

DN: Well, don't look at me!

AW: Maybe it's possible without suffering, but I doubt it. I think we're wrong that suffering is to be avoided. I don't think so. I actually don't think we can avoid it anyway. So you learn how to do it. Jesus said, "learn to suffer, and you will not suffer." Gnostic gospels.

DN: That was in a different Bible, but go ahead.

AW: That was in the one I really like.

DN: I've written a few of my own books of the Bible that I like better too.

AW: I'm sure. But it's important to know that this whole thing we think about trying to avoid suffering—like don't let that happen to me, I can't, blah blah blah—you know, suffering has a use like everything else. And in my opinion, if it doesn't kill you, even if it feels like it for many years, it is really trying to deliver something very important to your understanding and the growth of your compassion.

Don Winslow

DN: Your books and your short stories did well, but it was when *Savages* came out, that's when you got the world's attention.

DW: Yeah, that was kind of a bust out. It was very different in style for me and probably different in style for everybody. And of course they made a film of it, which changes the trajectory.

DN: What I love about *Savages* is you were afraid about what you were writing. I think you had even confessed you weren't sure you even should finish it. What was the problem?

DW: It was so far away stylistically from anything I had ever done. I was really just writing that to play with language. I wanted to play with a certain kind of southern California language. The book is set in Laguna Beach, and wondered if I could pull that off. I sent the first fourteen pages to my agent and said, either this is either really great or I'm crazy. He wrote back right away and said, drop everything else you're doing and finish this, which I did.

DN: The lesson there is sometimes the thing you're most afraid to write or the most afraid to pursue, that's really code for this is what you have to do.

DW: It was certainly the case with *Savages* and very much the case with *City on Fire*.

DN: Because you hadn't written about your hometown before—was that the reluctance?

DW: I left when I was seventeen, left that culture and went out to the Midwest. Then I wandered the world for a long time. I think there is still is a part of me that feels like I betrayed people by leaving. You grew up with that sort of tribal loyalty in this fishing village where you play hockey and a lot of the kids my age went out in the fishing boats. Three of my classmates died out there in the fishing crew. And so I got out and I had all of these sort of wonderful experiences. And I think I've always felt a little guilty.

DN: So did it feel weird to go back and walk those shores and streets as you were writing about it and recreating it?

DW: I would describe it as evocative. My wife and I started to go back really to take care of my aging mother, as one does. I'm sure people are familiar with this experience. We started going back for longer and longer periods of time as necessity dictated. That was in some ways a sad time, but also I began to rediscover the soulfulness of the place, the beauty of the place, which is undeniable. I'd go down Matunuck Beach Road on this sliver of Rhode Island and I got juiced, I got excited.

DN: Did you then have this sense of, "I've got to write about this place."

DW: Yeah. Look, I wrote the first sentence of this book twenty-seven years ago. I would pick it up. Put it down. I'd pick it up, I'd put it down. It was always sort of there. In the interim I wrote this big sort of drug trilogy, which was never intended to be one. And a book about NYPD and some other stuff. And then Covid happened. And I just felt, ok, I think something's talking to me. Now's the time.

Anthony Doerr

DN: After *Molluscs*, you wrote something for a high school short story contest with another one-word title, "Avalanche." But before you submitted that story, you did what all of the characters in your novels do: you went to the library.

AD: That's right, Dean. Good interviewer.

DN: What did you find there in the library before you turned in your short story called "Avalanche?"

AD: I looked for a book, but I was looking for how to write books. We didn't grow up going to writer's symposia, is that plural?

DN: Yeah, symposia. That's correct.

AD: It wasn't a family where we're like, "Norman Mailer is coming over for dinner," or something. I thought writers lived in Paris or Buenos Aires or were dead.

DN: Those are the options?

AD: I thought you'd have as much chance of becoming a writer as you would have of becoming a blue whale or something.

DN: So you go to the library for directions on how to become a writer.

AD: I probably asked the librarian because I wasn't good at using the catalog, and I found a book, *How to Write Short Stories.* The author had a few rules, but my instinct—this is when I was an adolescent—was to try to invert every rule that was given me. Things like, "Short stories must only have one protagonist. They must stay in a single point of view. There must be clear rising action, falling action"—can't quite remember his rules. But at that age, you're just like, read the first four pages and think, "I'm going to resist all these rules." I was worried because "Avalanche" had a dog character. It was from the point of view of a dog. I wrote a very serious short story that did not win the short story competition in high school.

DN: Here's what I love about what you said about this: "I wanted to make big sprawling jungles, but the author of that book said, 'I ought to be growing little bonsai trees.'"

AD: I probably misinterpreted him, but yeah.

DN: I think you've got the last laugh because all of your books are big sprawling jungles.

AD: Well, you oscillate between making the little leaves that make up the jungle. I mean, most of your time you're like creating these little jewelers' works, and then it's only when you take time to step away that you're like, "Oh, right, there's a whole story I need to tell here. I just spent four hours retooling what this girl's bedroom looks like." And you don't even realize maybe three months later you cut that scene where you describe her bedroom. You're always oscillating between using your loop to look at the microscopic layer of things, like, "How do my sentences look and work and feel and breathe and sound?" And then you step away. You take a walk or do the dishes, and you're like, "What is the larger narrative here? What is the whole shape of this thing I'm making?" So I want to make the jungle, but you have to make each individual piece inside the jungle. It's like building a house, but you have to build everything in the house. You don't get to call the plumber who brings in the prefixed toilet. Prefix—that's a mixed metaphor, though—"prefix" the toilet.

DN: You started out writing short stories, then you had a science column in *The Boston Globe*. Science has always been a theme: there are radio waves and gemstones and mollusks and snow crystals. I'm guessing because your mom was a science teacher, and the trips to Florida, that had something to do with your fascination with science?

AD: I think so. I was never taught to think in terms like, "You should now choose when you're 18 years old, whether you want to go to the art building for the rest of your life, or the science building. Make a choice, Jimmy. The science building will make more money!" I never had to think that way. I went to a Montessori school through seventh grade; maybe that was part of it. Mom was definitely part of it. I think of science and even theology and the arts as all ways of just investigating this wild, mad, amazing life, this chance we get to be here on this planet—if we're lucky eight decades, and then it's gone. Why not learn as much as you can, and who cares what you call learning? When they asked me to write the science column for *The Boston Globe*, it was on science books written for the layperson. I said, "You understand I'm totally unqualified to write this." But that was the point.

I loved that job. It was back when people read physical newspapers. I feel like that was an amazing grad school after grad school those ten years, because every four weeks I'd have to read three or four books. Sometimes string theory, sometimes new challenges to some element of the theory of evolution or something that would really keep me abreast. I miss that, even though the deadlines sometimes can wear you down.

DN: You wrote this collection of short stories, *Shell Collector*, everybody goes wild over it, and you follow it up with a novel *About Grace*. Why not stick with what got you all the acclaim, which is short story? Why try a novel when you know short stories are working?

AD: Dean, you've got to get on the phone with more literary agents. They're like, "Oh, these are great little stories. When is your novel coming out?" There's a whole debate in academic circles, the chicken or the egg, because publishers don't expect short story collections to sell; perhaps they don't promote them as much. But the truth is, in the days of Edith Wharton and Fitzgerald and Hemingway, when people were tired at the end of a work day, you would open the Saturday Evening Post and consume 7,000, 8,000 words of fiction. And now, it's pretty easy to fire up your machines that give you Law and Order or whatever, some Netflix thing on tennis, and you're like, "Bloooop!" and you do that, and that's your story fix. Humans are still just as addicted to narrative as ever, but there are a lot more shiny ways to go get it.

There's a little more interest in novels because that's a form of narrative that humans can't quite get anywhere else. Although long-form TV is starting to infringe in some ways, in interesting and really great ways, but some narratives take you nine to ten hours to consume. I think humans still really like to find that in written, printed texts.

N. Scott Momaday

DN: Were you thinking of yourself as a novelist when House Made of Dawn was published? It seemed to me that you were thinking of yourself as a poet and you also had done this novel, even though you weren't a novelist?

NSM: Yes, that was very much on my mind. I did write poetry exclusively when I was at Stanford, with one exception I did write a short story, but mostly poetry for three to four years. I found myself in a corner. I wanted elbow room, so when I got my first teaching post at Santa Barbara, I began the novel and it was a wonderful thing to do with this change of pace, and so I became a novelist. That was not what I set out to be, but there it was.

DN: You had written yourself into a corner as a poet?

NSM: I got tired of writing poetry because that's all I did for those four years. I came out of Stanford thinking, I'm going to try something else, so I did.

DN: Winning a Pulitzer for your first novel, especially when you didn't consider yourself a novelist, could have put enormous pressure on you.

"I'm the Pulitzer Prize-winning N. Scott Momaday." But it actually worked the opposite for you—it just freed you up to do what you wanted to do after that. Is that correct?

NSM: Yes. Once I had the novel under my belt, I felt free to go back to poetry. I still consider myself a poet rather than a novelist, but I've written in so many different forms, plays, travel literature, essays, and two novels, and a good deal of poetry. That's fine with me, I like that production.

DN: It didn't put too much pressure on you?

NSM: I don't think so. The novel put some pressure on me because when I finished it, I began getting, suddenly, invitations to women's garden parties, and invitation to write for different publications and so on. So it saved me from the publish or perish necessity and gave me a freedom. But there were some pressure, too. How do I follow that? I think it slowed me down for a time, but it didn't matter in the long run.

DN: You have evolved as a poet. You said in recent years, you've been freed up a little bit from rhyme and meter, from what you had been doing before. Is that an evolution that you like or do you sometimes still play with needing to go back to rhyme and meter?

NSM: I go back to rhyme and meter quite often, but I'm very pleased with having brought elements of the Native American oral tradition, especially into my writing. It's valid. It's wonderful. It's not English verse, but it's a kind of expression that is based upon repetition, largely imagery, and more important than anything else, faith, as an understanding that what you're doing is sacred.

DN: I love this line of yours where you say if just one poem stands the test of time, that's something that justifies your existence. A poem that stands the test of time. That's an accomplishment.

NSM: It can be a great accomplishment, like Tuckerman's "Cricket," for example. That's one poem that justifies his whole existence. You can say that about very few poems.

DN: Do you have a work that you point to that, other than the Pulitzer, that you feel justifies your existence, that's going to stand the test of time?

NSM: It doesn't have to justify your existence to anyone but yourself.

DN: Fair enough, but which one of yours does that?

NSM: There are two or three candidates for that. There's one called "Before an Early Painting of the Crucifixion." I spent a lot of time fashioning that poem. It shows the concentration I put into it. There's another called The Bear, which did justify me to other people. It was given the Academy of American Poets Prize at Stanford. I wrote it very soon after I got there, maybe the second year that I was there, and it is a syllabic poem. It is one of the best poems ever written, I think.

DN: Do you look back at that and say, "I did what I set out to do?"

NSM: Yes. I did it. I did it. And what a great satisfaction that is.

DN: You started painting well after you had written novels and poems and screenplays. What creative urge is going on there that you're working with brushes and ink and charcoal?

NSM: I had a long experience of drawing and painting when I was a child because my father was a painter, and I used to watch him work. I wasn't interested in becoming a painter until I went to Russia. That opened the door for me. But I watched my father work and I think I learned a lot by osmosis, just watching. Finally I came to the point where I needed to express myself in those terms. When I was in Russia I felt isolated. I was very conscious of my distance from my native land, so I began to draw and paint. That was to relieve myself and to give myself some sort of anchor, which worked. It was successful.

DN: But you're a different kind of painter from your father. Your father's paintings are very specific lines, straight lines, yours are a little more—

NSM: Messy.

DN: I wouldn't have said messy—I would have said less defined. So why that approach? Why these smudges as opposed to straight lines? I didn't mean that an insulting way, it's just that I can tell you're doing different things with the brushes.

NSM: He did kind of painting that I cannot do. I don't have the talent for doing the fine brushwork that he did, the two-dimensional, fine lines, as you say. I want to get done and start creating things that come out of my mind that are not in confirmation with any particular idea of painting. I just express what is in my view to paint. I'm much more spontaneous than my father was.

7

Worldview, Pessimism, and Optimism

How Does Your Mindset Affect Your Writing?

It's very dangerous to become cynics.

JOSEPH WAMBAUGH

Our writing is shaped by many factors: what we read, our life experience, our ancestry, where we were raised, the circumstances in which we were raised, our experience with pain, our experience with joy, whether we were loved well—if at all. These things contribute to how we see the world, and then how we express ourselves in our writing.

Many of us have witnessed brutality AND love. The writing that speaks best to me is when a writer captures that brutality, but punctures it with love or mercy or grace. Because, for me, that is the most accurate portrayal of real life. It's a mess. It's chaos. Yet occasionally it's breathtakingly beautiful.

Writing that shows the tension of pain and love is a good indication of the writer's view of how the world works. If you read Don Winslow, for instance, you see that crime is everywhere, every human heart is corrupt, and we're all headed for a murderous showdown. But there are glimpses of exceptions. Flickers of light. Faint reasons to hope. I asked him about this when I interviewed him, and he smiled at my assessment. He agreed that his main character is motivated by love, but he does some terrible things.

In my opinion, that is Winslow's view of humanity. Each of us has the capacity to love, and each of us has the capacity to be awful. We live in that tension. At least that's how I interpret his worldview through his writing.

Alice Walker and I talked about something similar. Her characters are also motivated by love, even though they are surrounded by hateful forces. Life for her characters is a struggle. That struggle, however, is buoyed by acts of mercy and compassion, sometimes from complete strangers. This is also a worldview. Given some of the injustices and criticisms she has faced for her writing, her characters and her skin color, one could presume that her novels would be infused with rage and hate. Some of her characters do exhibit rage and hate, but that's not the overall tone of her writing. Why not? "Because I'm free," she told me. That freedom was shaped by her life experience, her religious practice, and her view of the world. As I read Walker, love ultimately emerges, even from the most despicable circumstances.

All of us have a worldview. We may not be able to articulate it very well in conversations, but it will come out in our writing. That's where the rest of us will see it.

Joseph Wambaugh

DN: The *New York Times* said you used police writing as a way to express your views of society. Is that an accurate statement?

JW: Yeah, I guess if I'm that pessimistic and cynical, I guess it is.

DN: Are you pessimistic and cynical?

JW: My characters are pretty much, aren't they?

DN: Are you that pessimistic and cynical?

JW: I probably am.

DN: Did the job do that to you?

JW: I know that the job did. Definitely. I was much more romantic and optimistic, as a young person is, or should be. And police work did warp me a bit. I just hang out now with dogs.

DN: A police officer sees the worst side of human beings.

JW: Sees the worst of people and ordinary people at their worst. That's more damaging, I think to the cops. Seeing ordinary people at their worst makes him or her prematurely cynical, and young people shouldn't be as cynical as we became. It's very dangerous to become cynics.

DN: So out of that did you develop a worldview—and what is it?

JW: I did, yeah. That's what I write about. I write about young people who are cynics and have to operate in a world where people do not necessarily love them. I mean, if you want love, you should become a fireman not a cop. That's glib, but you do want love. And you don't get it. In fact, people actively dislike you sometimes. And the better you do the job, the more they dislike you.

DN: However, I think your worldview changed from *New Centurions* to *Floaters.*

JW: I got old.

Chitra Divakaruni

DN: In *Sister of My Heart*, one of your characters says, "That's the thing about us human beings. When we really love someone, we can be happy even when our heart is breaking." I think you've just defined the human experience with a statement like that. Is that your philosophy? Or was that one of those "true to the character" kinds of things? The whole world spins on a statement like that. Where did that come from?

CD: The primary impulse was that it came out of the character, and her situation and her understanding of the situation. But I think I do agree with that, and I'm glad to see that you do too.

DN: I think that sums it up, that you can have both experiences simultaneously.

CD: That's one of the complexities of human emotion and human loving: that you can love, in the best cases, in the most unselfish cases, you can be unhappy, *and* happy at the same time, because you can put someone else's life in front of yours, which is what Sudha and Anju keep doing for each other in *Sister of My Heart*, in spite of the fact that they often exasperate each other and they're often not agreeing about things.

DN: They put themselves at risk for the other to such an extent that it causes them tremendous anguish and grief. Is that your worldview right there, that this is what human beings do?

CD: I think I would say that. That's my view of, or my hope, and my understanding, that human beings can do that. It's not that we do that often. We do that rarely. But when it does happen, it's wonderful. And it's definitely worth celebrating.

Luis Alberto Urrea

LU: I told a friend of mine recently that I felt that I wrote the saddest comedies, or the funniest tragedies, and I couldn't tell which that was.

DN: They are both.

LU: I don't know why that happens. I think we all go through a real ration of crap in our lives, every one of us. I'm trying to honor that in everybody. I'm trying to really remind myself to keep my heart open to other human beings and what they're going through. I don't think it's monochromatic. People are astonished when they go to the Tijuana garbage dump that those people are funny and loving, and can be kind. I worked with a photographer from Harvard named Jack Booth—very good photographer—and I took him to the dump where he started photographing.

One day a cliff collapsed and covered a woman, and he dropped all his cameras and helped them dig the woman out, and thought, "My cameras are gone." But he went back to see, and the workers had set the cameras on a piece of cardboard out of the dirt on the bluff. He was astonished. We mentioned it to one of the women who worked the trash dump, and she said, "It's a workplace, you have to take care of your tools." It never occurred to them to steal it. They could have gotten a lot out of it. So those moments of our shared humanity mean a lot to me.

DN: Do you think you recognize that better because of your own personal pain that you had gone through? I mean, think about the diseases you had as a kid. German measles, Scarlet Fever, tuberculosis, you were abused. Do you think there was something out of that pain personally, that makes it so that you can recognize that condition better?

LU: I don't sit around saying, "Ohhhh, my pain!" But everybody here has felt pain. Everybody here has had some heartbreak. Everyone. It was hard for me to understand that everybody I meet at some point in their life has lived in the Tijuana garbage dump. It may be a much better dump than I can imagine. What was that you said to me today? About the guy who broke his back?

DN: Tim Hensel said, "Pain is inevitable. But misery is optional."

LU: Misery is optional. That's amazing. To me, it's all about choosing to live in joy, choosing to do the work that's required of you to fully enjoy the goodness that we have. Because it's very easy to keep dwelling on the badness, and I've done it, and it takes you down to the bricks, it takes you to your death. As an artist, I feel that I want to represent real people in all of their glory and foolishness, shame and pain, too. I'm trying to learn in my own life that your shame does not make you shameful; it's part of your being heroic. The things you have been handed that are difficult, are not what put you down, are not what diminish you. They're what ultimately lift you up and make something greater of you.

DN: In one of your books you say that your writings are the scars, but they're also the blossoming of the difficulties and the pain that you have experienced. They're both!

LU: I think so, but that's across the board. Think about any immigrant writer, for example. It's part of the American tradition of literature.

Chris Bohjalian

DN: You have a character in *Sandcastle Girls* who is forced to make a really, really difficult moral call at the end, and it causes her unspeakable grief, but it spares her husband from unspeakable grief. So I want to know a bigger question from you: do we all die with our secrets?

CB: Most of my books are about regret. I didn't realize this until I had been in San Diego this past January.

DN: You regretted not moving here from Vermont in January?

CB: I was being interviewed by a reporter from the *San Diego Union-Tribune* about *The Sleepwalker*, my most recent book, and he observed that the epigraph for my previous novel, *The Guest Room*, was a quote from one of my favorite doorstops, Dr. Zhivago, and the epigraph is this: "I don't think I could love you so deeply if you have nothing to lose or nothing to regret."

And while it might be dread that causes readers to turn the pages of my books, the operative emotion for the characters, I realized in that interview, was regret. So, when I think of the decision that Elizabeth Endicott makes in this book, it is something that maybe she will regret, maybe she won't, but yes, it is, like for so many of us, one of those secrets that is best, *best* going to the grave. There are moments when honesty is great, and there are moments when you just smile and say that you really love mushrooms on your pizza.

DN: But that secret emerges generations later.

CB: It does.

DN: So again, I'm just wondering, is that your cosmic view, that ultimately these things find the light?

CB: Can I tell you a story that takes about two minutes to tell?

DN: I would love to hear a story from you!

CB: This is a story I think about a lot when I think of the secrets of the Armenian Genocide, and a story I think about a lot when I think of how there are echoes from the past that will never be silenced. You can't kill one and a half million people without there being mass graves. Eastern Turkey, Syria are awash in unmarked mass graves. In 2013, I was with my great friend, Khatchig Mouradian, and five other Armenian-Americans, and went to one. The history books say that over a three-day period in 1915, 10,000 Armenians were marched to the edge of this 350-foot ravine and every single one of them was killed, bayoneted, slaughtered; their bodies thrown unceremoniously to the bottom.

After we paid our respects, we went to see the remains of the Armenian church and monastery, and they're gorgeous. When we're leaving, a Kurdish gentleman knocked on our van door and said, "You can't leave, you have to meet my mother-in-law. She's 98." This was 2013. We did the math; she was born in 1915. So, we went to meet her and thank goodness we did because in this case, the history books were wrong. Not *every* Armenian was killed in that cataclysmic three-day period. There was one young woman in the line who was so beautiful that a member of the Kurdish killing party pulled her from the line and married her. She had in her arms, her newborn baby girl, an infant, and he raised her as his own, and that's who we met that day.

Here's why the story is important. Going back to your question of secrets, and whether they ever lay buried forever. At one point when my friend was interviewing her, she looked at all of us and she said, "You're Armenian, you're Armenian, you're really Armenian." And that's when I got it. Her son-in-law was a good man, a very good man. It wasn't that he wanted us to meet her, he wanted her to meet us; to see that while she's the last living Armenian in the area, the race continues. We live on, and she's still alive today—102. And, in fact, you know, when I've gone back, I brought my wife and daughter so that she could meet yet another generation of Armenian-Americans. She, and her stories, will live on.

I wrote about her for *The Washington Post*, and I tell the story to anyone who will listen. I don't know what they were thinking in 1915, whether anyone would know, or why it was in any way okay, to kill 10,000 women, children, and men. But the fact is, she lived, and her story lives on.

DN: Through people like you.

CB: And people like you.

DN: *The Sandcastle Girls,* in the middle of all of this horror, the brutality, the unspeakable stuff that goes on, here are people trying to do good;

they're showing mercy, and they're showing grace, and they're showing love, and kindness. Is there a worldview coming from you that says, "This is what humanity is like as well"?

CB: Absolutely. There's a very important reason that two of the most morally righteous characters in this book are Turkish. There's the physician and there's a young Turkish soldier named Orhan, who disobeys a very specific order. He's named after Orhan Pamuk, the Turkish Nobel laureate who was tried in Turkey for defaming Turkishness for acknowledging the Armenian Genocide. The fact is that there is an awful lot of horror in this world. I mean, my gosh, I don't just mean the natural horrors, I mean, the horrors that we inflict upon each other as human beings; the genocidal horrors, the war horrors, you know, nations chemical-weaponing their own citizens. But there are also enormously beautiful small acts of goodness and kindness. I'm sure if you look at ravaged Key West after a hurricane—or Key Largo and Houston, or Aleppo, Syria after Bashar al-Assad's attacks on his own citizens—you will see the individual heroes whose names will be forever lost to history, but who do good, who rescue seniors, who rescue infants, who are caregivers. That is who we are too.

DN: That is humanity's story as much as the other.

CB: We are not just genocidal maniacs, there's also good in our heart.

Alice Walker

DN: Which is more effective for getting things to change—writing or violence?

AW: For me writing.

DN: Now why did you just say "for me"? Do you think that's not always the case?

AW: I can't say for sure. I can only really speak for myself. It's something I had to learn through real rigor. There are insults to the soul—apartheid is such an insult. It is a major insult every day. You feel like you need to protect your soul, just from being destroyed, and writing is what helped me. Of course I have felt violent. It's a natural human instinct when you are oppressed, obviously. Martin [Luther King Jr.] I'm sure at times felt violent. What is so wonderful about his greatness, as with Gandhi, is that turning away from that, and doing the effort to transform a culture in a different way without violence, is very very challenging. And it's why we love them.

DN: There are some things in your writing that deal with hate. You said, "I found, in my own writing, that a little hatred, keenly directed, is a useful thing. Once spread about, however, it becomes a web in which I would sit caught and paralyzed like the fly who stepped into the parlor." Can hate be directed or harnessed a little to accomplish something?

AW: Yes, I think so.

DN: Like what, for example?

AW: Well, my hatred of plastic in the ocean.

DN: The reason I fixated on hate is because there are a couple of places, like in "*The Third Life of Grange Copeland*," the character disrupts church services that are teaching about love, and he shouts, "teach them to hate, teach them to hate, if you want them to survive!" That just sounded so powerful.

AW: It's powerful, but it's not a good thing. He knows what he means. But actually when you teach people to hate, you're teaching them to wound themselves. Because hate is like a very sharp knife, and you can easily cut yourself. That's why love is actually better. Even though we suffer so much trying to change society by using or having love, hatred is not really controllable. You can feel that you can sometimes hate one person, but it grows like anything else.

DN: But, that character, Brownley's wife, you describe her as having a weakness for forgiving people. "A stupid belief," it says "that kindness can convert the enemy." It didn't work out that well for her in your book.

AW: You know, you're reading a book I haven't read in thirty years. I hardly remember it.

DN: Then I can tell you pretty much anything that's in there! You won't know! Do you want to talk about forgiveness?

AW: Well, I think forgiveness is essential.

DN: But it killed her!

AW: Well, it killed her. But *not* forgiving may have killed her as well. And it may have killed her before she died.

DN: I want to ask about your philosophy. I'm taking this out of "The World Has Changed." "The way I see it, life is about growth, struggle, and trying to expand your love of self and of other people. Also, to really try hard to not cause harm, to cultivate a way of life that is harmless. This is likely to take all of your energy, for your entire life. And if you harm some folks along the way, well that's why the apology was invented."

Is that still the case?

AW: I think so. We're just bound human beings, really. Some of us, for whatever reason, are just not up to par at certain times, and that is why the apology is still useful. And we should not be afraid to use it.

Don Winslow

DN: When I got to this particular page in *City on Fire*, I thought the whole thing comes down to page 302. This is where you get philosophical. You write, "The nuns used to say that the devil comes disguised as an angel. That the worst thing you'll do, you'll do for the best reasons. The most hateful things you'll do, you do for the ones you love the most." This is the main character's conflict. He's remembering this from his schooling. And you keep ratcheting up the pressure on this guy. I think it comes down to this dialogue between Danny and his accountant.

DW: Okay. I'm with you. I'm fascinated.

DN: I promise, I know where this is going.

DW: I trust you.

DN: Danny is talking to his accountant and discussing what Danny is about to do, and Danny says, "This is a one-time thing." And the accountant says, "Your soul is never a rental. It's always a sale." The accountant said this. What do accountants do? They're the ones who see the true cost. It wasn't a priest, wasn't a nun, it wasn't his wife, wasn't a family member, it was an accountant who was saying, this is what it's coming down to. Then Danny prays, not for forgiveness, but for strength to do something awful. Oh my gosh. There, in my opinion, is where this whole thing hinges. You've built up this character and now we've got him on the precipice. He knows he's about to commit something for which there is no forgiveness.

DW: Exactly.

DN: That's pretty philosophical, don't you think?

DW: For a crime writer.

DN: A crime writer who never finished journalism school.

DW: Failed photography twice.

DN: The Danny character has this saying—"If you want to build a new life and a clean life, you can't do it on top of sin." So he has this redemptive moment, but then that sends him in a whole other direction. That's where book two and three . . .

DW: Books two and three come in. Very perceptive, very astute of you. I carry that theme through the three books. Here's this guy, who out of love for his family and his friends and his community, his neighborhood, does some terrible things. And then he has to run. And then he tries to leave his past behind him. He's a basically decent guy, but you know, warning: Objects in the rear view mirror may be closer than they appear.

Anthony Doerr

DN: There's such a morality in your characters. They all have these moral quandaries, and yet there's this kind of fundamental drive to do—I hate the cliché, I know it makes me sound lazy—but to do the right thing. They struggle with what they want to do and what they end up doing, and then they usually do the right thing. Is that part of your own kind of sense of humanity that we all have this fundamental morality to us that we're going to do the right thing?

AD: I would answer that differently depending on what news articles I've read most recently.

DN: That's fair.

AD: In *Cloud Cuckoo Land*, I explored this end-of-history illusion where people always seem to think they're living at the end of history. I think about my parents crawling under the desks getting trained for atomic warfare. They're growing up with this idea that civilization could end any minute. Some of the book is set in the fifteenth century—these people in Constantinople in 1453 as this enormous Islamic army is coming to take the city. The city walls had stood for 1,000 years at this point. They genuinely believed that the world was ending, like history, the final period was being put on history, and that the second coming was there. That's what all these Christians believed inside the city. And, of course, history has just kept going.

I find hope in that. Each time you read more about any historical period, you're like, "Okay, we've been through this before." You can feel despairing about that, but you can also feel hopeful, like people keep finding ways.

DN: I know you have some Catholic upbringing, but I don't know that that's what's informing you now necessarily. You're tapped into some kind of spiritual or transcendent stuff when you write. Just the way you embrace mystery and wonder. You've got this line where you say, "Writing is better understood as kind of a prayer, an inquiry, something best done over time, repetitively, day after day." I read your stuff and I feel spiritually uplifted. Is that just a by-product, unintentional, or do you know you're tapping into some transcendent or mystery?

AD: No, I'm like eating a donut, just barely trying to get a sentence out.

DN: That's not to say donuts—

AD: There it is. The path to the universal is through the donut.

DN: There could be a Eucharistic quality.

AD: There are days when literally I'm like, "Just make it to 10:00 a.m., and then you can walk and get a donut." That's kind of my goal. I'm sugar motivated. I do think that I feel very acutely maybe because of Grandma, maybe because of losing a couple friends when I was young, like maybe I overestimate the threat of mortality, but man, we barely get to be here. The Earth is four-and-a-half billion years old. Humans have only been harvesting and collecting crops for 12,000 years maybe. Writing has barely been around. I get to participate in this thing.

Amor Towles

DN: This is my favorite line in the novella, and it's toward the end, where the Charlie character says, "If we don't stare down the thing that makes us want to look away, then the world is just a mirage."

AT: Yeah.

DN: Is that true in writing for you—that that's the thing you have to write about is the thing that you would rather just look away from?

AT: I probably don't do that enough. It's a very interesting question because I'm not a writer who is, for instance, saying, "What are the challenges that we face as a society right now? What's going on politically? What's going on as we tackle issues of race or gender or generationally or right-wing, left-wing?" I am absolutely not that person, that writer. So, it's so funny that Charlie says that because he's probably right. For me, it has to be a different version of that, which is that it has to be the willingness to look at the way humans behave and interact and to look at them very closely and with generosity so that you can see, because we all have our limitations, and we all have our strengths. To bring characters to life accurately, you really have to embrace the variety of human experience and the variety of human personalities and give them each their due. That's the thing that I really try to achieve.

Alice Walker, 2020

Amy Tan, 2003

Joseph Wambaugh, 1997, in the first Writer's Symposium interview

Joyce Carol Oates, 2015

Mary Karr, 2011

Nikki Giovanni, 2016

Peter Matthiessen, 2005

Pico Iyer, 2020

Dean Nelson, horrified by something Ray Bradbury said, 2001

8

When the World Says No How Do You Handle Rejection and Criticism?

> You can't learn anything and improve from positive reviews, so you can learn something from those bad reviews if you can find a way to read them and not be too emotionally distraught.
>
> ANTHONY DOERR

I'm sure I'm not the first person to tell you this, but success has very little to teach you. In my interview with Billy Collins, he told me that he sent several poems to Poetry Magazine when he was a teenager. The editor wrote back and suggested he keep writing poems, but to stop sending them in to the magazine.

Peter Matthiessen got a rejection from an editor who said that James Fenimore Cooper had written a similar novel, and that Cooper's was much better.

Chris Bohjalian's writing professor suggested he go into banking instead of writing.

Anchee Min grew up under the dictatorship of Mao Zedong who publicly despised writers. A chef or a butcher was of much more value to society, Mao said.

And yet here we are. They kept at it.

We've all heard the stories about how long J. K. Rowling worked on the Harry Potter stories, how many rejections the Twilight series received, the rejections for Anne Frank's diary, as well as for *A Wrinkle in Time*, *Gone With the Wind*, and on and on.

But, as Stephen Marche says in his book *On Writing and Failure*, the stories of famous books being rejected "are about as useful as lottery ads are to retirement planning."

"What I find strange is that anyone finds it strange that there's so much rejection," he writes. "Nobody needs a manuscript" (p. 23).

Sometimes the rejection comes from within our own heads. A lot of writers I know begin with an idea and they are carried by the passion within that tells them not only that the idea is awesome, but that THEY are awesome. Before long, though, a different drumbeat emerges—the one that says not only does the idea suck, but that THEY suck. It's hard to get past that.

All of the writers I talked to below know the tension of wondering whether the story they're writing is any good. That's why it's important to have good editors, agents, people invested in your life, who can give you honest feedback, even if the feedback is negative.

A question all writers must face is, Who am I doing this for? Is the goal to get published? To reach some level of acclaim? To prove something to yourself or your community that your writing is worthy? Maybe the most worthy reason to continue despite rejection is that the writing is itself the purpose. Whether it achieves "success," depending on how you define it, is less valuable than the fact that you created something that didn't exist before. And that the next thing you write will be even better. On this topic, take particular note of Elizabeth Gilbert's experience below.

In his book *Letters to a Young Poet*, Rainer Maria Rilke responded to the young writer's question:

> You ask whether your poems are good. You send them to publishers; you compare them with other poems; you are disturbed when certain publishers reject your attempts. . . . I suggest that you give all that up. You are looking outward and, above all else, that you must not do now. . . . There is only one way: Go within. Search for the cause, find the impetus that bids you write.

Put it to this test: Does it stretch out its roots in the deepest place of your heart? Can you avow that you would die if you were forbidden to write? Above all, in the most silent hour of your night, ask yourself this: *Must* I write? Dig deep into yourself for a true answer. And if it should ring its assent, if you can confidently meet this serious question with a simple, "I must," then build your life upon it. It has become your necessity. Your life, in even the most mundane and least significant hour, must become a sign, a testimony to this urge. (pp 10–11)

Elizabeth Gilbert

DN: Are we ever going to see your novel that's based in Siberia? Will it ever see the light of day?

EG: I believe in my heart that it will. It's not up to me. More and more in life, stuff's not up to me. What's up to me is to create the thing and then to listen to what is the next right action. I wrote this big, fat, juicy novel that was supposed to be published this week. Actually, I don't even want to say it was supposed to be published, because clearly it wasn't supposed to be. It was scheduled to be published this week.

DN: YOU thought it was going to be published

EG: It's set in Siberia in the middle half of the last century, and it's called *The Snow Forest*. I wrote the novel and I made an announcement about it on social media saying this is set in Siberia in the Soviet Union and everybody was all excited about it. A few days later there was this coordinated outrage and injured response from Ukrainian readers. I have a lot of Ukrainian readers, because Ukraine has big readers, and I've been publishing there for years. There was this massive, "We're canceling this book." And they did. They got on Goodreads and gave it six or seven thousand one-star reviews.

DN: Even though they hadn't read it.

EG: It doesn't matter. They were like, "how could you right this minute write a book that is centered on Russia?" Like, "Please don't do this. Do you not see? Please, don't do this to us." It's such an interesting spiritual experience because at first I felt terrified and attacked. I mean, it was trending on Twitter. I felt like I was being assaulted. What did I do? I'm so careful. How did this happen? Nobody saw this coming. I had a bunch of Russians read it to make sure it was cleared for Russians. That's the danger of writing about a culture you don't know anything about because there's stuff you don't know what you don't know. Ukrainians have had it up to here with the West's infatuation with Russian arts. Like, "Could you stop being in love with Tchaikovsky and Dostoevsky? They're killing us forever. Please."

I was in a hotel room in London because I was doing prepublicity for the book, and all of a sudden the entire internet was screaming at me. I got on a conference call with my publishers, and I had this horrific moment where they were looking at me and they were like, "Well what are we going to do?" And I'm like, "Where's book daddy to tell us?" Who's the authority? Like, I'm the fucking authority? This has never happened to me. I could feel that I was having this trauma response. I had just enough spiritual practice at this point to say, hey, I'm having a somatic reaction right now. I know myself well enough to know I have never made a good decision from this emotional state. So can you just give me an hour, and I'm going to get away from all the noise and the chaos? I need to sit and I need to ground and I need to pray, because I don't know what to do.

So, I just sat and I was shaking and considered What am I experiencing right now? What is the belief I'm having that is causing me to have this reaction? I found it and the belief is that I'm being attacked. So, well let's work with that. Is it true? And my ego was like, it sure feels true. I almost got my book canceled, shut down, and the *New York Times* is saying, what's it like to be attacked right now? *Wall Street Journal* is calling and my publisher is saying that I'm under attack. The people who are attacking me are saying they are attacking me. So, it sure fucking feels like I'm being attacked. Everyone seems to be in agreement on this.

And then this other part of me was like, just because everyone is in agreement doesn't make it true. We know this. So is it true? Try to have an open mind. Is it true? I sat like this for twenty minutes. Is it true? And then I started laughing because Oh, it's not true. I'm literally sitting in a five-star hotel room, wearing a plush bathrobe on a beautiful spring day in London with my room service tray next to me with my cappuccino, with money in the bank, a home to go back to.

DN: Just brutal . . .

EG: If Martians came down right now and said, what's happening right here and I said, "I'm under attack," they would be like, "Could we get some of that attack?" Because this is what being attacked looks like? I realized I'm not under attack. I'm fine. I'm well. I'm safe. All my needs are met. I am healthy. My family is safe. Everyone I know is doing fine. Nothing bad is happening to me.

Then you do the turnaround. Oh, the people who are attacking me, oh, they actually are under attack. They are literally under attack. They've lost everything. And their family members have been killed. And their country is being destroyed. And when a people who are being oppressed and attacked take a break from being oppressed and attacked because they feel it is so important to rise up as one voice and say to me, please don't do the thing you're about to do because it's going to be harmful to us. Why don't I just listen to that? I, the one who's not under attack, listened to the ones who are. I read things people were saying on Twitter. And then I was like, oh, I super see what you're saying. Cool. We're good. We're going to postpone this book. This is not the time for it. And I called everyone back.

I feel like there's a way to publish it that's respectful and appropriate and that is not this week. Someday, and I feel in my heart that that day will come, and it will be very clear when that day will come.

This is the other thing about really what it means to be an artist—you must make things and release the outcome. When I told that to my editor, she said, you worked for four years on this book. It's devastating because you worked so hard on it, it's such a waste. Only somebody who doesn't love their work would ever think that four years of work is a waste. I already got the best part of the experience. There is no better part of the creative experience than the creation. Nothing can compare to that and be as good. Ukrainians have bigger things to worry about. Go back to trying to survive, I'll see you later. You don't need to be worried about that now.

Joseph Wambaugh

DN: *The New Centurions* started out as a short story, right?

JW: Yes. And I sent it everywhere. I started out at big magazines and descended to the penny, three-cents-per-word magazines. Playboy was particularly cruel. I sent one of my short stories there and I got it back quickly. I sent it back six months later thinking they never read it the first time. And I got a letter this time. First letter I ever got and it said, "It's no better this time, schmuck." Many years later I was asked to give Playboy permission to do a serialization of one of my books. I searched for that letter everywhere. My "dear schmuck letter." I couldn't find it.

Peter Matthiessen

DN: You got a pretty heady start as a young writer. You sold your first short story to *The Atlantic*. You know, nobody does that! And yet, you were brought back to reality by an agent, responding to a novel you had sent in. You remember what the agent said?

PM: Yes I do, very well. It was burned into my brain. I sent this novel in, as my first novel, and I got into about 150 pages, and I thought, "This is the great American novel, clearly. And it's time that I shared it with the populace at large."

DN: This was after publishing one short story, right?

PM: Two.

DN: Okay. Well, *then*!

PM: I waited around the post office like a village idiot for days and weeks, waiting for Hollywood to call. And this package came back, an ill-wrapped package at that, and I realized it had my manuscript in it. I never wanted to see that again. I thought it was on its way to Metro

Goldwyn-Mayer, you know? And this note—this is the entire note: "Dear Peter, James Fenimore Cooper wrote this 150 years ago, and he wrote it better. Yours, Bernice."

That was a smart pill. In a way, that probably was a great novel. But she really knocked me right off my perch. I put it on the shelf and I don't know where it is. I never went back.

Billy Collins

DN: I read somewhere that you sent some poems to *Poetry Magazine*.

BC: When I was eighteen or seventeen, yeah.

DN: They were rejected. How long did you wait before you sent any more to them?

BC: Over twenty-five years, I think. When I was *ready.* I actually got a nice letter back from Henry Rago, the editor of *Poetry Magazine*. I was a high school senior and he actually wrote a nice letter encouraging me *not* to send in more poems. He was very clear about that, but to continue. It was something like twenty-five years later that I thought I was ready, and sure enough I was.

Anne Lamott 2014

AL: I wrote my first novel about my father's brain cancer, and it was published on August 26. The first review I ever got was from Pete at *Publisher's Weekly*. It says almost verbatim, "Whatever meager charms this book possesses. . ." Not that I memorized it! ". . .whatever meager charms this book possesses are marred by the author's constant show-offy overkill."

DN: Yow.

AL: It changed me, because it was true. What I needed people to do was to see that, yes, I write about very serious stuff, I write about loss, I write about true things, I write about our true heart experience of being human, but, "No! I'm not depressed. I'm not a buzzkill. I'm this fine, happy-happening girl!" It took a long time to be able to claim my humor, since I didn't want to use it to convince people that I wasn't a loser.

Joyce Carol Oates

DN: The reviewer in the *New York Times* didn't think much of *The Sacrifice*.

JCO: I think that she was basically defending her own territory.

DN: As I understood her review, she was asking why a white woman would write from the perspective of a race or a gender or an economic class that wasn't her own. She was challenging why you would create these kinds of points of view. But isn't that what you've been doing your entire writing life?

JCO: Oh, well, that's true. But there's such a thing as identity politics, and people who believe in identity politics don't think that one should be able to write about anything other than one's self. I think that literature and art are very open just to the imagination. So if Shakespeare wants to write about a woman or a Black man or an elderly person, I think that's great. To me, that's what art is. Faulkner writes about Black people. But I've often written about people very different from myself. It just seems that somebody didn't believe in that. But most of us don't feel that we should just write only about ourselves; it can be very narrow. It's an ideology, a political ideology. Some would say that men probably shouldn't write from the point of view of women. I would not say that. Some people believe these things passionately because they are ideologues.

DN: You took a bold move by replying in print to that reviewer. Essentially, you said that you didn't write the book she wanted you to write. You wrote the book *you* wanted to write.

JCO: I don't think ordinarily one should respond to reviewers. But I felt it was so unfair because she hadn't actually read the New York State Grand Jury report on the Tawana Brawley case, she hadn't read the basic primary document, and if she had she would've known my novel was completely different. So she was chiding me for writing about something that actually I wasn't writing about. I just thought, if you're writing for the *New York Times*, you should do the basic research. And it would only take an hour. It wasn't that hard to do the research. But the reviewer didn't know that, because she hadn't read it. So she attacked me.

DN: Some amazing things were said about women writers back when you were getting started. One headline in particular from the *Detroit Free Press* said about you, "Detroit Housewife Writes A Play." Did you just boil when you saw that?

JCO: It's amazing. It's amazing and it seems amusing now. I don't know that I had any strong feeling, I was probably just bemused. "Housewife" . . . well . . .

DN: You were a college professor.

JCO: I was a university professor at the point, yeah. But much later than that, *People* magazine did a whole story on me. And this was ten years later. I was a full professor at that point, and I had a large lecture hall. And the reporter came to the lecture. But then when it came to the actual magazine, the headline was "Shy Faculty Wife." Because my husband was a professor.

DN: But so were you.

JCO: I was a professor, too. But I was the shy faculty wife even though this person had seen me giving my lecture and so forth. It's just the way women had these things said about them.

DN: One interviewer said that you write like a man. What does that even mean?

JCO: Oh well, Norman Mailer said that. Or, I think it was Norman Mailer.

DN: Well, he was certainly comfortable with his identity, wasn't he?

JCO: I like Norman Mailer very much. He was just *brimming* with male chauvinism. It was just so exuded, the whole macho, that it was almost endearing. Because he had no hypocrisy. I mean, other people might pretend to be feminist and so forth. Not Norman. He actually did like my writing. He introduced me at Lincoln Center one evening, and he was just going on and on about my book on boxing, and he said, "It was so good, I thought I'd written it myself." He got all this laughter, and he didn't know why people were laughing.

DN: Do you think you have a pretty thick skin by now?

JCO: That's an interesting question. When you think of the great writers, some of them were extremely sensitive, some of them seemed indifferent, and yet it didn't—it doesn't seem to affect the actual writing. I think many writers feel that if they read a vicious review or even a mildly negative review, it will sap their energy and they won't have the enthusiasm for working. It's like being hit in the stomach. You just don't have the energy. That may very well be the case for everybody.

Some people just don't read any reviews, even the good reviews. I don't read a lot of reviews. One of the writers in classical American literary history who was the most sensitive was Hemingway. Extremely sensitive to criticism. I mean, really really sensitive to criticism. Even though he was a great writer and had written great work and probably knew he was a great writer. But yet, he was very vulnerable. So it would be better for him not to know about it. He got in actual fights with people. I mean he actually hit people.

DN: Have you done that?

JCO: Oh, no. I just don't have that kind of personality. I'm more resigned. I write reviews myself and I try to temper. If I'm disappointed in a book, I basically don't want to write the review, so I tell the editor that I can't write the review. But I try to temper it, and it's all subjective, really. James Joyce got horrible reviews. His first book, *Dubliners*, a beautiful book, was burned in Dublin. So that was a pretty bad review.

DN: What's the Henry James quote that you have on your desk?

JCO: "We work in the dark—we do what we can. Our doubt is our passion and our passion is our task. The rest is the madness of art."

Robin Jones Gunn

DN: You wrote stories for the young female audience, had the girls in your youth group check them out and give you suggestions, you made those corrections, and then sent them to a publisher. What did the publishers say?

RG: "We just don't see a market. We don't think this kind of a romance would really sell."

DN: But you knew that was wrong because you had these. . .

RG: Girls in the tent! I wanted to tell the publishers, "Go look into your daughter's bedroom! What is she reading?" I know there is this whole audience that is just sort of submerged; they're underground. We need to get to them.

DN: Did you feel like, "I got my signals crossed somewhere, because I know these stories work, but publishers are saying, 'Forget it.'" Were you tempted to just say, "Ehhh."

RG: Of course, I was tempted to give up and I felt like, "I don't know what I am doing. I will just copy these stories and give them to the girls and I will be done." But there was a fire in my belly to get it beyond there because there were other girls in other tents and other states and other places. I knew they were looking for the same kind of book.

DN: Later in your career you had some books sent back to you by editors.

RG: Yes I have.

DN: You had been writing and publishing for a long time. How did that feel?

RG: It started with that second *Christy Miller* book, and I started all over—

DN: But it's happened more recently, after you had done dozens.

RG: Right. So that first time I felt like, "Okay, I'm trying to figure this out. No shame; on we go." Then I wrote, I don't know, maybe it was like twenty-five or thirty books. I published and wrote the *Glenbrooke* series and got to book seven in the series, and when I wrote book eight and turned it in, the editor said, "I know you can do better. I want you to start over."

DN: That had to sting a little.

RG: Absolutely.

DN: Was she right?

RG: She was right, and I would tell her that gladly now. At that moment, I thought, "What do you know?" I mean, just: "How dare you!"

DN: "Don't you know who I am?!"

RG: Yeah, but just that feeling of, "You don't get what I was trying to say!" And there's such a crazy thing that happens with shame, where we hide, and we close in. This was the biggest challenge in that experience, to just keep saying, "Shame off, shame off; grace on, grace on" and then to not close in or give up but to move forward, and learn, and dream a new dream, and try again, and be humble and open. Then it happened again. The worst one that happened was, I had written a Christmas novella, titled *Finding Father Christmas*, and actually, this was the fastest book I'd ever written; I think it came out in about two weeks.

It was kind of crazy, because we were in Hawaii at the time in August and it was very hot, and I was writing about Christmas in England in the snow. But I'd read that Jack London had written *To Build a Fire in Honolulu* in August—

DN: Good enough for him.

RG: I thought, "Okay, your imagination really has to be engaged to do this." So that first one I really loved the story. It came right out, won an award, and then they said, "Would you write another one?"—*Engaging Father Christmas*. "Yes," and I wrote it and I turned it in and the new editor said, "It's not romantic enough. We really wanted a romance. Could you go back. . .?" "Okay, sure." It was just really plodding along. So I got the second version out. "Ugh, that was really hard!" and then I sent it in. She goes, "No, I don't think this is it. I think you need to really work at it. This is what I'd like to see: *this* and *this* and *this* and *this*." So I wrote a third version, and I worked really hard and just tried to get that third version just right. I sent it in. I had to put off other books. "No, I think I liked the second one better, but not enough—could you write. . ."—so I wrote it a fourth time entirely. After I wrote the fourth one, she said, "You're just so off-track, I'm just going to publish the second one and be done with it." I don't know what I learned from that.

DN: What to do with anger mostly? All that wasted effort . . . or was it wasted effort?

RG: Nothing is ever wasted; everything's redeemable. There's always a purpose for it. But then what's so interesting is that there's a film producer that has asked to do the two books together: *Finding Father Christmas* and *Engaging Father Christmas* as one story. It's been almost four years in process and the contract is signed. So we'll see how the production goes and when it actually airs, but if I'd given up—they needed that romantic story and the second one to pair with the first one and if I just said, "Forget it. I'm not even able to do this anymore." It would have deterred this from happening.

Chris Bohjalian

CB: *The Sandcastle Girls* was gestating for twenty years. This isn't the first time I tried to write a novel of the Armenian Genocide. I tried for the first time in 1993 and 1994, and I wrote the entire manuscript—392 pages—and when I finished reading it, I realized it was a trainwreck: utterly unpublishable.

DN: What was wrong with it?

CB: It was all a young Armenian-American's anger. It wasn't a novel. Moreover, about this time, Carol Edgarian had published her remarkable novel of the Armenian Genocide, *Rise the Euphrates*, and I remember thinking to myself, "Why in the name of heaven does anyone need *my* take on this story when we have the work of Carol Edgarian, Peter Balakian, and Franz Werfel's magisterial epic, *The 40 Days of Musa Dagh*? So, I sent that manuscript to my alma mater, where you can read it if you are a scholar or a masochist.

DN: Yeah, pardon the redundancy there. . .

CB: It's a bad book.

DN: Do you ever think about the person who ran the writing program, who told you that you couldn't be a part of it?

CB: I do, some days.

DN: Do you remember what she told you to do instead?

CB: I do. At my illustrious alma mater there was a writer in residence whose work my mother loved. I read one of her books, and it was pretty darn good. To determine who would be among the few, the proud, the chosen in her creative writing program, you had to submit a short story, so I did and I was then summoned to her office. There was the short story on her desk and she looked up at me and she said, "You're Chris. I'm not even going to try to pronounce your last name." She beckoned me in and I sat down and she slid my short story across this expanse of mahogany as if it were roadkill and said, "Well, Chris, I have three words for you. . ." and I knew this wasn't going to be good. She said, "Be a banker."

DN: Ouch. And it did take a while. I mean, 250 rejection slips, before you published anything.

CB: In all fairness to this professor, that short story was probably pretty terrible. But yes, I amassed 250 rejection slips before I sold a single word. I was sending these very Scott Fitzgerald-esque short stories to *The New Yorker*, and *Harper's*, and *The Sewanee Review*, and being summarily and consistently rejected. When I got number 250 I thought to myself, "Hmm, Plan A, not working. Time to try Plan B." So, I gathered six months' worth of *Cosmopolitans* together because *Cosmopolitan* was still publishing a lot of fiction. Then I tried to write the perfect *Cosmo* short story. It's about a female supermodel who lives in lower Manhattan, married to a fabulously wealthy arbitrage trader, but their marriage is kind of dicey. So, on weekends, she goes to their equally cool beach house in Fire Island to see if the marriage can be saved, but instead spends the entire time playing scantily clad, beach volleyball. *Cosmopolitan* bought it!

It's in a rather historically important issue of *Cosmopolitan.* For a magazine that we sometimes say is kind of sexy, only one time has *Cosmopolitan* had nudity in it, and that was that particular issue that had my short story in it. It was the now-infamous, *Build Your Better Bust* issue. My mother was so proud.

DN: Beats banking doesn't it?

Anchee Min

DN: In your book *Becoming Madame Mao*, you quote Mao Zedong and his view of writers: "I don't take bookworms too seriously. What do they know, dictionaries? What is a dictionary but pages of dead words anyway. Can they tell the difference between rice shoots and weeds? What could be easier than being a bookworm? It's harder to learn to be a chef or a butcher. A book has no legs. One can open or close it at any time. A pig has legs that can run, and a pig has vocal chords that can wail. The butcher has to catch it and slaughter it. The chef has to make the stinky meat taste delicious. Those are real talents." And yet you became a writer?

AM: It's unbelievable. When a nation is illiterate, Mao's quote, he's our god. You just worship his words.

DN: So being a person of words was a dangerous thing?

AM: Definitely. But we did not know Mao was the person of words. We were incapable of thinking. So you're incapable of learning and incapable of being a human being. So we were . . . we're humans without . . . I don't know how to put it.

Alice Walker

DN: Your books have been banned all over the place. In the California state standardized tests, there were two of your stories that upset people because one story looked like it was about anti-meat eating, and another story was anti-religion, in people's opinion. But here's the great timing. This is happening while you are being honored by the governor of California as a literary treasure. That's just too rich.

AW: Yeah, and basically that's why you need not pay any attention to any of it. You just basically live, do your work, head for the hills when you want to. They're going to be coming for you whatever you do. Your job is to just keep going, one foot in front of the other. This is actually in one of the great Buddhist texts, which is so remarkable because it's so old. But basically what it says is, no matter what you do or say, they are going to talk about you. They are going to drag you down. It's part of the human condition. And so what you learn, what I have learned over the years, is basically, I can't say that I'm not wounded—we're all wounded somehow—but I get the arrow out. And I keep going.

DN: But here's the thing about those stories that were banned, and the people that had trouble with "The Color Purple." The critics hadn't actually read the stories.

AW: You know, I don't even have a place in my brain for conceiving of the kind of mind that would be so violently opposed to my work. So I don't know if they read them or not. I mean obviously they didn't read them the way we would read them. You know, with intelligence.

DN: Here's what you've said about banning and censorship. You said, "They are attempts to avoid the pain of encountering subjects that frighten or hurt. In order for understanding among people to evolve, we must continue to learn to sit with one another's truths, which to me is the real meaning of the first amendment." That's good. Your biographer, Evelyn White, in the preface of her book said the reason she was drawn to you was this question: "What was it about Alice Walker and her work that always seemed to generate such intense emotion?" What do you think that is? What is it about you and your work that just generates all this stuff?

AW: What do you think?

DN: Oh no no no no no. You're not my therapist. Although I like you better than my therapist!

AW: Well that's good. Honestly, I don't know. I write with the passion that I feel, and what I'm grateful for is that I have the skill apparently—sometimes anyway—to make it connect. To have it connect with other people. I see it as a gift; I see it as something that comes from a long line of artists who were not permitted to be artists, and writers who were not permitted to be writers. So I feel it intensely as a responsibility, and I think all of that is transmitted to the reader.

DN: It makes a lot of people uncomfortable.

AW: Which is good for them!

DN: Your writing is a form of activism, but you've also personally done some activism. You call it "paying the rent of being alive and on this planet." You've been arrested plenty of times, but the account that I was so moved by was one of the times you were arrested in Washington at a women's march, and you and the police officer who arrested you became friends. How'd that work out?

AW: Well, I maintain that the police are also the people. Since the police are also the people, even this person who was arresting me, it was his job. I was trying to help him—actually I didn't know which way the hands went. But I just saw a brother. I just saw my brother, really. He was wearing the uniform, but he was a human being. This is sort of a tangent, do you mind?

DN: No!

AW: Well, when the hurricane hit New Orleans, some friends and I took a lot of books down to the Astrodome, where some of the people who lost everything were. The police were there, and I could tell that some of them really wanted books. And I had a lot of books, and the regular people who I was giving books to said, "You don't have to give them any because they're the police." But I could see clearly that they wanted to read. The people said, "Don't give the police books, just give books to the people," and I said, "But the police are people." That is incredibly important I think to remember. Even with all the horrible things that are being done in our communities by the police. We will lose so much if we forget that the police are the people also.

DN: There's a great image of this police officer on his knees in front of you helping you put your shoes on.

AW: Oh yeah! And he was also telling me that his wife was not happy that he arrested me. It was wonderful, because I just felt my sisterhood with her. I just felt like, yeah you just go give it to him good, you know?

DN: Here's another reason why people have intense emotions about you. You've been a vocal supporter of Fidel Castro in Cuba, Daniel Ortega in Nicaragua, First Americans—you've appeared with them at different protests in North America. And more recently, Palestinians.

AW: That's not recent, that's old.

DN: Well, okay, and you've got this conspiracy theory guy—

AW: David Icke.

DN: Are you just trying to find a way to upset people? Because you've got a lot of people saying—because of David Icke and your pro-Palestinians are people—you get accused of being anti-Semitic and hating Jews. What's that about?

AW: The foundation, funnily enough, is in my marriage. I married this wonderful Jewish man, a lawyer. After the Six Day War, when Israel took all the land that they had "conquered" and refused to give it back, we had an argument. I thought that the land should be returned to the people. And he thought it should not, and he thought that because I thought it should be returned that I was anti-Semitic and not in favor of Israel. But I tell you, there is something that is in this slur that is unfortunately growing in this country. It will soon be that whatever you say against the behavior of the Israeli government will be termed anti-Semitic. This would be very dangerous, and we must not let it happen. You have a right to your feelings, your expressions, about anything. That's the foundation of that. But as with anything else, I accept that I will be blamed or accused of whatever, but I prefer to have done what I thought to be right to matter what the consequences.

DN: I think a lot of the concern is just the presence of David Icke on your website.

AW: I love David Icke. Take it or leave it.

DN: This is some of the criticism that really surprised me about The Color Purple. Critics felt sorry for the men in your story, but not for the women.

AW: Well, there we are. It was shocking, actually, to have men—often who hadn't read it—who said, "I haven't read the book and I haven't seen the movie but it's making us look bad." You know who also didn't like The Color Purple at all? Bill Cosby. He hated it. He thought it was very bad for our community.

DN: Because it made Black men look bad? It did.

AW: Well, there are a lot of ways to look at it. When you're in the trenches, as we have been for 400 years, it's really about freeing us. It's really about actually having a life. And to have a decent life, you have to look at some of the most awful places. If you don't do that you will never be free. I think the longevity of this story teaches us that you can actually tell the story in its harshest aspects, but also to show that you have these places of harshness and you can have redemption too. So the men in this story are redeemed. It's just that when you have a culture that insists that all men have to be a certain macho type, they just can't see the other men who are not like them. Part of what we need to do in many of our cultures is to be sure that we can identify people no matter what they're doing, no matter their behavior. They're still human beings. It was so painful to realize that many of the men who complained just completely missed Albert's transformation as a human being. I thought it was so beautiful.

DN: It ends so hopefully.

AW: Oh, I thought it was this beautiful thing to think that someone who was so controlled by his father, by the culture, by everything, and not strong enough in himself to have the woman that he loved, that he somehow managed to transform himself into the kind of person who could be her friend, his wife's friend, at the end. I thought this was lovely, and so possible.

DN: Redemption was part of the theme.

AW: Exactly right.

DN: So similarly, with your book "*Possessing the Secret of Joy*," you went right after the topic of female genital mutilation, and the cultures that practice this had a problem with you doing this.

AW: Not all of them though!

DN: I thought they told you to stay in your lane. What's this Western woman—

AW: Some of them, some of them had that view. But honestly, when you get down into these communities where the children are really suffering and the women, when you help them even remember what it felt like, what had happened to them, they were very glad. Because after all, this is a movement against female genital mutilation that African women themselves were leading. It's just that they needed support from us outside the cultures to help. And I was happy to help.

Anthony Doerr

DN: One of the things I loved about the book *About Grace* was all of the interconnections with the characters, and through the natural world as well, which is one of the themes in so many of your books. But fundamentally, what you're telling us in that book is that we are connected to one another, and that even when we screw up, we sort of save each other. That's what I was getting out of that, and that's where the double sense of the word "grace" comes in. *The New York Times*, however, didn't think as highly of it, as a collection of your short stories. Did that affect—

AD: Oh, this one person at *The New York Times* . . .

DN: Yeah, one reviewer. So did that affect you?

AD: Of course, yeah. I mean, there's a few writers who I believe, like Marilyn Robinson once said, "I don't read reviews and they don't bother me." She's an extremely wonderful writer, and I believed her. But most writers, when they're like, "I don't care about what anybody says about my work," (*fakes smoking a cigarette*) I'm like, "Right." (*rolls eyes*) If you worked for months and months or years and years on something, it's human to be interested in what people think of it. We had two babies at the time that review came out; we were living in Italy. My wife was doing most of the work, but I was in the trenches, and you're like, "I've got this book coming out; I have to go to these European countries to promote it." Then your publicist is like, "Also, *The New York Times* reviewed it today," and then you're like, "Well, what did they say?" So yeah, that stuff can sting. Do I remember the name of the writer who wrote it? Yes.

DN: I read the review, and I felt like there was something else the reviewer is saying about that book. I thought he was also saying it was too well-written. Honestly, that was the sense I got from it that the writing was so beautiful that it was distracting.

AD: It's been a long time since I read it, but I remember some of that. I think it was like, "It's cold. The book is cold." I mean, the whole book's about snowflakes, so I was like, "Well, kind of a compliment." In the end, you can't learn anything and improve from positive reviews, so you can learn something from those bad reviews if you can find a way to read them and not be too emotionally distraught. By the time a book comes out, you're making something else, maybe twelve months or ten or six months into a new project. So your happiness is more dependent on creating things and not getting too attached to the reactions to something you made before.

N. Scott Momaday

DN: Your second novel, *Ancient Child*, was not as popular as House Made of Dawn. Did that bother you that it didn't reach that same level?

NSM: Yeah, it did, because it's a fine novel, I think. It's a great novel. I like it and I got a bad review in the *New York Times* and that did hurt, but the reviewer wanted me to write another book and I didn't write the one he wanted, so he was kind of hard on me. It was not as well-received as *House Made of Dawn* had done certainly, but I'm proud of it. I think it would make a great movie and I haven't convinced anybody of that yet.

Nick Hornby

DN: What's your take on the book banning that's going on in libraries?

NH: It's horrifying and heartbreaking. I live in England, which is a post-Christian country. No one has any strong religious views there. So a lot of the debate in the United States is very alien to us; the evangelical stuff I don't follow or fathom. But then the second aspect of it is what they call the culture wars, the war on woke, which we do have to a certain extent, and certainly we have conservative politicians who were trying to import your war on woke into the UK, and it's just as depressing as the evangelical stuff. It used to be called politically correct, and when I was growing up in England in the '60s and '70s, there was no such thing as politically correct, and it was horrible. You could see racist jokes on the BBC on the channel that the government pays for, and that was pre-woke, and everything about that stuff, woke and political correctness, seems to me to be a welcome antidote to some of the unthinking and awful antisemitism and racism and certainly sexism and misogyny that I was force fed on television when I was a kid. I'm very reluctant to go back there, but that seems to be what these people are after.

I was asked to write a little bit about *The Kite Runner*, which is also being banned in some American schools. The problem with that book from the censors' point of view is that it features the male rape of a youngish boy. It's horrific, but to read that and say, "I don't want my children to read this. . ." The book is about how no one's child should experience that. It's the central event in the entire book. No one takes it lightly; it destroys the narrator for complicated reasons. And to just take that incident out and say, "We mustn't see that" means that you can never understand what other people are enduring in the world, and that makes you very stupid as a nation. You can go to war with the Taliban, but if you're denying women's rights at the same time as you're banning books, you think, "Really? You've got to make more of a distinction than that."

9

More Than Words on a Page What Do We Mean By "Craft"?

I was trying to attack with a flamethrower, and this required more of a scalpel.

LUIS ALBERTO URREA

When I was growing up I had a toy called "The Visible V-8 Engine." There were dozens of pieces in multiple colors, and the instructions had you put together each component of a car's internal combustion engine. Here is the carburetor, here are the spark plugs, here is the fuel pump. The outside of the engine was clear plastic, so that when you had all the pieces in place and turned the small crank at the back, you could see how the engine worked. The cylinders rose and fell, the belts turned just so, and you could witness what made a car move. I still know things about car engines because of that experience.

Talking about the craft of writing is a little like that.

Just like with most engines, most stories have some elements in common. In most stories there is a main character. That character usually wants something, and the story involves the many things that keep the character from getting what they want. In the Harry Potter series, the boy wants to know who his parents are. There are multiple events that try to keep him from getting what he wants. That's the conflict. So character and conflict are components in making the story work.

How well we know that character will have an impact on whether we care about them. The presentation of the character will involve description, action, motive, relationship with other characters (like other engine parts), and more. Setting, which is the atmosphere in which the action takes place, is part of the craft. Is it raining so hard at such fierce angles that the seals around the windows surrender and let the water in, almost as if it were invited? Or is the breeze blowing softly through the bedroom window, lightly ruffling the powder blue curtains, almost as if they're waving, or even applauding?

Concrete and significant details are part of this engine, too. How the story begins, how it resolves—or doesn't—are all part of it.

Most writers I know don't spend a lot of time thinking about craft in the first draft or two. At the beginning stages the writers are trying to get the ideas moving, and are trying to get a sense of what this story is about. Then they can pay attention to craft. Amor Towles, as you'll see below, is a bit of an exception to what I just said. Because he spends so much time on his outlines, those outlines are a kind of first draft for him. Revisions allow him to pay attention to craft much more quickly.

But most of us are putting the components together as best we can, knowing that we'll come back to it over and over and over, looking for a better image, a better metaphor, a better description, so that the reader has a smooth ride.

This chapter is a version of The Visible Engine.

Amor Towles

AT: Even in a novel with a large ensemble of characters like *The Lincoln Highway* or *A Gentleman in Moscow*, to ultimately do a good job of writing the story and bringing the characters to life, you have to fall in love with all of them one at a time. In a novel, the biggest difference between Draft 1 and Draft 2 is that in Draft 2, I tend to be shrinking the amount of words that are dedicated to, say, the three or four central characters, and I tend to be adding space for Characters 5, 6, 7, and 8. This makes sense if you think about when you're writing the book—you're going to overwrite the main characters because it's so important to have them fully imagined, to have their events fully described, to have their emotional lives and their ideas shared with the reader, but you end up overdoing it. The reader doesn't need to know all of that, and you've over-explained it like I'm doing now.

Part of the editing process is to take the same amount of emotional intellectual material, the same vibrancy of those characters, but reducing the amount of language that you're using to describe those events and those experiences. Here's a paradox of writing, which is that, as you shrink it and take away excess words and sentences and explanations, you're actually increasing the vitality of the character. The characters can get killed by the overbearing descriptions that a writer can bring to the story. That's happening in the editing process—shrinking them down, providing better economy, making them sharper in a way, the central characters.

But simultaneously, as I'm rereading, I'm like, "Oh, man, this is a great character who I have not done justice to. We have not heard enough from them. I did not draw them as accurately and in as much detail as they deserve." And so, suddenly in the rethinking of the revision, those characters start to express themselves. They suddenly are in the conversation that they had been left out of, or they have a chapter suddenly dedicated to something, how they're processing whatever the events are. That's this long way of saying you have to keep falling in love with each of these individual characters, with the goal of bringing them fully to life.

DN: But the short story is taking even a bigger ax to all of that.

AT: Yes. I've written short stories since I was a kid. And I think most novelists, we grow up writing short stories at whatever age you start because the short story is the best form in which to master elements of craft, and you do that by writing all kinds of different stories with a different approach to setting or a different approach to characterization, a different approach to dialogue, a different tone for the narrators. You just keep experimenting in different stories with different topics set in different places about different people, but telling them in different ways, and slowly, but surely, what happens is mastery of craft, you hope.

When I was in high school, the teacher who had the greatest influence on me, probably, was a guy named Dick Baker—he was a great intellect, taught very rigorous English literature classes. When I would get my essays and stories back from him, the most common comment that he would have in the margin was the initials S-U-G, and SUG stood for "sweeping, unsupported generality." And he meant that as a criticism. As it turned out, it was my superpower, so it all worked out in the end.

DN: So, you developed that even further?

AT: Yeah, I just kept going, took it another step further. So, I'm going to share with you a sweeping unsupported generality right now. And the sweeping unsupported generality is that one major difference between the novel and the short story is that in writing a novel, an author consciously or unconsciously is very concerned with orientation. As you enter the world of a novel, the writer consciously or unconsciously has to orient you in that world by establishing When is this taking place? Where is it taking place? Who are these people? What is their relationship to each other? What class do they come from? What are some of the events in the recent past that have bearing on where we're going? Who are the critical players? Maybe even some glimpse of some of the themes that are going to play a big role later in the novel. This is a very important part of novel writing: providing this sense of orientation.

If you take your favorite novels and read the first fifteen pages, I think you'll be amazed if you think about it this way of how much information is there. Now that you've read the whole thing, you go back and look at it and say, "Oh, yeah, there's so much there to get me started." Because we as readers need that orientation in order to go into the adventure of the novel with confidence so that we have an awareness to then follow the tale in a way that is meaningful.

In a short story, you do not have this. You do not have the time to lay that out. And so, the job of the writer and the reader changes radically. You're not going to be about orientation. Instead, it's about disorientation. It's exciting to write in that form. As a reader, I'm not going to get set up. I'm not going to have everything explained to me. I'm going to be dropped into something. I'm going to have to figure out where I am. We can have quite a deep response to the story, even though it is only a glimpse of life. I think the story provides a different satisfaction but a great one.

DN: You wrote a book that you didn't think was very good. Are we ever going to see it?

AT: We're going to go that way? We're going to go there?

DN: Yeah. Are we ever going to see it?

AT: No, you'll never see that.

DN: What was wrong with it?

AT: The best way to describe what was flawed in that book is by talking about how I approached *Rules of Civility* differently. The single most important difference in the two works was that I had not outlined that failed book. Those of you who have read my work probably have a sense of this, which is that I'm very interested in how a novel as an art form can be very cohesive, where it has all these elements which are building and then coming together at the end in some culmination of events that feels all fated and predestined, and where the imagery has played out over the course of the novel, and the formatics have built, and the nuances have played with each other. A novel can be like a symphony. You might have motifs that repeat. You may have a particular phrase of music which repeats, but it is interpreted by different instruments. Here by an oboe alone, then suddenly by the entire string section, and then played for a different mood at a different tempo at a different volume over the course of the symphony.

But then you get to the end of the symphony, and it all comes together in this great culmination. When they hit the final chord, we in the audience are like, "Oh, that was it. That's perfect." And so, I like to achieve that in the novel—that's what my aim is at any rate—and you cannot really do that if you don't outline because to try to bring everything together in this cohesive way without planning, it's just going to be impossible. In that unplanned book, I could look back at it and say, "Oh, at the end of it, now I understand all the elements that I would wish were coming together now," but it would require going back and writing the whole thing from Word 1.

DN: Let me see if I understand what your process is. First, you get an idea, and you sit with that idea for a couple of days. Then you start to create an outline. Scaffolding, I think, is what you called it.

AT: Yep.

DN: But that could take years. Right?

AT: Yes.

DN: And then you write the novel.

AT: I'll expand on what you're saying, because it is true. Usually, an idea for a story or a novel is very brief. It's a sentence. It might come to me because I see something. It might come from me out of the ether. Like, "a guy gets trapped in a hotel for a long period of time." That was literally the sentence that I started with, and I was like, "Oh, that's an interesting idea for a story." I was in a hotel in Geneva when I had that idea. I took the elevator upstairs. I checked into my room and immediately took out the hotel stationery because—and this will often happen with something that really grabs me—within a matter of an hour, it's really within a matter of minutes, I'm like, "I know a lot about it." So, that man trapped in a hotel? I know a lot about it and that I was like, "Oh, this could be in Russia. It'll be an aristocrat. He could be sentenced to house arrest in a fancy hotel across the street from the Kremlin. It could start after the Revolution and go all the way to the Cold War." I knew all of that for *A Gentleman in Moscow* in the first few minutes. And then in the course of two hours, I filled maybe five pages of handwritten notes, which was the scaffolding, which was basically all the key events of the story, how it would play out. But then what happens, what really grabs me is I will spend two, three, four years designing the book. I'll take notebooks, and by hand in a whole series of notebooks, I will imagine everything that happens, all the characters, their backgrounds, their personalities, the various events, the settings, some of the conversations, a lot of the tone, some of the philosophical components, just working through the idea by hand.

DN: This is all before the narrative begins?

AT: Yeah. I may be experimenting with the things that are going to be a part of the narrative, like the opening of a chapter or an actual scene, to try it out and see how it's going. But basically, it's this design phase. I might do that four different ways. Then at the end of that, now I know everything. So, then I make the outline, which for a novel might be thirty or forty pages long. And then I start writing Chapter 1. With a short story, it's the exact same thing but just compressed. I still have an idea that might be a sentence. I might dwell on it and start to design it and imagine all the components, the people, the events. I'll build an outline, but the outline might be on a page, and the design phase might be three months instead of three years.

DN: So, how close is the final product to the outline? Is it really close, or do you leave room for, "Oh, I think it needs to go this way."

AT: There are enormous changes. The scaffolding parts tend to be very close. I've always known the end of the book immediately, and that has never changed in any of the draftings. When I say, for those who know *A Gentleman in Moscow*, let's say Nina: day one the idea was always there. He becomes a waiter. His nemesis is going to be the Bishop. There'll be this guy from the KGB, Osip, and they'll become friends, and that was always there. Anna Urbanova, that's always there. So, those key things are there. What's changing is incidents, or the character, the personalities may be shifting as I'm getting a better sense of who they are. Certainly, the poetry of the language is changing a lot as I'm taking different approaches to telling the story.

DN: You made me late for several appointments when I was reading your stories.

AT: Good. Yeah, good.

DN: I would be reading this and thinking, "I can get the next chapter. I can work that in before physical therapy. And it never worked. There was this gravitational pull from one chapter to the next, and it was so skillfully done. And then I read this, what *The New York Times* said about you: “Beneath his coiffed prose, Towles is a master of the shiv, the bait and switch. We see the flash of light before the shock wave strikes often in the final sentence.” And that’s exactly how that novella hit me. It was superbly crafted.

AT: Thank you.

DN: I was impressed, but really, really angry. It’s a conscious thing on your part, clearly, to pull the reader from one thing to the next to the next to the next. Visually, how are you seeing that when you’re doing it?

AT: It’s an interesting question. I do think that fiction can benefit from having some internal momentum. I don’t mean it in the suspense story sense, although it’s a cousin to that. But a novel that is feeling the compelling need to go further and further into the story, it’s a valuable thing if you can figure out how to do it. I’m not even sure I know what it is. But it’s constantly following the thread of human development. As something is happening, people are changing and getting a glimpse of the fact that they’re changing; you can see the stakes are changing, and the person’s changing. What they were going to do next is suddenly up for grabs because of what’s just happened. And they might now say something totally different to their spouse than they would have said the night before. Anything could happen. But you can have all urgency in narrative.

DN: You’ve compared your writing craft to Andre Agassi’s tennis. How are these two things similar?

AT: It’s not so much that I’m comparing myself to Agassi. But it’s about mastery of craft, trying to explain how the mastery of craft works in writing, and I do it by analogy. What I mean by it is that Andre Agassi does not have a great forehand. What Andre Agassi has is 100 great forehands. Because over the course of his young career, what he’s doing is he is trying to master, certainly, how to return high-speed serve with topspin across the center of the net. But he’s also trying to master how to do a soft shot when he’s approaching the net from mid-court, when he’s reeling back on his feet from the baseline into a lob, doing a shortcut. . . . Wherever he is on the court, wherever the ball is coming, wherever he needs to send it, that is a different forehand, and each one needs to be mastered. He wants to get to the point where he doesn't have to think about it. Instinctively, when he's in that spot, the ball's coming in that direction. He is going to do the perfect swing to send the ball where it needs to go to win the point.

Writing is very much like this in the sense that ability and dialogue and setting and characterization and using metaphor and using allegory or illusion, it is not one of any of these things. The writer, you don't go and master one of these things with one approach. Instead, what you need to do is master each of those elements in all kinds of contexts. Because when you shift what a story is from an aristocrat in Russia 1920 to a bunch of eighteen-year-olds in America, 1954, everything has to change: the way the plot unfolds, the way the dialogue unfolds, the way that setting is described, the way that metaphors are used or not used, the way that allusions are done or not done, the poetry throughout the language. All that has to be different to fit with these characters in this context at this time.

In the case of *The Lincoln Highway*, it gets more complicated because you have eight different characters who are telling the story from eight different perspectives, and each one of those has to sound different to the reader and should because it has to be an expression of the inner life of Sally or Woolly or Duchess, depending on whose chapter it is. Each time you make that shift, all the elements of craft in a way have to re-adjust to be an expression of that character's internal life. Then, again, that's one of those things that gets you that pull of going on because you really feel like, "Okay, I'm with this person, seeing the world through their eyes and what's happening from their angle, end of chapter. I'm going to have to now revisit all of that through Emmett's eyes to see what he thinks or what he feels or what might happen to him under these circumstances." Anyway, the tennis metaphor is really about that.

DN: It's remarkable all the different shots that you've mastered. In *A Gentleman in Moscow*, that's a thirty-two-year period in that book. *The Lincoln Highway* is ten days.

AT: Yes, and that's a very different type of writing. There's a lot of differences between those two books, but the biggest difference is the one of duration. The reason that's such a big difference from a writing standpoint is that when you write a book that spans thirty years, like *A Gentleman in Moscow*, it is going to be significantly about evolution. Because what's happening over thirty years is that the main character, the Count, is going through changes, and he's evolving as an individual. The relationships are evolving: him and the actress, or him and Nina, him and the people in the kitchen. That's evolving. Russia is evolving. So, when you read a story that spans thirty years, almost certainly the evolution of these elements is going to be a central aspect of the story in terms of how it's told and in the thematic impact, the emotional impact for the reader. When you shift to a story of Lincoln Highway that only has ten days, you don't have the luxury of describing evolution in that fashion. So, what I have to do in that case is figure out how am I going to take this narrow aperture of human experience, this brief moment of time, and give glimpses of the past and a sense of the future in such a way that the reader still feels like, in only ten days, that they still somehow took in the totality of life, not simply just a moment in time. That's a different challenge from a writing standpoint.

Nick Hornby

On Dialogue

DN: I think one of your strengths as a writer is dialogue, which makes sense since you do so many screenplays. But it is so precise, and it reveals the character. When you think about how does a character get revealed in a fiction work, it's usually appearance, how they move, how they interact with the setting, how they speak. Almost all of your character revelation is in how they speak and then how they think about what they've just said. I wish I could talk the way your characters talk because they're so funny and they're so deep. Are you always listening and eavesdropping, and hearing stuff that you're thinking, "Oh, that could totally work in a dialogue," or is this just coming out of you?

NH: I am really nosy. So, if I've got headphones on the top of a bus, and I can see there's something going on between two people, then I'll turn the music off and keep the headphones in so it looks like I'm not listening. There's nothing that goes directly into a movie or a book, but the rhythm of it and also the specificity of what people might argue about. They never argue. . . It's never like, "You don't love me. Yes, I do love you." It's always there's some warp and weft and weird detail in there that you think, "I must remember that." Not that particular detail, but you can replace it with something else, and it will sound pretty good.

People have been nice about my dialogue, and all I can say is it's so easy for me that it's not a talent I value. The stuff that's harder for me, I think, "I did that—I got through it." But the dialogue, I don't have to think twice; I can write it very quickly, and really the problem is being disciplined about it. You can write too much, and you think actually they're just talking, and maybe it sounds good, and maybe it's realistic, but it's not getting me anywhere. It's taking me further away in fact. Then I've got to go back and start cutting and pruning.

DN: But you can do it from so many different points of view. I made a list. You capture voices of young men in your books, of a female doctor, of a woman who falls for the neighborhood butcher, a sixteen-year-old boy who just got his girlfriend pregnant. They don't all sound the same. You're doing this from all these different points of view, and I just marvel at your ability to do it.

NH: Well, thank you. But I've got kids. I've got sisters. I've got wives. I've got friends. I've got friends' kids.

DN: Wives—that was plural wives?

NH: I've had wives plural, yes.

DN: Just to clarify.

NH: Never more than one at a time.

Joseph Wambaugh

On Endings

DN: When your books end, they don't end with a "made for television resolution;" they resolve, but the characters don't always know they resolve. *Floaters*, for example.

JW: They don't end with a bang but a whimper, huh?

DN: Sometimes it resolves for the reader—we know what happens, but the characters are left just as clueless as they were. What are you telling us when you do that?

JW: That's kind of the way I did police work. I never knew what was going on at the end of things. I was a detective and it seemed at the end of every case I was never sure what the hell happened anyway. It's probably natural because of my investigative history that I would write that way. Things never tied themselves up in ribbons. They were never resolved to my satisfaction, and I guess I came to feel that life's the same way. We don't really know too much the end of things, we just sort of stagger on. That's the way I've written all my stuff. Just staggering on.

Chitra Divakaruni

On Involving Senses

DN: You involve a sense of *smell* in all of your work. I've never experienced it as strongly as I have in yours. Is that intentional? There is always the smell of sandalwood, of very specific flowers and spices.

CD: It's a couple of things. Partly, it's intuitive. I like to write in a way that involves the reader's senses, because I like reading things that do that. The second thing is that the tropical world, the Indian world that I often write about, is a world of very vivid smells: the tropical flowers, the spices, the sweat, and dust, all of that. That becomes a big part of the Indian world, and therefore, when I'm describing the American world,

I'm looking for correlations, and therefore, I'm looking for smells that would describe the American world as well.

DN: What are the dominant smells in the American world?

CD: Chinese takeout.

Ray Bradbury

On Creating Characters

DN: You say that in writing there is a difference between thinking and feeling. You aren't real big on thinking first.

RB: No. First of all, you can't imagine the story and you can't think it ahead. You have to live it. These people who sell you on plotting in the books, constructing the screenplay—constructing the screenplay? What the hell is that? That's why so many screenplays are lousy, aren't they? You can just see people sitting at a meeting saying, "We'll do this next. We'll do that next. Why don't we try this? Why don't we try that." That's all intellectual crap. It's all masturbatory. Everyone trying to one up someone else. You can't do that.

Look at writing as a snow field. It's pure and you have your characters that you believe in. Each of them has a destiny. You've got to know what each of them wants, madly. And then you fire off a gun and send your characters running out in a field full of snow pursuing their dream, their desire, their want. And after they run you look in the snow and see their footprints. There's your structure. But you can't imagine that. You gotta run first.

Peter Matthiessen

On Taking Notes

PM: When I'm in the field working, I have my little note-taking system. I always wear shirts with two big breast pockets. If you go to a surplus store, you can usually find old *Fish and Wildlife Service* notebooks that are rain-proof. They're great. But even if you can't find them—those square Husky notebooks—keep two of them. All day long, you're putting down little things. If you're like me, you have to write them up that night, because you won't be able to read them by the next day. Especially if it was raining, you know, you lose them. You don't know when you're going to use it.

I heard a line, and used it in my Watson novels. I was in the Okefenokee Swamp studying Sandhill Cranes. I was in this old boat and ran into an old guy in a rowboat. He was going the other way and you saw his old flat-bottom skiff. It was a homemade boat if I ever saw one. It had old beer cans rolling around the bottom, and his baits were all dried up there on the seat. He obviously hadn't had much of a day out there with the fish. As he was coming along he rested on his oars just to coast past me and he said, "You seen any fish around here might care for a ride in my boat?" I didn't know how I was going to use that, but I did.

Luis Alberto Urrea

On Addressing Painful Experiences

LU: In college after my father died, I did not know how to deal with this event, and I tried to write about it. You don't know how to express profound feeling, except maybe by overstating it, when you're a young writer. If I had had musical skill, I would have been in a rock band. So then I could have joined a death-metal group and sung in the cookie monster voice, "I hate God! I hate God!" But I didn't have that. I was trying to write this torment out and I couldn't do it. I kept turning in these pieces. And this very staid and respectful gentlemanly, old-school professor—his eyebrows would go up. Finally he said, "It's just too much. You can't make me suffer. I'm not going to let you hurt me." That was some of the best writing advice I ever got: "Let me feel it for myself." He basically slapped me and said, "Get a grip!"

DN: What does that mean when somebody says—"get control of your work"?

LU: In my case, it was a kind of advice. I'd been taking many poetry classes with him. We'd been reading people like Eliot, Stevens, all these great poets. For me, it meant to get control, not only of my language, but my approach. I was trying to attack with a flamethrower, and this required more of a scalpel. It had to be put in context. He didn't understand what was happening. He didn't understand what was going on in Mexico. He didn't understand my feelings. So what I wanted to do then was to try to get that experience into a controlled piece of art that had some stateliness to it. Chaos and hysteria didn't honor my father or my own words. Perhaps the professor was thinking more of a minuet than a death-metal song. To have this technical mastery of what you're trying to do, the science of the piece, and that if you get control of the science of the piece, then some of the emotion and the pain in the flame can be carried in it. And he was right.

Chris Hillman (Interviewed by Karl Martin)

On Parameters in Songwriting

CH: Writing a song, you're basically doing a short story in three and a half minutes. And you're opening with the opening line, your plot, your closing, and then your repetitive chorus sort of summarizes the whole story.

KM: But in a song form, you're also working within rhyme scheme, so it seems like you're very aware of a song form that you inherited from a tradition.

CH: I am trying to stay within the parameters as every songwriter does, but I also subscribe to the no rules theory. But the no rules theory is limited because you're not trying to fool the listening public. You're really writing from your heart, and you're following your heart. Keep it as simple and to the point. That's what I've tried to do.

Billy Collins

On Imagery

DN: There's so much vivid imagery in what you write—is this just one of your gifts, or do you really work at images like this one from the poem "Aristotle." "Disappointment unshoulders his knapsack here and pitches his ragged tent." That's a beautiful line. Did that just pop out or did you really work at that?

BC: I don't remember writing much, to tell you the truth. I wouldn't remember where that came from. I don't know. I think that Michael Longley, the Irish poet, was asked, "where do your ideas come from," or "where do your images come from?" and he said, "Well, if I knew, I would go there and I wouldn't come back."

If you were to picture disappointment as an allegorical character, what would he look like? In this case, he's a hiker. I don't know why though. You just go with these out of instinct. You don't want to make perfect sense.

Lysley Tenorio

On the Importance of Conflict

LT: I start with "What's the story here, what is the beginning, middle, and end, who are the individuals who would find themselves within this dramatic space and how do I make them believable and how do I make them interesting and how do I make them complex?"

The root of all good narrative is conflict. If you're not a writer who is interested in conflict or trouble, it'll be very hard to write a good story. Nobody wants to read a story about a couple who goes on a picnic and has a perfectly lovely day and the sun is out, there are no ants, and they enjoy their meal, they end up engaged, get married, and live happily ever after. That would be the most boring story of all time. We may want to live that but we don't want to read that. We want to read about trouble.

DN: I've heard the line "only trouble is interesting."

LT: It's true. Only trouble is interesting in fiction. Maybe we don't want it in life but we want it in what we read. It's a common thread in my stories. A story has to have stakes. If characters dream big from the very beginning, the stakes are automatically high and there's something that is worth fighting for and hopefully worth a reader exploring page after page after page.

When someone points out—your stories are funny, does it take a long time to develop humor in the work?—I don't really think about developing humor in the work. I think about what is emotionally true in the moment. So you may have a very silly moment in a story where a woman thinks she's about to receive a beautiful present from her boyfriend or her lover and she opens it up and it's a wolf mask and he says, "I want you to star as a creature in my movie." That is a funny moment, but for these characters, to her it's tragic. She's thinking that I thought he was going to give me a really meaningful, beautiful gift that would be some symbol of love. Instead, he has given me this ridiculous costume he wants me to put on.

That's not a moment of me thinking I have to make this a funny scene, because humor in fiction is not a joke. Humor is actually just another side of the truth. So the humor in that moment is truthful to these characters. To another person, that moment is tragic because you see all her dreams being dashed. To me that's what emotional truth is. It's many different kinds of truth competing with each other. That's where you get tension. If it were purely funny, you'd just have a joke. If it were purely tragic or sad, you have nothing but pathos. That kind of single note in fiction is too flat. I don't think it will work.

Nikki Giovanni

On Rhythm

DN: A lot of your poetry doesn't have any punctuation in it whatsoever. That's got to be intentional, so I'm wondering why, but I'm also wondering if that's so whoever's reading it can read it however he or she wants to read it, with whatever cadence, whatever pauses?

NG: My poetry works on the breath. Now, I only have one lung, so that might affect my intake. You know, the stupidest thing on television is that one where the grandfather's sitting with the two little girls. And he said "the wolf huffed and he puffed," and the little girl said, "like you do grandpapa!" you know, don't you just want to reach in and slap the crap out of them?

But my poetry is on a breath. It's like a song. The poetry is available if anyone's kind enough to read it. It's available to be read as they understand it.

Robin Jones Gunn

On Believable Characters

DN: I felt that readers would be able to identify with this Christy Miller character right away because she feels like she doesn't fit in, everyone was cooler than her, she didn't like how her body looked, she felt very awkward. That's a universal feeling for teenagers.

RG: Absolutely! When I finished writing the first *Christy Miller* book, *Summer Promise*, I showed it to my grandmother, and she was in her eighties. She read the book and said to me, "That's exactly how I felt as a teenager!" I thought, "Grandma! You were born in 1902, and you lived in the Midwest—how? Why would you feel just like Christy at the beach with the surfers?" But it's that same universal question of every young woman coming of age: "How am I ever going to fit in? Why do I look the way I do? Why am I so clumsy?" These *Christy Miller* books were written quite a few years ago. Just last night, I met with some girls that were twelve and thirteen, and they had just read the *Christy Miller* books, and were telling me all the things they liked about it. I said, "Wait, I have to ask you, did you notice that Christy did not have a cell phone? Was that a problem for you?" "No, we didn't notice that, but you know, when *this thing* happened, and she felt like 'everybody's looking at me', I felt that way just last week." So as they read in this generation, it's not for technology, it's just more for the feelings and the reactions.

DN: You captured how people feel about themselves in the very first page or so. I assume that was intentional.

RG: No, not at all. When I started writing, the story began where Christy Miller is on the farm in Wisconsin, and her parents come in and say, "Okay, you're going to your aunt and uncle's for the summer, but don't do anything you'll regret later." Then Christie gets on the plane and she's sitting and looking out the window, and then she gets to the airport, she meets her uncle and they go out to dinner [pretends to yawn]. I went to a writer's conference and turned in the first three chapters to an editor. After he'd read it, I sat down across the table. I could see on the first page a red line; the next page a red line, and he went: *page, page, page, page, page, page, page* [pretend to turn pages] and then he stopped and he had a big red circle. He goes, "This is where your story begins." That circle was on: "'I hate you! I hate you!' Christy Miller shouted."

DN: Because she's talking to herself in the mirror, right?

RG: Wadded up her beach towel and threw it at the mirror. The editor said, "That's where I got interested." Nobody needed to hear about another airplane ride. I needed to see Christy. I had the advantage of writing that part first so I can feel closer to her.

DN: Well, as the creator of the character, you needed to know how she got from Wisconsin, or wherever she was, to California. You needed to know that, but the reader—

RG: Yeah, it was kind of off stage.

DN: So, "start with the action . . . "

RG: Apparently, that's how you're supposed to do it.

DN: Also in that book, early on, there's this really funny moment where she goes to a party, and she's just looking for a soft drink, and she goes and asks for some coke. And it gets misinterpreted by everybody.

RG: It happened to one of the kids in our youth group, and I overheard them telling their friends and I was like, "Oh!" [pretends to write on a notepad]. I'm always writing things down. One time, we were on an outreach trip to Mexico, in Mexicali, and all the girls who are sleeping on the gymnasium floor, you know, our sleeping bags and suitcases all tucked in these little rows. I got in my sleeping bag, and the teenage girl next to me rolled over and said, "Oh, this boy I liked said this. . ." And she stopped, mid tears, and said, "Wait, I'm not going to tell you any more because you're gonna put it in your books." I said, "No, you can tell me."

DN: As you're reaching for your notepad . . . For writers, everything is potential material, right?

RG: Yeah, it's all open season.

DN: Writers are always paying attention.

RG: That's why we put in the front of every novel, that this does not reflect any real human or is not based on any true circumstances, because it's a mix of it.

Chris Bohjalian

On Believability

CB: In 2008, I published a novel about one German family's complicity in the Holocaust, *Skeletons at the Feast*. I didn't need to do any education in that book, because all of my readers knew about the Holocaust. In 2010, when I started *The Sandcastle Girls*, most of my readers knew nothing about the Armenian Genocide, so that meant an educational component. I began by creating a female version of me, an Armenian-American novelist in midlife, who knows far too little of her own ancestry.

DN: But my observation of people who start with big ideas for a novel: "I'm gonna write a novel about the Armenian Genocide!"—they get so preachy, and it's just propaganda. Somehow, you avoided this by creating these really believable characters. It's a love story, but I'm also in the middle of this horrific thing that's going on here. Did you ever find yourself saying, "But I got to hammer this point home about the genocide" or did you just get caught up in the story?

CB: I have a great editor at Random House named Jenny Jackson, and there were definite points when I would be sending her chapters, and we would be talking on the phone, and she would say, "I get it. You just did some more research. You need to dial your anger down."

DN: Why a female protagonist? You've done this in a number of your novels, where you've written from the perspective of a woman. Why is that?

CB: What links 1915 to the present is a photograph that the character Laura finds. It's one of those classic Ottoman photographs of Armenians dying in the desert. In this case, it's one particular woman dying in Aleppo, and Laura risks her entire emotional equilibrium to research who that woman is in the photograph, because there's just a tiny inkling that they might be related. I wasn't sure that a middle-aged man would be likely to risk his entire sense of self over one photograph, the way a woman would. When we look back at the women and men who survived, those women were unbelievably strong. My grandmother is a case in point. My grandfather had always assumed that they were going to live forever in Paris after they wed in the 1920s. As soon as my grandmother was pregnant with my father, she made it quite clear to my grandfather, "No, not happening, we're going to America."

DN: So this was kind of built into your family lore, to be hearing stories from a female perspective.

CB: Yes. Whenever I'm writing a book, I depend upon my characters to take me by the hand and lead me through the dark of the story. I never know where a book is going, and when I started *The Sandcastle Girls*, I had absolutely no idea where it was going or how it was going to end. All I knew was that every chapter needed to have an educational component and that was Laura, to put the Armenian Genocide in perspective, and to explain to readers in Denver, *this is what happened and this is why.*

Jane Smiley

On Creating Characters

JS: The reader's greatest right and privilege when he or she is reading a book is to say, "this is bull____" and toss it aside. The writer has to know that. The writer has to know that the reader can always look away, and so the writer has to draw the reader in in some way.

DS: You have said, "What is difficult is not to write something new, but to write something interesting and true."

JS: True in the eyes of the *reader.*

DS: So the reader just has to suspend his or her disbelief to go with you.

JS: Yes. You just have to be true to yourself and your own imagination, and there's a lot of ways to do that. For example—let's say I decided I was going to rewrite King Lear.

DS: What an idea!

JS: When I finally decided that I could do that, the spark of inspiration was about setting. The setting that inspired me was a place in northern Iowa called the Pothole Prairie. We were driving south on I-35 from Minneapolis, and it was late in the afternoon in about March or some damp, dark, depressing time of year. I was looking around and said "you know, this drive should set that Lear book."

And Bingo. It all came to me. What came to me was the setting.

DN: We're talking about *A Thousand Acres,* for which you won the Pulitzer Prize. But you tell it from one of the daughter's points of view.

JS: When I said, "this is where I'm going to set that Lear novel," I had known for years that I wanted the daughters, Goneril and Regan, to say what their side of the story was. Because I remember, even from the first time I read *King Lear* in high school, I was annoyed that they didn't get to say anything. Lear just kept babbling on and on and on—complain, complain, complain.

I kept a chart in *Moo,* because *Moo* is the one that takes place at a land-grant university, and I knew that I wanted to talk about a lot of people in the university. The thing I had to keep track of was, were they showing up enough? So the chart I made was a grid with the number of the chapters across the top and the names of the characters down the side. If they showed up in a particular chapter, I would check off the ones who showed up. Then I would look at the grid and see who was missing. I also knew that every so often, I had to have a lot of them. So there had to be a party. They had to show up at a party.

For the last *Hundred Years* trilogy, I never got any of them mixed up. I knew that the reader would and the publisher knew that the reader would. But for me, it was like members of your family. Why would you ever get any of them mixed up? They're so weird. And so much themselves.

DN: In that *Hundred Year* trilogy, you describe a baby named Frank. I admired your ability to describe how a baby acts and reacts.

JS: I had three babies! I'll never forget when the second one was born, and the doctor put her in my arms, I knew instantly that she was different from the first one. Just by the way she relaxed. The first one remained this kind of self-contained package. She continues to be self-contained to this day, and so she was four years old when the second one was born—they're both girls—and I knew the first one really well, and then the doctor handed me the second one, I said, "this is a different kid!"

It didn't matter what baby books I was reading, none of them said, "OK, they're born with an inherent temperament, they're born with an inherent way of being, an inherent way of perceiving the world, and you have to take that into consideration." They just said, "train her this way, train her that way. Train her this way, train her that way." Didn't work! That was part of the inspiration for starting with Frank's infancy. I wanted to show the difference between Frank and the brothers and sisters.

DN: You have this line about families that I thought was so disturbing. The main character says, "when my father asserted his point of view, mine vanished. Not even I could remember it." I've seen a lot of families like that.

JS: What's that from?

DN: *Thousand Acres.*

JS: OK. So I always say about *A Thousand Acres*, "Uncle Bill told me to do it."

DN: This is Shakespeare's fault?

JS: Yeah, Uncle Bill Shakespeare. That line—all of the stuff—the goal in *A Thousand Acres* when I set out to do it was to adhere to the plot of *King Lear* as plausibly as I could and still make it plausible in our day. Which meant there couldn't be a war. And because it was Iowa, there also couldn't be a gun battle. And there would have to be legal stuff. That was the only way; I tried very hard to make that the only way I veered away from the play.

Everybody my age knew somebody who had those parents, I didn't have those parents, but everybody knew somebody who did. The very authoritative parents.

Nnedi Okorafor

On Word Choice

DN: You have this great scene in *Zahrah the Windseeker* where the main character encounters a gorilla, who tells her to turn off her electric compass. The gorilla says to her, "you should learn to use what you have in your mind. It's much more reliable and far less irritating." Maybe a reference to cell phones?

NO: It might be, or it was just me imagining what a gorilla would say to a human being.

DN: I'm intrigued with how you revised *Who Fears Death?* because originally it was twice as long, maybe two volumes. Is it true that you took the pages out of order and read those pages in isolation to see what stayed and what went? How do you revise that way?

NO: It was tough. *Who Fears Death* took me six years to write. When I finished the whole thing, it was two books, 700 pages. I took that to my agent, and he read it and he said, "This is great, it's gonna win awards, it's African science fiction and it is very rare. You need to make this into one book without changing any of the plot elements." I was like "What?"

My agent also writes books on writing, and he taught me this technique where I was to go through the whole thing, the whole narrative, and take all the weak phrases and make them into strong words. So "very big" would become "huge," stuff like that. So what I did was I printed the whole thing out.

DN: You printed out 700 pages?

NO: Back then we had Kinkos.

DN: You killed a few trees.

NO: But it was for a good reason. I printed it out, then mixed up all the pages. And then threw it on the floor, mixed them up some more, and then went through each of those pages out of context, one by one, and went through all the words. All the words. And also took out all the inner thoughts, because ninety percent of inner thoughts were mainly redundant. So I took all of that out.

DN: Because the action would reveal what they were thinking anyway.

NO: Exactly. It took two years to do that and got it down to 389 pages. That was the book. So now it reads very fast and smooth and there's no fat on it at all because of that process. I've applied that technique to everything I've written from that point on.

DN: The other point that is useful for writers is to go ahead and write long in your early draft because you can always take stuff out.

NO: Yes, and it's easier to work with something than nothing. For me, the editing process is a lot longer than the initial genesis phase, when you throw it down on a page first.

DN: I'm curious by your word choices in some of your titles. When you titled *Akata Witch*, you knew you were stepping in it with those words. The Nigerian press wouldn't publish those words. Why would you use words like Akata and Witch knowing how inflammatory they are?

NO: There is a part of me that is chaos.

DN: Granted.

NO: It's not that I like to make trouble, but I like to start conversations. I like to stir it up and then run away.

DN: But the Nigerian press wouldn't even go there.

NO: No, they wouldn't. The word Akata is a derogatory term for African Americans and those who are like me who are born outside of Nigeria. There is a whole conversation around this. Some Nigerians will say, "Oh it's not a negative word, it's not negative at all, it's just a word." No. Anyone who's been called Akata knows it's not a nice word, we know. It's purposely inflammatory as part of the book. The main character is called that and has to deal with it. Then there's the word Witch—also very problematic in Nigeria because the word Witch has a lot of negative power and a lot of fear around it. So in Nigeria they had to change the title because people wouldn't buy a book called *Akata Witch* for their kids to read. Things have changed a lot, because Nigerian readers have gotten used to me. They know I write that juju stuff, and they're kind of used to it. They know what I'm about.

DN: "Oh it's her."

NO: Exactly. She's at it again, okay let's read it anyway.

DN: You describe her as growing up and making her own decisions. That doesn't strike me as sci-fi or fantasy—that's like right now.

NO: Science fiction doesn't have to be completely foreign. My favorite type of science fiction is woven in with now. It doesn't always have to be concerned with the technology. Sometimes it can just dwell in the vicinity of the technology. Sometimes it can just be in the future, and it can just be a narrative that happens.

DN: You're suspicious of novels that come too quickly.

NO: Definitely. It should be like a wine. I think time is required. It's not optional. It needs to simmer and mature and grow and evolve. You can't rush it. If something does form and it forms quickly, fine, I'm willing to accept that. But I would definitely be suspicious. I think that time is a factor in a good story.

Katie Manning

On Thinking Visually in Poetry

DN: You pay so much attention to how the words appear on the page. The poem "The Belly of The Whale" is spaced in such a way that looks like the side view of a pregnant woman. And in your poem "How I Measure Your Body," you have four squares of words that look identical as far as length. I counted the number of words in each square and, within one or two, there are identical numbers of words in those squares. Why is the visual component of your poems important?

KM: Thank you for counting my words. I didn't count them—I was just looking at the visual squares.

DN: You're at sixty-eight per square.

KM: I do sometimes count words and syllables. I'm really interested in numbers in poetry, and I've presented on math poetry panels.

DN: When you're writing a poem, are you thinking visually while you're writing?

KM: Oh, absolutely. I think visually and I also think sonically, so I read to myself a lot while I'm drafting because I want the sounds to be there, but I definitely think about the visual also. I usually let myself handwrite in a really messy way to get ideas out, sort of getting the clay, and then when I'm actually bringing it to the screen and starting to craft and do the visual design of it, that's where I'm forming something. That's where I'm actually making something that's useful or beautiful. Hopefully.

DN: Now the clay is on the wheel. Once you've gotten the big glob of clay, the craft part is now the shaping.

KM: Yes. That's where I spend more of my energy. The drafting is sort of frenzied, sometimes in multiple stages. Then I really craft the poem. That's revision, where I am creating a poem.

Don Winslow

On Word Choice, Description, and Structure

DN: One of your hallmarks is the simple declarative sentence. You are to the point, very spare, let the action speak.

DW: The way I put it to myself is that there are no freeloaders in this apartment. Every word has to pay rent or at least do the dishes.

DN: So many crime novels build up to what the conflict is. But for you, the inciting incident is on Page 1. Why that approach?

DW: It was just an image in my head, that this guy's lying on this beach where I've been since I was four years old, where I went after my dad died, where I walked some months after my mom died. And he looks out at the ocean and this beautiful woman is coming out of the water. And he has this realization that everything's about to change.

DN: And as he looks back, he says I wish I would have taken her back into that water and held her under.

DW: If I'd known then what I knew now.

DN: But that's page 1.

DW: Well, why waste time?

DN: Many people who have read *City on Fire* say the themes are about loyalty and respect. I think it's a lot deeper than that. I think this has a lot to do with a character who feels trapped and he wants to do good things, but he has to do a lot of bad things so he can do the good things. That's his dilemma, right?

DW: Absolutely. I think it's page two.

DN: This is a very short book.

DW: We're going to read the entirety of it to you today.

I often like to point the compass at true north and then kick it a little slanted, so you get that slightly askew point of view.

DN: There's such good description in this book. You're talking about this storm as the character's looking at the surf: "White caps that look like beards of sad, old men." I read that and I thought, ok, now that did not come out in the first draft.

DW: No. It did not.

DN: I'm relieved. Or the one character's looking at another guy and says, "strands of his white hair remind him to stop at Rite-Aid for dental floss."

DW: That's pretty funny.

DN: But then the Danny character is having to make decisions, and you have the setting contributing to what's happening on the stage. The surf is being vicious, "big waves crashing on shore like bombs." That's his head. That's his heart. That's also what's going on in the surf. I think I know enough about writing that when you go back and revise, that's when these types of descriptions start to get some light.

DW: I think for the most part that's true, and every once and a while you get lucky on a first draft, and it just goes. I wrote a novella that starts off with the sentence, "No one knows how the chimp got the revolver." That just wrote itself, like zoom! But to get to your more serious question about craft, I write first drafts very fast. There's an old martial arts saying that I think applies to writing. It asks the question, how do you carve a tiger? The answer is, you get a big block of wood, and you carve away everything that doesn't look like a tiger. That is the process, but first you need that big block of wood. You need that first draft that I need to write fearlessly. No judgment. Nothing. You can't sit and judge yourself as you're writing. There's too many people in the room. You can't have that Jiminy Cricket character on your shoulder, "Ah, it's an adverb!"

DN: I haven't thought of Jiminy Cricket in a long time.

DW: Happy to bring it back. As drafts go by, eight, nine, ten, fourteen, then, all I have in mind is the reader.

DN: Who do you have in mind in that first draft?

DW: Me.

DN: You just want to get something out.

DW: It's just selfish. It's just entertainment for me.

DN: Then you look at it and say, is this anything?

DW: Yeah, and sometimes it's not. You've had that experience, right? It's Tuesday, you think it's great. You look at it on Wednesday, you realize, well it's garbage. What was I thinking? But you know that a novel's going to be a long-term relationship. A trilogy is going to be especially a long-term relationship. My drug trilogy featured a guy named Art Keller. I've spent more time with Art Keller than any real person in my life. Just hour after hour, day after day over the course of twenty-three years.

DN: Do you chart out who the characters are ahead of time? Or do you do like Ray Bradbury said he worked, where you shoot the starter's pistol, set all the characters off on a race with snow on the ground, and you just follow their footprints?

DW: That's great. I'm more in that line. I don't outline, which causes immense problems late in a book. In that drug trilogy, which is thousands of pages, I'm writing book three and I'm thinking, did I kill that guy?

DN: I need a reincarnation scene.

DW: Exactly! Like, it's a miracle! But this would actually happen to me. It's like two or three days of writing and I go uh, wait a second, madly flipping through book one, oops. No good.

DN: Every writer has to figure out their own way to do it. Teachers will say you need an outline, you need to know where this thing's going. I've never been comfortable with outlines. I feel like it's like a polaroid picture that starts to emerge as you're writing.

DW: I know myself well enough, little Irish Catholic boy that I am, that if I did an outline, I would stick to it slavishly. Right? You know, A B 1, Sister Mary Theresa.

DN: Standing there with a ruler.

DW: Right there. I want to be surprised. If I'm surprised, the reader is going to be surprised. I like painting myself into corners because then you have to get out. If I'm painted into a corner, the reader's painted into the corner and it's a fun experience for us both.

DN: You have said you "write badly until the good stuff comes." You have an interesting mix of ethnic heritage. One side is Irish, and one of your characters refers to "Irish Alzheimer's," "where they forget everything except their grudges." You know my family!

DW: I come from Irish on one side. I'm very waspy on the other. So waspy we never had confrontations. The way we communicated was to leak memos through a third party.

DN: Let's keep talking about craft. The longest paragraph in the entire book . . .

DW: Hmm, I know where you're going.

DN: Why did you choose to write it that way? Everything else are these genial, short, declarative sentences, no adjectives, no adverbs. And then you have two pages of mostly one sentence that just unloads. Why that?

DW: I wouldn't let the copy editor touch it, either.

DN: I'm sure you put a note on that and said, I know what I'm doing here. Leave it alone.

DW: I said, "This is it. I'll write commas if I want." The segment you're referring to is a stream of memory where Danny is mourning his closest friend who was virtually a brother to him. And he's remembering their childhood of these three boys who grew up so close that their name was one name, PatTommyJimmy. I grew up like that. So, those are direct memories. I wanted to go into that sort of, this is pretentious, Joycean stream of consciousness because I wanted a certain rhythm for the reader.

DN: But you disrupted the main rhythm by doing that.

DW: For that segment I wanted the reader in this lyrical stream of memory that they couldn't get off of. I wanted to put the reader into this stream, this river, and say you can't get to shore until we're done with this little segment in this stream. Because I thought it was more evocative the more emotive.

DN: It was jarring to me to think I'm really reliving this guy's childhood. I'm with him on this little journey.

DW: It needed a different perspective than the rest of the book.

DN: So how do you revise?

DW: I have some weird tricks. Once I finish the whole manuscript, I'll go away from it for two or three days and work on something else. And then I come back and I read it from beginning to end. Then I proofread, then I'm carving the tiger. A lot of the things I'm going to be doing are structural because I realize a scene I had on page 301 probably should have been on 101. I do a lot of frontloading, trying to structure it, building that tiger. As we get through more and more drafts, I pay attention to the way that the words fall on the reader's ear and eye. We think of reading as just a mental activity, but it is a physical activity as well. So, I'll read dialogue out loud to myself, because I won't hear the right notes, but I'll hear the wrong ones. I'll stand back from the screen so that I can't see the words, but I can see the shape of the page.

DN: The visual matters to you.

DW: Very much. With the example you just gave, there's no white space in that segment because I wanted to grab the reader by the front of the shirt and pull him or her all the way along until I was ready to let them go. Other times, though, I want to focus the reader's eye on one or two words that might stand for a lot more. In that case, those words need white space around them. They need negative space. The look of the page is really important to me because I think it's important to the reader. They don't realize it. It's not a conscious thing. But it's me directing the rhythm of their reading.

DN: This is illuminating how intentional you are about the visual component of it.

DW: A syllable can flip a chapter. Sometimes if a word ends at the block end of a line, I might not want it to be an end. I might want it to lead into the next paragraph or the next piece of dialogue. So I might play with adding or subtracting a syllable if it makes sense to move the line to the next line. So there's white space and continuity.

Anthony Doerr

On Chapter Length

DN: You structured *Cloud Cuckoo Land* similarly to your other books, with really short chapters. You use an image in explaining why—that it's like you're launching a projectile. While it's still in the air, you change chapters, and the reader is having to keep that projectile in the air at an unconscious level, knowing that it's moving until you come back to it a few chapters later. Is that still how you feel about it?

AD: Yeah. If I do a good job, or if a writer does a good job—sometimes you can fail—and they'll kind of forget, and the spinning plate will fall off the stick. *Suspend* is Latin. "Pend" is inside; the word "pending" is inside that. *Pendere*: to hang. And it's this metaphor of if you leave something hanging at this moment of its highest trajectory, a reader will be dying to see that thing come down. So a reader might keep turning a few more pages just to see that thing come down. It's kind of a trick; you can get her to turn a few more pages. That's been the trick of narrative forever. The bards in Ancient Greece would walk around town and sing *The Odyssey* for wine and bread. They would leave cliffhangers. They'd be like, "Well, if you guys feed me, tomorrow you'll hear what happened to Achilles." You leave him hanging up there so that you can eat.

10

When Enthusiasm Fades

How Important Is Discipline?

I don't feel well if I don't write.

RAY BRADBURY

When my daughter was little, I would occasionally take her to a skating rink near our house. One time, after we had watched the winter Olympics on television, she decided to spend most of her ice time in the center of the rink doing spins and balancing on one skate. She would watch some of the other skaters nearby who were practicing routines, and she would try to mimic them.

When we were done, we sat on a bench and unlaced our skates.

"Did I look like Michelle Kwan out there?" she asked.

"Not yet," I said. As my daughter remembers it, I said "No." But I added, "With practice, though, you could be good at it. You have the balance and coordination." She was silent. Then, in the car, she declared, "I suck at skating."

A lot of would-be writers see themselves in a similar way. They get an idea, they try to write it, and it's not very good. Then they hear what some of their peers are producing and they get intimidated, which leads them to the conclusion, "I suck at writing."

To them, good writing just falls out of the sky on some of the lucky ones.

Maybe it is just for the lucky or the strong. But maybe it can happen when we lace up the skates again and put in the work.

I know a lot of writers who say they will start writing when they have more time. Maybe when the kids are grown, or the job pressure eases, or when they're no longer taking care of their parents. Maybe when they retire. Or when they're inspired.

Robin Jones Gunn's example below is a great lesson for us. She had two little kids, a job she didn't like, was trying to help her husband in his youth ministry job, and she felt like she had stories to tell. But when? Then she read a reference to C. S. Lewis getting up before dawn, making a proper pot of tea, and getting his work done. She bought a teapot, got up at 3:00 a.m. a few days a week, and did her work. She did that for more than fifteen years.

Remember Christopher Buckley's question, "Do you want to be a writer, or do you want to write?" Those are two different things. Those who say they want to be a writer are going to struggle with the discipline of getting up early, of writing regardless of how they feel, and of writing badly for a long time before it gets good.

Writers write. Sounds like a cliché, I know. But it is true. Stephen King said, "Amateurs sit and wait for inspiration. The rest of us just get up and go to work."

Jack London said, "You can't wait for inspiration. You have to go after it with a club."

Joe Wambaugh said it's the hardest job he's ever had—and he was a cop in Los Angeles, a member of the Marine Corps, and worked in a steel mill before that.

Sometimes the first drafts come easily. Then the real work begins. One of the myths about writing is that after the first draft you can cruise. But it's only then that you, in the words of Annie Dillard, go at your work with an ax.

Some people have legitimate reasons for why they don't write. But as I said in the introduction, your excuses are just not that interesting. We all have excuses to not write. Yours don't impress anyone. Writers write. So write something today.

Joseph Wambaugh

DN: A columnist asked you if anyone had said to you, "That book was such a natural, it must have written itself." Do you remember your answer to him?

JW: No. What did I say?

DN: "And I gave birth to myself one winter day back in East Pittsburgh when I had nothing else to do."

JW: It's the hardest work I've ever done. I've only had three jobs in my life. I was in the Marine Corps for three years, I worked in the steel mill for two-and-a-half years, and I was a cop. I've never had any other jobs. I'm sure there are jobs that are very tough, but I've never had a harder job than writing. It never got any easier. As a matter of fact, it got harder. My last books were much harder to write than the first books because the first books were based on my personal experience and things I had to get out. I wasn't a professional writer. I just had to get things out. And they came out. In my later books, I guess I'm a professional writer, and I have to do the job. It's harder. Much harder. So, sorry if you think it's going to get easier. It isn't.

DN: However, when I read what you write, it seems like you're having one great time writing this.

JW: Boy are you wrong. I have a great time having written it.

DN: Do you remember your answer to the person who said you seem to have so much fun writing and asked if writing was fun?

JW: No.

DN: "About as fun as my hemorrhoidectomy."

JW: Sounds like something I would say.

Chitra Divakaruni

DN: You have said that "you have to be prepared to give things up for writing." What kinds of things do we need to be giving up? What did you have to give up?

CD: The X-Files? There were a lot of things that I enjoyed doing, but that weren't really giving me things that were important in return.

DN: What do you do with writer's block?

CD: When you're really blocked and just can't write, and even reading wonderful inspiring people just makes you more blocked because they're so wonderful, read some really bad books. Then when you see how bad those writers are, and still they got published, you will *really* be inspired.

DN: I have heard people say that there is no such thing as writer's block, that it's only a lack of material, a lack of paying attention to the world, a lack of eavesdropping on conversations around you. What do you think?

CD: I think those people who said that weren't writers. I constantly have writer's block. We all go through dry periods, and then periods when we are very productive. Often what's happening during our periods of writer's block is that we're probably processing things, and we're not ready, and we don't know how to express them. They're very painful and frustrating periods, but one needs to work through them.

Ray Bradbury

RB: You must write every day. Every day of your life. If you don't write every day, you'll get sick. Writing is a process of cleansing yourself as well as all the other things. You don't know how it works but it does work. I haven't gone mad yet. I've never used a psychiatrist. I've never used a psychoanalyst. Good writing is automatically a cleansing of the soul. If you do honest work, passionate work and deal with your real fears, you can have a pretty good life and not need help from outside. Maybe it doesn't work that way for everybody, but it sure as hell has worked for me.

DN: Here's the analogy you like, borrowing from Jascha Heifetz: If a musician doesn't practice one day, he knows it. If he doesn't practice for two days, his critics know it. And if he doesn't practice for three days, his audience knows it. You say that writing is the same way. After a while, if you aren't doing it every day, people will notice.

RB: I've never given them a chance. The most I've gone without writing is sometimes when I travel, but even there you got a pad and pencil with you and you can get your work done. I don't feel well if I don't write. A year ago I was in the hospital for a month. That was a real endangerment not only to my life, but to my writing. It was really bad the first week because I didn't have a chance to write. After the second week I began to dictate over the phone. It's not good writing. Dictation is only 50 percent good stuff. But writing with a typewriter is the real stuff, so I came the closest to being really depressed a year ago in the hospital. As soon as possible, I began to teach myself to type again. Then I was back in shape.

Amy Tan

AT: I think we all have this happen where you picture your life being the same way that it is at that moment for the rest of your life, and you always pick this when you're in some miserable funk, thinking I'm going to be changing diapers for the rest of my life, I'm going to be writing this for the rest of my life, and that's what I figured. I decided I needed to do something for me. I was working ninety hours a week. I decided I should cut back to about fifty and then I'd use the remaining forty to write fiction.

DN: I didn't know there were ninety hours in the week.

AT: They were billable hours. There were ninety billable hours in the week because I billed ninety billable hours. That's how much I was working. I was crazed. I could not stop working and I needed to find a method that would work to get me to stop. I would allow myself to work fifty billable hours then I'd have to spend the rest of the time writing something that would not make me any money whatsoever. It would just have to do with writing for myself.

DN: Has that compulsive, non-stop writing translated into your fiction writing?

AT: In the beginning, it certainly did because people like you didn't ask me to come to this esteemed place to come to talk to you all.

DN: I hear that all the time.

AT: I would be home instead of here. I would be home by myself and in my study writing. And I did. I wrote every day from about eight in the morning until seven in the evening when my husband came back from work. It was a wonderful time of solitude. Things changed after the publication of *Joy Luck Club,* and they really haven't been the same since. But I love those moments where I have nothing to do but write. My time is a lot more fractured now.

DN: I want to read a sentence or two from *The Bone Setter's Daughter* and ask you a question from it. We're talking about a family that makes ink in this setting:

"Good ink cannot be the quick kind, ready to pour out of a bottle. You can never be an artist if your work comes without effort. That is the problem with modern ink from a bottle. You do not have to think. You simply write what is swimming at the top of your brain and the top is nothing but pond scum, dead leaves and mosquito spawn. But when you push an ink stick along an ink stone, you take the first step to cleansing your mind and your heart. You push and you ask yourself, what are my intentions. What is it in my heart that matches my mind?"

I bracketed that and thought you just described the writing process in general, didn't you? I don't know if that was an intentional thing on your part, but that's you describing: writing.

AT: It was my intention to write about what it's like for me to sit down and write. I know nothing about ink making except what I've done through research so I could write this scene. It's not the factual details that matter as much as the emotional truth, and when you get that down, it's believable that the person there is sitting with the ink stick and is thinking very seriously about what she needs to write and why.

DN: But it goes beyond that, according to this. It can't be the first things that come, the thin stuff at the top.

AT: Right. That's also a little bit from my parents. My mother especially. If it's too easy, it's not worth pursuing. It has to be more difficult than that, and I find that to be true with writing. People often say you have to dig a little deeper and take the things that you love too much and throw them away and see what really remains. All the stuff that's fancy. All the stuff that you think is going to show you in your best light—take that away and see what remains. You strip it down to the bare essentials, to the bare truth. I try to do that, and as simple as it's stated there, it is very difficult to do.

There is so much pond scum on the top of my mind when I begin. Part of it has to do with people's expectations. You have to get rid of that. Any writer has to get rid of that. When you're writing for yourself, when you're writing literary fiction, you have to be aware of your absolute purest intentions and not be swayed by what you think people want to hear. Unless of course, you're a political speech writer. You cleanse yourself in a way. I like the idea of the rubbing because it gives you the time to think about the process and how this is all going to meld the heart, the mind and flow into the hand and onto the page.

DN: But Amy, what you're describing is hard work!

AT: It's work for a long time and then there reaches a point that's magical, and this is what every writer wants to feel. You get a sensation that is the most wonderful, overpowering emotion and everything comes together and suddenly the writing seems effortless. It's not effortless but it just comes. You know what it is, and when I reach that point—it happens only once or twice during the entire writing of the book—it makes the entire writing of the book worth it. I have little moments of it in pages, but the big essence of where I know what I'm writing about and it's all clear and it all comes together happens maybe once in the writing of the book.

Garrison Keillor

GK: We write not in order to express ourselves, but we write in order to find out who we are and what we think. You can sit down at a piece of paper or a blank screen, you can sit down with no idea what you are going to do, and you can still find something very useful to do. You don't need to wait until you have something fully formulated or even vaguely formulated in your mind. That's why the habit of writing is very useful to develop. It may seem like a waste of time, but so what? So what? Time is meant to be wasted and it will be good for you, no matter what you wind up doing. I think the habit of sitting down and writing at a regular time is a wonderful habit.

DN: I've talked to several people over the years where they say you write out the Lake Wobegone stories you tell on the radio, that you know exactly where they're going. But others say, no you just a have a general framework of where this story's going to go and then you just riff off of that. Which is it?

GK: You want to know exactly where you are going. You really do. You want to have something written out. It alleviates panic.

When you write, you want to give yourself some freedom to let things flow out onto the page onto the screen. You don't want to interrupt yourself. You don't want to start editing as you are writing, though your mind is at work. Your internal editor is at work in arranging things. But you want to get to it quickly, and you want to do it bravely. If you're writing prose, any sort of prose, it helps to read it out loud. You can hear things. If you are writing on a computer, fine, but you really need to print it out as a hard copy. Print it out as a hard copy, double spaced, even triple, leave yourself a lot of room. The act of looking at it in a different medium really, really, really helps. Look at it with a pencil, and make your marks. Then you type it back into your computer and fool around with it some more. It's a process that can go on and on. One has to learn to love doing that and not to rush it. It's the pleasure of taking your own thoughts which you've invested something in, that's you, that's your writing, and the chance to take it and advance it and to eliminate the wasted motion and to eliminate the vanity and purify it and scorch it and melt it down a little bit. It's meant to be pleasureful, and not painful.

Chris Hillman

CH: In songwriting it's not something I sit down and say, "Today I'm gonna write a song and it's gonna go here and here," and it just comes out. Sometimes it comes out quick, and sometimes it takes a long time. You agonize over it.

Lysley Tenorio

LT: That first year when I started sending out work I managed to sell two stories. One was in the Atlantic and one in Plowshares. But it was another two or three years before I sold another story and I realized, for some writers it's a long process. I wish that I could write more quickly, and I wish that I could write more decisively, but as I'm writing I'm also editing in my head so as you move forward there's also a lot of backtracking. For all the moments of inspiration and the fun that writing can be, it's incredibly labor intensive. It just feels like you're working with these bricks and constantly arranging them in a big way, but also in a very very small, very fine-tuned way. Especially once I started writing on my own outside of school, I realized, oh boy this is a lot of work.

There are some days when there are a million things I'd rather do—I'd rather do the dishes than write sometimes, but when I finally force myself to the desk, when I'm at the keyboard or working with pen and paper—let's just say I nail that paragraph or I get that sentence right that has been troubling me for two days prior, it feels like a small victory. You will want to do the football touchdown dance. Is that the sport where they do that? I don't know. But you kind of just want to high five the air. That's what keeps me going.

For one story, I wrote early drafts in graduate school and I felt like I was always really close to getting it done, but I could never get it right so I would put it away and pick it up two years later and I would think maybe I could do something with this and work on it. But I couldn't get it right, and I would put it away. Normally when I would do that I would just throw the story away. I've written stories that I've finished and they don't work and I toss it. But I cared about this story and if I cared about it I knew I had to keep working on it.

One day I was working on it and thought, maybe it needs a new beginning. How do I start this? The family I'm writing about is moving to Lemoore, and I was just saying Lemoore to myself and I realized, I don't even speak French, but Lemoore, L'amour, they sound the same, that means love, and Isa is a girl who dreams of love. She dreams of sweeping romances. She's a teenage girl. Not that all teenage girls think that way but she's that kind of teenage girl. So, I thought, if she thinks she's moving to a city that's named for the French word for love, then she thinks, ah that's my destiny, that's where I want to be. So what a let down when she sees it's called "Lemoore" and she doesn't know what that means.

DN: But then she has the identical experience with a boy where she thinks, this is what love is. She has the same experience with the name of the town as she does with this relationship with this boy and that doesn't work out either. What a story.

LT: Thank you. It took a very long time to write so I was very very happy when it was published. I felt like I could go to sleep for a while.

DN: Your writing process has changed over the years. You used to be one of those who could blast it out, twenty pages in a night, a caffeine-filled writing experience. You don't write like that anymore.

LT: No. I'm tired. I can't write until four in the morning anymore. I teach full time and that takes up a lot of time and admittedly I am doing more self-editing than I was before.

DN: Is that a good thing?

LT: It can be but often it's not. Sometimes I just need to allow myself to be messy on the page because you never know what kind of material you might generate. But because I feel as though my time is so fractured now, I hesitate to devote my free time to bad pages but sometimes that is what you've got to do. So I am not as fast as I used to be, but I mean hopefully I'm a better writer.

DN: You're working a novel now, but you're a short story guy. What's that like?

LT: It's a whole different monster to tame. I hear more students who tell me they're going to write short stories and then move on to the novel. This idea of moving on seems like the next natural step, as though the short story were some kind of training ground.

DN: Like you're in the shallow end of the pool.

LT: Right, and maybe that's true for some. But for me the short story has its own set of demands that the novel does not. When I'm writing a short story, by virtue of the genre or the form, it's got to be short. If I'm heading into thirty-five pages, I'm thinking this is too long and it would be hard to publish. So I'm working with compression and I'm working to see how much mileage I can get out of one paragraph, one sentence because it's got to do double or triple duty. With a novel you have the luxury of space, but what's seemingly luxurious is also quite daunting because now I'm writing a scene and I'm thinking this scene has gone on for seven pages—when does it end? Will somebody end this madness now? It's harder to feel tamed and controlled by the parameters of brevity when a novel can go as long as it wants. I'm still trying to figure that trickiness out.

DN: That's a completely different mental discipline because you've got these boundaries that you're used to and now you don't. How is it working so far?

LT: It's slow. I'm a slow writer. I really, really am. I've been working on a novel for a couple years and I took a sabbatical a couple years ago. I'm a full-time teacher but had sabbatical for a year, and I managed to write the first draft of a novel. It was a terrible draft and I was fine with that but after finishing the draft and sitting with it for a while, I had to accept that that's not the story I want to tell. I'm certainly not the first writer that has happened to, but nonetheless it still bums you out. Now I'm back into the story and it's a story that I not only understand better but that I actually care about.

Destin Daniel Cretton (Interviewed by Karl Martin)

KM: A writer of a screenplay—more so than a writer of a short story or a novel—has to be willing to collaborate, because as you said, the screenplay is not the finished product—the film is the finished product. You have to have this give and take with actors. How does that work?

Are you open to characters saying, "I think I'd do it this way," or improvising scenes?

DDC: That's my favorite part. If I was one of the Coen brothers, then I would just be like, "I am an amazing writer and you will say my words," but I'm not that type of writer and I never think anything I write is perfect. Not because I'm insecure, but because I'm always hoping that it will be better. I'm always hoping that it will come more alive than what I am able to do in words. I love actors and what they do. I don't understand it—I have no idea how they do it, but it's extremely exciting to me. It's the same excitement I get from doing documentaries. There's something so thrilling about happening to be in a moment in time when you have a camera in your hand and you're recording something that will never happen again and it just happens and it's in your frame. That happens on a set when your actors feel free enough to just go with it, or go off-script, or maybe do something that even surprises them.

There were so many moments when we were shooting "Short Term Twelve" when people would do things that would surprise themselves. One scene that was not written in the script at all is when Marcus comes in with his shirt off and he sits down. It wasn't in the script that his shirt was off and I was in the other room looking at the monitor. I was like, "What's going on—why is his shirt off?" But then it was, "Oh that looks amazing!" so we shot the whole thing with his shirt off.

KM: How did you get involved with writing a screenplay based on Jeannette Walls' memoir *The Glass Castle*?

DDC: The producer Gill Netter had seen my films "I Am Not a Hipster" and "Short Term Twelve" and brought the project to me. I read the book and just loved it, tried to pitch what I would do, and then had to go to Lionsgate. First, I had to pitch as a director, so I tried to tell them how passionate I was about it and the way that I saw the movie. Then I asked my friend Andrew Lanham to co-write it with me to help adapt this book. We were hanging out and I was telling him about the book. He had read it and I told him some ideas, and he had some ideas and it felt so fun, so I asked him to do it with me. We went back to Lionsgate and we had two giant white boards that we had mapped out every sequence and every scene, and color-coordinated it. It looked very impressive, just all these color-coordinated words in outline form. I was super nervous, but it was kind of fun doing it that way. It was just us, the executives and our producer in a big conference room, but we were all huddled around these white boards, and we were just like "and then this happens and then this happens," and they were just like "mmmm." We went through the whole movie like that. They signed off and then we started writing. It was one of the toughest things I've ever done, but it was also pretty fun.

KM: So you're working with another writer, but you're also working with an existing story. There's a certain boundedness to that, where you have to stay true to this and decide what episodes will translate well to film.

DDC: Totally. It's not just because it's a book, but because it's a good book, we had to do our best to stay true to it. That whole process was scary because I love the book so much. It was scary once we started getting into it and realizing how little space you have in a screenplay, how much we had to get rid of. It was a huge realization as to why you constantly hear people say, "I love the book and I didn't really like the movie." But the most freeing thing we had to remind ourselves of, which was something Jeanette was so wonderful and gracious about, was reminding us that this is a new piece of art. It's called an adaptation, and it is, but it's a new thing. And it should be a new thing, and they should not be compared because they are incomparable.

We had to constantly to remind ourselves, "What is the heart of the story and how is the scene that we're writing connected to that? Does it feel like her voice, and is this screenplay doing the same thing that the book did?" Sometimes sacrifices need to be made in order to keep the whole thing feeling closer to the truth of the book. If we just went through the book and pulled out every great amazing scene—because there are so many amazing, tragic, moving scenes, one after another in that book—if we tried to cram them into a movie, it would be true to the book scene-by-scene, but as a whole, it would not be true to the book at all because it would not flow. It would just be a bad movie.

Finding the balance between looking at this screenplay as a whole and whether it is truthful to the heart of the story as a whole is definitely a big learning curve.

I'm incredibly undisciplined. I try to write every day, but for the movie I'm doing right now, I had to do quite a bit of research. A lot of that was reading, reading a whole book to find out that there's nothing in this book I can use, and spending a whole week doing something to find out that it was completely pointless. But it's not pointless, it's just process of elimination. Part of it was volunteering at certain places that allowed me to gain personal experience in the world that I'm researching. A lot of it was interviewing people who are going through similar things through the characters that I wanted to experience. I'm watching a lot of documentaries and going on YouTube—there's a lot of good stuff on YouTube. It's a combination of all that stuff, but it is difficult to know when to stop. At some point, I felt like, okay I know I don't have everything, but I don't know what else I need specifically because I don't know what's going to fit into this screenplay. So I did enough for a couple months to do an outline of what I wanted the characters to be going through emotionally, and now I'm trying to get through writing it. In places that I don't fully know the research, I generically write it or leave notes like "figure this out."

Joyce Carol Oates

JCO: I look out the window a lot. It's very important to me to have a view out the window.

DN: This is part of the creative process for you, walking, running, looking out the window.

JCO: That's what I say to myself. I might just be looking out the window. We have this fantastic place on Panoramic Hill in Berkeley. We have a view going down toward San Francisco and the Bay, and we can see the Golden Gate Bridge, and a fantastic, ever-shifting display of light and color as the sun sets. It's quite mesmerizing. Closer in are eucalyptus trees, and all sorts of Steller's jays, which are not known on the East, and they're all flipping around. And it must be mating season for the squirrels, because the squirrels are *everywhere*. And they're big, bushy, red-tailed squirrels that are scampering all around and clattering over the roof. One of them, or maybe it's not always the same one, he's always looking in the window at me. He's sort of wondering, like, am I a squirrel? I mean, what's he looking for? He's looking with his little eyes. So I spend a lot of time dealing with all this.

DN: It's important work.

JCO: I'm just sitting down to my work and I hear the click, and it's a squirrel. He's wondering what I'm doing. I guess it's mating season and he couldn't find a real squirrel or something. He's there every morning. I don't want to disappoint him, but I'm not going out with him.

DN: You need to think more highly of yourself than that.

JCO: Well, I'm not going out with that squirrel. I stayed in and did my work.

DN: Maybe the squirrel's a writer, and he's just killing time looking in your window.

JCO: I think that might be possible.

DN: Looking out the window notwithstanding, you're a pretty disciplined writer. I think it's interesting that you can get the work done, and yet a lot of the characters you write about are these chaotic individuals, they're just sort of the . . . not you.

JCO: Well, I give the impression of being disciplined, which is all you have to do, you know.

DN: You describe the process of writing a novel as: "obsession, excitement, anxiety, then melancholy when done, and fear that nothing will ever mean that much again." Do you still feel that way about writing novels?

JCO: I like writing on a daily basis, and there's a lot of satisfaction in writing. And probably I was just being a little funny, in that. Because there's a lot of positive satisfaction; it isn't all just these negative things. I do miss some novels that I put a lot of my life into. When I think back on them, I sort of wish that I was writing them again or that I could go back and have that time in my life again. But of course it all moves on, and you can't do that.

Carlos Ruiz Zafon

CZ: I have to work very hard at my books. I would like to believe that they choose me and then they whisper in my ear, and then they use me as a medium or something. But in my experience, I need to hammer them down and fight against them continuously to put them on paper. Maybe there are writers who are fortunate enough to have ideas that they don't know where they come from. In my case, I need to force everything into being. If I don't do it, I wouldn't do anything, I would just be playing the piano and writing music, which is a way for me to have fun, or reading, or working, or traveling. So I need to force myself to work. It's not necessarily a pleasant process.

DN: Really?! Writing is hard work? Seriously?!

CZ: Hard work is being at the harbor bringing crates out of ships. So when I complain about it, I feel embarrassed because you're there in a nice office, playing music, sipping caffeine, and squeezing your brain to see if there's something useful in there, trying to work the language and rewriting everything to death. In many ways, you're working with the things you like and enjoy, so it's a luxury occupation. Still after many years of doing it, I find it hard work because it's a pure abstraction. You're creating something from scratch. There are a lot of creative endeavors where you are reacting to material, where something pulls you through the process. When you're writing, there's nothing. You have paper and ink and a huge nothingness staring at you all the time. You have to create creatures that are going to be interesting, and you have to create a universe, a world, a story. At least in my case, I need to work hard at it. It doesn't come easily, even though with years you develop experience, and you develop the craft and you do it easier, and way better.

Robin Jones Gunn

RG: There was a season when I was trying to find time to write and I couldn't. With two small children and my husband doing youth ministry, I was always helping him out and working part-time with various little jobs. I read in C. S. Lewis' *Letters to an American Lady*, she has something about how he got so much work done, and he said something to the effect of, "I love the still dewy, cobwebbed hours of the morning, and I rise before dawn, make a proper pot of tea, and get all my correspondence done before breakfast." And I just closed the book and thought if it worked for Jack, I'm going to buy me a teapot.

I literally bought a teapot and started drinking tea, and I set the alarm and I got up at three in the morning, three days a week. Those are the best hours; no one ever called, it was quiet, and I could write and write and write. I did that for years for maybe fifteen or eighteen years, because that was the only way to get the work done.

DN: You've got this great quote in one of your books where you say, "What good would it do to say, 'One day I plan to write a book,' unless I set my alarm, get up in those cobwebby hours in the morning, and actually start with chapter one, page one."

RG: I hear from so many people that that's been a dream for a long time, and they just haven't started, so they write to me to say, "How do you get started?" It's very simple: you just get up, you get started, you start someplace and then you show up and keep doing the hard work, and keep working, and rewriting. It's hard work!

DN: I'm impressed with how you became a student of the publishing world. You talked to bookstore managers, and asked, "What are people buying? What are they interested in?" That helped shape you as well.

RG: Absolutely. When I was writing children's books, I had a job at a bank. I hated that job. I don't like numbers, I like words. So I had to, for five years, just to make ends meet, go and work with numbers every day. At lunchtime, I would sneak out and go down the street where there was a bookstore. I would go in with my notepad, and I'd ask the people working there, "What do people come in for? What are they looking for but they can't find it, for children's books?" Or "What is it that is selling really well right now?" I took notes and I'd read all those books and self-educated what the market was.

DN: Did that shift how you wrote your stories or the kinds of stories you wrote, once you had that information?

RG: It gave me a larger view of what was out there, because I think so many writers get into this isolation bubble where they have a great idea and so they just keep working on their idea, and they're not aware of how things are going in the market, and then they're so surprised that they can't find an interest from a publisher. Trends go up and down, and sometimes you have to put aside one project and start on another one. But I needed all the help I could get, so going to a bookstore was a good place to go.

DN: You have another great quote about the writing process: "The writing journey had befuddled, humbled, and amazed me in ways I had never experienced before." Why was it befuddling?

RG: The befuddlement was clearly on sitting down on the days where nothing would come, and you just knew you had to keep at it. Being so befuddled of—"I had so many ideas yesterday when I was at the grocery store—where did all those ideas go?" It's like running around with a butterfly net capturing the thoughts, and then you get home and you want to take the butterflies out and stick a pin in their backs, but they're all gone. You just have this befuddlement of, "I am so in need of the space as a creative person to get the emotional well filled up so that it bubbles over, so when I sit down to write I'm not just befuddled and feeling like there's nothing to draw from, but rather it's really full."

I don't take notes on my phone, but I always have a notebook with me or a journal, and I'm always jotting things and taking notes, and cutting things out, and putting them in binders. I'm a collector. I think all writers are collectors, sorters, and stackers. That's all we do. We gather it together, then sort it out and stack it up.

DN: And you do that physically? You have a physical binder that you put photos and notes in, then spread this stuff out and say, "I'm ready to write?"

RG: I always write a prayer of dedication to the Lord before I start, because I feel like this is something God's blessed me to be able to do, and I want to always say thank you ahead of time and dedicate every project to God, like, "This is yours, do with whatever you wish." So I write the prayer and put it on the first page, and then after that, it could be a variety of maybe something I cut out of a magazine and put on a piece of paper, or some notes that I took. Then when I start writing, I always write by hand, the first few pages, and put it in there.

DN: Why by hand?

RG: Because something happens in your brain and the tactile way of pulling it out of you is different than tapping it.

DN: It's too easy to delete on a keyboard, in my view.

RG: Maybe that's it.

DN: You're committed to it when you hand write it. I knew that was your practice, but I wondered if you knew why that was your practice.

RG: No, but someone can psychoanalyze that.

In one of my Christy Miller books I knew this plotline: "Christy is hanging out with friends and they're going to shoplift, they're going to get away, but Christy is going to get caught; she's going to end up at the police station, and it's on a trip to Palm Springs with her wealthy aunt and uncle." I was in Southern California at the time, and I drove to Palm Springs. I took my grandma with me—she's in her late 80s. So grandma and I went to Palm Springs, and I found a hotel and I went to the desk and I said, "I'm writing a book about some teenagers that stay here with their aunt and uncle, and I wonder if I could see your room so I could describe it?" They said, "Sure! Come see your room . . . here's our pool . . . would you like to have lunch on us?" "Oh, well, okay!"

DN: Note to self!

RG: My grandmother loved it. Then I went to the local drugstore and asked them, "If a teenager was caught shoplifting, what would happen?" "Oh, we would take them back here, and they have to sit in this room, and sit in that chair, and the police come and get them." I sat in the chair, the police didn't come to get us, but my grandmother and I went to the police station, and we had our thumb prints done.

DN: You got the photo?

RG: I wanted to feel that, yeah! They were so into it—"Oh, you can write us in your books. My name is Bob." I went home and the book just poured out because I felt it. I had never been in that experience as a teenager, and I hadn't heard anybody talk about it, but to make it to be Christy, I had to act it out so to speak.

Jane Smiley

DN: You said, "The only prerequisite for writing novel is the desire to write a novel."

JS: Yes.

DN: Then you go on to say, "It's the only thing that overcomes the handicaps to writing that novel." Those handicaps are—do you know the list by heart, or do you want me to read it?

JS: No, you can. I don't know the list by heart. I'd be interested to hear it.

DN: These are all the handicaps to writing a novel, according to you—perfectionism, low self-esteem, depression, alcoholism, diseases of all kinds, immense riches, economic hardship, deadly enemies, resistance of relatives and friends, laziness, retarded professional development, the regular responsibilities of adulthood, and even imprisonment. So those are the handicaps—

JS: Well, those are *some* of the handicaps.

DN: And you're saying the desire to write a novel overcomes those.

JS: It *can* overcome that. I'm thinking handicaps in terms of a horse race, where the horses have to carry a certain weight owing to how much they've won before. So some horses in the race are carrying more weight; some horses in the race are carrying less weight. It's supposed to even out the field. So I'm thinking of those kinds of handicaps, not physical handicaps.

DN: You're not looking at them as impediments necessarily?

JS: Well, they can be impediments, but this feeling of desire—and for me, that's a sense of curiosity—that's the thing that overcomes what is holding you back. For me, the thing that's holding me back is laziness.

DN: Wait a second, you've written dozens of books. You've written more than a library could hold, and *you're* saying you deal with laziness?

JS: I do deal with laziness. But it's not laziness about just writing, it's laziness about everything. There's laziness, and there's addiction. Laziness is where, "Yeah, you don't wanna do it, you're not gonna do it, why should I do it?" But then you do it, and feel great afterwards. Addiction is where you're saying, "Oh, I wanna do it, I wanna do it, I wanna do it," and then you feel terrible afterwards. So it's better to be lazy than addicted.

DN: That's carried you this far, hasn't it?

JS: Well, there are people who love it, and want to write, and want to write, and can't stop themselves from writing, but then they're dissatisfied with what it is they wrote. One of my other quotes from *13 Ways of Looking at the Novel* is that every first draft is perfect, because it never existed before. That's the thing you have to tell yourself when you're working on the first draft of any book. You have to just get to the end. I've known so many writers who have lots of talents and skills, but as they were going along, they say, "Ugh, that chapter's a piece of _____. I don't know what I'm doing with my," blah blah blah. A friend of mine said it was the committee talking to you.

DN: Stephen King calls them "the boys in the basement."

JS: One of the things you have to learn to do is just ignore that and keep going. Because you don't know, as you're writing, what part is really good and what part isn't good. But when you finish and you come back after a few months and read it over again, the reader brain—the brain that's read all these books, way more books than you'll ever write—kicks in and says, "that's working . . . that's working . . . nah, that doesn't work, you need to fix it." The reader brain is not as judgmental as the writer brain. And it's also more knowledgeable. So you just have to get through that rough draft, put it aside, and let the reader brain take over as you work on the later drafts.

Nnedi Okorafor

DN: You've said that people should write unapologetically, which is how you've approached your craft. But for people who aren't you, what does that mean?

NO: It means turning off those voices that say the story you're writing isn't good enough or interesting enough or can't be understood by everybody. Those voices stop things at the door. Those voices can be outside and inside, because you know you could have people on the outside saying things and then you can also have those inner voices as well. A lot of writers are looking for instant validation quickly, when they just need to shut up and write. I can be a little harsh.

Christian Wiman

DN: You're big on memorizing poetry, aren't you?

CW: I started memorizing poetry when I was younger, when I first started wanting to become a poet. I didn't understand the poems that I responded to, and it was an attempt to completely understand them, and partly because I wanted to own them, like possess them. When you're young there's something very predatory in the way that you read, you're always trying to get something out of it. As you get older, I find that my reading habits are driven more out of sympathy. I want to make connections with somebody. I read in order to make connections. Like my wife will be reading something so I'll start reading it for that reason. It's simply wanting to make a connection. Now I memorize out of love. I want to carry it with me and I want some sort of refuge from the chaos of the world all the time. The noise, the blab, I want something clear and clean.

DN: Do you have a hall of fame of poems everyone should memorize?

CW: Not really, no. What I tell my students is, make sure you memorize something that you love, that you really want to have in your head. Make sure it's good.

Alice Walker

AW: Writing is a struggle. It's daily. This is one of the reasons why meditation is so good. There are all kinds of ways of being with yourself in quiet.

DN: In *The Temple of My Familiar*, you say you relied on the guidance of synchronicity; dreams, insights, intuitions, they all seem to help you. A lot of us would just call that being in the zone. You're pulling all these forces from all these places—including your dreams—and you even called it a circle of magic. Does that happen every time you write?

AW: Not like that book. It was an extraordinary experience. Do you want me to give just a brief little introduction to this circle?

DN: Of course!

AW: I had bought a house that was twelve feet wide, so really small, and one night in a dream I woke up. I went downstairs and there were many floors, and I finally got to the very very bottom, and there were people from this other realm visibly creating beautiful things. I was just like, who are these people, how did they get in my house, what does this mean? They were speaking Spanish, and I have no clue how to speak Spanish.

I realized that in order to get to know who they were I had to learn the language well enough—still very terrible—I had to go to a country where they spoke the language and they made these things that they were making. So I ended up going to Mexico, where I've now been for thirty years, for part of every year. I started writing *The Temple of My Familiar*, and they came. I feel like I had the help of whoever these beings were. Worlds of information, and worlds of past activity on our planet became incredibly available in a way that I could not imagine happening before this journey. That's what I mean about a circle of magic, because I just relaxed into it and tried to find a way to get to where I could make it real, to create something that I could hand to you, and you could read, and you could have this same experience.

DN: You seem to write better after you've gone through some kind of a trauma.

AW: Well, that's part of what traumas are for—

DN: Wait a minute, what?

AW: That's part of what they're for. You may not write out of it, but you learn a new dance step, or you decide to go to Timbuktu. Apparently, what happens down here, out here, wherever we are, is that we inevitably go through major, painful, horrid, terrifying experiences. What to do with them? What are they for? I think, and choose to affirm, that they are ingredients for creativity.

DN: You have also said that poems present themselves to you, and they present themselves to you in bunches.

AW: It is like a visitation, but it's also like a guest. You prepare for it, you feel like there is something gathering, something happening. It's like you live the work of it. It's not coming from above, it's coming from a life deeply lived, sometimes a lot of struggle and pain and loss. But eventually all of this turns into a kind of gold. And then what happens is you have to find a way to present it, to be there, present, for it to come so that you can present it as a gift to the world—which it is!

DN: You seem to have this open heart. Even the titles of some of your books are *Now Is the Time to Open Your Heart*, *The Way Forward Is with a Broken Heart*, *Taking the Arrow Out of the Heart*. Are you seeing a pattern here? What is this about? What is this heart?

AW: It seems to me that one of the goals of our existence has to be about having an open heart, and learning to even know what that is or what that feels like. I maintain that the feeling of the open heart, and it's not like an open window exactly, but the sensation of love in the heart is one of the aims of the human life, to be able to actually feel your heart in the activity of loving. It's not all about when you fall in love; that's when most of us feel our heart. It's hard to describe it. I have seen paintings of the sacred heart, where there is this light coming out of the heart, and that is what it feels like. To be able to create at a deep level of compassion, and love, without considering at all that they may just kill you for doing it, is to awaken that feeling in your own heart. And it's really worth anything, to be able to feel that. It's incredible.

DN: You've tried to take sabbaticals from writing.

AW: Yeah, I failed.

DN: How come?

AW: In the church that we used to have in the south they would say, "He ain't finished with me yet." My sense is something similar. I think that when I am done, my sabbatical will go into eternity. But until that moment, I'm just doing what I'm here to do.

Katie Manning

DN: It seems like you are constantly submitting your poetry to reviews and websites and blogs and then, in your spare time, you started your own review publication, the Whale Road Review. Obviously, the publishing part of poetry is important to you. How important is it?

KM: There's the not pretty answer, which is that I'm a professor of poetry, so I need to publish for my job.

DN: That's fair.

KM: But even if I were not, I would still be pursuing publication very actively. It's the human connection that drives me more than anything.

DN: The fact that you started your own review says you're providing a space for other writers, almost as an act of gratitude for the space that had been created for you over the years. I assume that's rolling around in there too, right?

KM: Oh, absolutely. One of my greatest joys was when we had one writer who was in his nineties and one writer who was a junior in high school who both had poems in the issue. I love bringing wide age ranges into the journal and bringing people who are from all different backgrounds. We have writers from all different continents, and I do think of it as paying it forward. It feels like good literary citizenship. It makes me happy to do it.

DN: Where does the time to write come from?

KM: I have blank notebooks, I have one at my desk, I have one by my bed, I've got one in my purse, so anytime I get an idea or I see something or hear something that seems like it might be interesting, I'll scribble it down so I can get back to it later. I also have scheduled time for myself. It is on my calendar. I've been meeting with a group of friends on Friday mornings, and we have a two-hour block where we just are writing together. Giving myself that permission and scheduling it for myself has been really helpful.

Some people require themselves to be drafting in order to feel like they're writing. Anything I'm doing in the service of writing, even submitting for publication or anything else that I'm doing around the work of writing counts as writing. So I never feel like I'm having writer's block or "Oh no, I'm not writing." Any of those things count and feel like I'm being productive in that way.

Margarita Pintado

DN: How do you still do it? There are so many reasons for why you could avoid it. Everybody thinks you have to have these big blocks of time and a retreat in Santa Fe or something.

MP: I do it while making breakfast. I have a little notebook on the window right there in the kitchen. I am very intentional about welcoming poetry. Most of the writing occurs in my head, and then everything else is editing. I'm surrounded by notebooks. Every now and then I leave the kids and I come to the bedroom quickly and type as fast as I can, a poem that I just formed. I love it, and it's happening more often. Or at the playground—I have a little notebook in my purse. This is the thing that gives me more joy besides my children and my husband. It's stealing time from other things that the world tells you are more important, but you know they are not.

DN: Are you as confident writing in English as in Spanish?

MP: Absolutely not. Or speaking. I write in Spanish, everything pretty much. My English writing is limited to emails. I speak English more than I speak Spanish, but I write mostly in Spanish. I had just begun writing a few poems in English and feeling more comfortable. It's way easier than translating my poems from Spanish to English.

Don Winslow

DN: Do you write a certain number of pages a day?

DW: No. I treat it like a factory job. I write by the hour.

DN: What if nothing gets done?

DW: Then nothing gets done. Everyone has days like that. I start work at 5:30 a.m. and work until mid-morning and then we usually go for a four-to-six-mile hike, come back, have a little lunch, have a siesta. I said one wonderful thing about living in the southwest is you can call it a siesta and not a nap.

DN: You feel kinda smart when you do it that way?

DW: Or European. Distinguished. And then I go back and work until about 5:30 p.m.

DN: So it's writing and hiking for you?

DW: Pretty much. That's when we're here in Julian. When we're in Rhode Island it's a little different because we're a mile from the beach. I start at 5:30 on the old porch of our house because when I first started on these books, I didn't want to wake people up. So I'd sneak down, make a quiet cup of coffee, go out to the front porch and write. I just like it now. Then I work until 3 in the afternoon and then we go down to the beach until about sunset.

DN: It sounds so idyllic, and yet the stuff you write is not. I would never have guessed that your stories came from a guy who said, "Oh, I just go to the beach, go for walks."

DW: I'm paraphrasing Flaubert who said, "I lead a common, placid life so that I can commit chaos on the page."

Anthony Doerr

DN: In your *Four Seasons in Rome* book, you say, "To write a story is to inch backward and forward along a series of planks. You are cantilevering out onto, into, the darkness, plank by plank, inch by inch, and the best you can hope is that each day you find yourself a little bit farther over the abyss." Is that how the writing process is for you? That's how it is for me.

AD: As you get older, you have to forgive yourself if you're a few inches back from when you started. If you're like, "Oh, I'm five inches back towards the shore," that's okay. I used to really be hard on myself: "You need to make progress." But it sometimes means you don't have great writing days.

I think we're so trained as Americans to love efficiency, and I'm trying to learn to accept inefficiency. Sometimes you learn so much from your failed projects. Sometimes just going to take a class on quilting or surfing—even if you don't become a professional quilter or surfer, that's okay. But there's so much pressure on us as young people to be like, "Well, how is quilting going to inform your career as a cardiologist, Timmy?" The best cardiologists are obviously amateur quilters.

DN: Your only nonfiction book, *Four Seasons in Rome*, is, in addition to telling you about your year in Rome with newborn twins, it's about the history of civilization, the frustration of trying to write a book with two newborns in another country. So it's a book about writing a book, or more accurately, about all the things that kept you from writing a book?

AD: I wrote it as procrastination from writing *All the Light We Cannot See*. It's a total work on procrastination.

DN: I loved *Four Seasons in Rome* for a variety of reasons. The John McPhee influence in me was paying attention to the structure of that book. It was a clinic in structure. Main character heads off on an adventure, has all sorts of trouble, keeps seeing glimpses of hope and reasons to continue. All the while this is giving you a chance to tell about Rome, and nature, and architecture, and graffiti, and loads of your personal fears and reflections. When I finished that book, I thought, "This is how you write a book."

AD: Wow, thanks.

DN: Didn't that book start out as kind of a series of letters?

AD: I had kept a notebook. I've kept a journal since I was 16. My high school English teacher had us start keeping a journal, and it just stuck with me. It's always been a place to work out stuff, language. You can describe people in an airport. To have a place once you become a published writer where you can write unpublished writing is a really helpful thing. It's also a way to keep the muscle of translating the big pulsing magic of the world into language, like doing your sit-ups. It's a way to kind of stay fit.

DN: But you were writing *All the Light* . . .

AD: I was given a prize to work on that novel in Rome. But the journal pages started to overwhelm my fiction writing because the city was just so interesting. I'm used to Boise where everything's familiar, and being in an unfamiliar environment generally makes the work of your senses so much more engaged, especially when you don't know the language super well. Suddenly, I spent three hours writing about the Piazza I had just been in that would be regularly flooded to pose mock naval battles to entertain the populace. And you're like, "That's more interesting than the book I'm writing." And then the pope died. I had published a few letters in this site called *The Morning News*, and they had gotten tons of attention. The city is about three million, but seven million people *came* into the city. You go to the corner bar to get your specialty, and you're like, "There's Katie Couric, there's Matt Lauer," or whatever—he was still existing then.

DN: When it was okay to be Matt Lauer.

AD: So those letters, some editor was like, "Have you ever thought about turning these into a book?" And I was like, "Well, that would be less than 500 pages, and I already have some of it in my notebook." My brain was like, "Maybe I can finish this, unlike this World War II thing that's not getting finished."

DN: I love this line from *Four Seasons in Rome* where you say, "One minute, I think, "This here, this is a good sentence." Then next, I'm on the brink of throwing the whole thing away. But I'm used to this by now." That's the writer's life, right?

AD: The neurotic writer's life, yeah. My wife helps me through that all the time because there's moments when you're really like, "This is not working; this is not solvable." But experience helps remind you that if you get a good night's sleep, lots of problems can be fixed.

DN: You ascribe to the Murakami quote about running, about the importance of just getting going. Once you set the pace, he says about running, then the rest will follow. And here's his quote, "The problem is getting the flywheel to spin at a set speed, and to get to that point takes as much concentration and effort as you can imagine." Do you still have trouble getting to that?

AD: I don't, but I have trouble with interruptions. Sometimes there are interruptions I invite upon myself, like saying yes to invitations.

DN: Oh, really, we're interrupting?

AD: Big time.

DN: Really?

AD: Life interrupts you as every person here knows. Parents get older; kids need stuff. The Covid pandemic hits. You get the flu. You get the norovirus. You break your ankle. Things happen. Sometimes keeping that flywheel turning on any creative project, on whatever you guys are interested, that's incrementally how you build big things, by just picking the berries one berry at a time; you fill a huge bucket. If you stop picking berries for a few days, sometimes the berries get a little rotten. My metaphors got all messed up.

DN: No, that's not bad.

AD: Flywheels and berries.

DN: The violinist Jascha Heifetz said, "If I don't practice one day, I know it. If I don't practice two days, the critics know it. If I don't practice three days, the whole world knows it." That's like the huckleberries, right?

AD: Except I never think the whole world's paying attention to me.

N. Scott Momaday

DN: What I loved about the novel *Ancient Child* is that you did so many different things with time. You describe the character Gray trying to write, and you say her experience was laborious, confusing, frustrating, and maddening. Then here's the quote: "But once in a while, she would write something that pleased her, that seemed very close to what she wanted, and that satisfaction was like no other that she knew. It was the satisfaction of having done what was in her to do, of having reached the best that was in her, of having been true to her purpose and herself." I'm guessing you're describing your own experience, right?

NSM: Exactly, yes. That's the way I feel about things. Writing can be laborious and very difficult to do, but if you do it to your satisfaction, there's no feeling that's better than that. That's the reward of writing.

DN: But for writers, how often does that satisfaction actually occur? Are you one of these guys who just carves this pearl every time and it's awesome, or are you struggling?

NSM: Once in a while, I write to my potential. I think I do anyway, and that's a great setup. That's what keeps me writing. That makes everything worthwhile.

DN: Wouldn't you think after all that you've written over all these years, it would be more than once in a while?

NSM: Well, I suppose so. It's happened a good many times to me and I'm very grateful for that. In the long run I'm not sure what of my work is really satisfactory to me. I achieve a certain level at times and if it's a high level, if it meets my expectations and maybe exceeds them, that's great. That's, as I say, the justification for writing, but I'm sure that I've written quite a bit that doesn't satisfy me to that extent.

DN: You've got another character in that book whom you describe as an artist, and you show him in a manic state. You say he's afflicted, headed for a nervous breakdown. He was trapped to produce what the public wanted as opposed to what he wanted. Has that ever been you?

NSM: Probably on occasion. I've felt that I was doing something that wasn't my ambition, particularly. There was an expectation that I would produce something of interest or value and probably didn't satisfy me as much as I would like. The character you're talking about is fascinating to me because he's a mythic kind of man. He's an artist. And he has this bear power. So at the end there's this transformation. He does turn into a bear—as I do on occasion.

DN: I've never seen you turn into a bear. I have read the account.

NSM: You don't want to see that. Run for your life if you feel that happened.

DN: It would be too much.

NSM: Too much.

11

Consider the Reader

Who Is Your Audience, Really?

I had a bulletin board in my little corner where I wrote, and I had all the photos of girls who gave me their school photos. This was my audience.

ROBIN JONES GUNN

Some writers see themselves as writing for young people, or primarily for women, or for men, or for readers with a particular identity. Other writers see themselves as just wanting to tell a story, and they assume they will eventually figure out who the ideal audience would be. Some writers just want to tell the story that's on their mind and don't think about the audience at all.

However you approach your writing, most of us want our stories to land somewhere, with someone. That means you go back over it and consider whether the reader who has emerged in your mind will get what you're trying to communicate. That may mean simplifying a few things, or complicating a few things.

The two things readers won't put up with are boredom or confusion. Readers will trust that you know what you're doing, and they'll stick with you—for a while. After a while, they'll drop you like a rock. There are too many other things to do.

I remember reading Ken Kesey's novel *Sometimes a Great Notion*, and being confused and frustrated for many pages, but I was living in Oregon and the setting of the book was Oregon, and I stayed with it. Eventually something clicked and I got on his wavelength and found the book to be astonishing. Same with *100 Years of Solitude*, by Gabriel García Márquez. I wouldn't recommend writing in their style of giving multiple characters the same name and toggling from past to present without announcing it unless you absolutely have to.

It's risky to ignore the audience. You don't want to pander to them, but you do need them.

When I read a story to my four-year-old grandson, if we get to a place where a character cries or is sad, he reaches for the book, gently closes it and gets off my lap. He's okay with a character who gets lost and then found. He's okay with a character who gets yelled at by a park ranger (thanks, Yogi Bear!). But he draws the line at tears. Whenever I make up a story for him when we're in the car, when I'm putting him to bed, when we're taking a walk, I make sure the main character isn't sad. I know my audience.

If we're trying to get published, the first audience is your editor. And she is, hopefully, representing the broader audience. So don't forget your editor!

Chitra Divakaruni

DN: One of the groups that takes a consistently pretty good hit in your books is men.

CD: You think so?

DN: I was almost offended. Are we really that bad?

CD: My books are admittedly woman-centered, and strong women are at the heart of the books, and the stories are told from the point of view of the women. It's their story. Therefore they're presented with greater sympathy and greater empathy. But I hope what I've shown is that the men are complex characters, they're caught in many social institutions and emotional baggage that they have carried for a long time. I certainly hope I haven't shown them as villains. Although maybe they're not the heroes.

DN: One of the things I thought was intriguing about all of the works of yours that I've read is that while men are not portrayed necessarily as heroes, I never got the impression that you were writing only to women. How can you make men look the way you do make them look, and yet not be so marginalized as a woman's writer?

CD: Because when *certain* men read my books, they say, "well, I'm not as bad as *those* guys!"

DN: I see where this is going.

CD: Then they feel better about themselves, and then they buy the book, and they give it to all the men-friends.

What I hope for, with my men readers—and I have great faith in this—is that there are many thoughtful men readers out there who are interested in reading a story from a woman's point of view, who are curious about how such a story would be told, how a woman would see a situation as different, and who applauded strong women. That is my great hope.

Nikki Giovanni

NG: My friends say that I assume intelligence. I like to think that I do. Dumb people don't pick me up, I can guarantee you that. Donald Trump is not gonna quote me. I'm relatively intelligent, so I assume intelligence. When I'm writing, I'm putting things that intelligent people can pick up. Like I said, very few dumb people quote me.

Robin Jones Gunn

RG: I had a bulletin board in my little corner where I wrote, and I had all the photos of girls who gave me their school photos. This was my audience. I pinned them up on the bulletin board. I would type it and look at them: "I am telling you the story." I knew who they were, and I knew what they wanted to hear.

12

What You Believe How Does Faith Affect Your Writing?

All of our writing is religious.

RAY BRADBURY

It surprised me a bit when Ray Bradbury made the statement above in my interview with him. When he explained further, it made total sense. In his view, creative people, particularly storytellers, are tapped into something beyond their ability to articulate its source. It can come out of a traditional faith, but it doesn't have to. Anne Lamott's Christian faith informs her writing now. But so does Bradbury's cafeteria-style faith, where he samples a little bit of these and a little bit of those and puts it together in his own style.

Not all writers claim a spiritual dimension to what they do. In fact, some are insulted by the suggestion, or at least they don't understand how the topic even comes up. That's fine. I have asked some writers about this and they have given me a blank stare, as if I had just spoken a foreign language—which to them it is. But when I think of creativity and spirituality, I think of them as almost the same thing. Similarly, some might claim that a belief in science eliminates spirituality from the equation, as portrayed in the movie Nacho Libre, where the main character's sidekick says, "I don't believe in God. I believe in science." As if it's one or the other.

Blaise Pascal, the great scientist AND person of faith, would say that his faith made his appreciation for science even greater. And vice versa.

C. S. Lewis's *Chronicles of Narnia* are beautiful stories that are informed by his faith. Tolstoy and Dostoevsky's novels and short stories are informed by their faith. We don't have to be afraid of it. Where the faith dimension can get weird is when writers start with a premise that their work must result in the reader "getting the message," or converting, or perpetuating a belief. That doesn't strike me as creativity as much as it is propaganda.

Maybe the better term for acknowledging the faith or spirituality dimension would be "mystery." We're not trying to solve the mystery or prove anything. But we're letting it be present, like the Iris DeMent song that says, "I'll let the mystery be."

Elizabeth Gilbert

DN: In your book *The Signature of All Things*, you have this exchange between the Alma character and her love interest Ambrose. They're having this conversation about nature and science and reason and suffering and God. And Ambrose says the air was alive with invisible attractions—electric, magnetic, fiery, and thoughtful. There is a hidden meaning of knowing. They go back and forth about evolution and mathematics. I read that section and I thought, this is your Grand Inquisitor moment. This is you talking to yourself. You've got the Alma character arguing on the science side of things—it's all explainable. And then you've got Ambrose saying, "Is it? Is it?" It reminded me of that scene in Brothers Karamazov where it's all an argument within the same mind. Were you arguing with yourself at that time?

EG: I was more on Ambrose's side. At that point in my life I was trying to convince Alma, because she was living in the totalitarian rigidity of pure logic. The reason he was so exciting to her and so fascinating to her was because he had left that arena a long, long, long time ago. You and I were speaking today in the car about another moment in the book that I think about all the time. This book is about evolution.

At the end of the book Alma meets Alfred Wallace who was a contemporary of Darwin's. They both were writing about adaptation of species.

Wallace really admired Darwin, and was an incredible scientist, and was a mystic who believed in spirituality. I loved something that my longtime friend Rob Bell wrote, where he says, "you don't have to call it God, but it doesn't solve the problem." You're still stuck with the mystery, right? You don't have to call it God but there's still an enormous mystery as to what in the world we are doing here, why we have this consciousness, why we know that we're going to die, why we have these heightened sensitivities. We can write operas and we want to write novels and we get incredibly moved and we murder each other viciously. We are so weird. We are so profoundly weird. Something very strange is going on here. In the end, all I can think, the only thing that will settle me when I'm in despair about the state of myself and the state of the world and the state of what I love is, there is a great and beautiful intelligence in the universe that wants to be in communication with us at all times. All I have to do to remember that is to get quiet enough to hear it saying, "Stay with me. I'm right here."

Anne Lamott

DN: In your book *Hard Laughter* the narrator says, "These are the thoughts I am left with: that romance is stupid, and sometimes worth it; that fellowship is risky, and always worth it; that I am ridiculous, and I am not." Has your view of things changed from that?

AL: Is that from *Hard Laughter*?

DN: Yes. Do you remember writing that?

AL: No.

DN: So I could really be saying anything.

AL: Yeah, you could. This could all be Danielle Steel.

Everything changes when you convert, because suddenly, you're not entirely insane and all alone and without a guiding light. When I wrote that book I was in my early twenties, and my father, who I couldn't live without, was dying of brain cancer. I basically believe all those things you read, but I believe so much more, now that I've gotten sober.

Having survived a lot, and having been transformed by a lot, having watched God do a lot of alchemy with all that stuff, loss and disappointment and bad romance and shattered dreams and all that, you go, "Gee, isn't it interesting, this box that I've been lugging around, I couldn't care less about it anymore. It actually doesn't matter. I can toss it off," because you want to fly a little lighter, and a little lighter.

DN: You've also written about the importance of grief, and that one of the things that you wanted to do in *Crooked Little Heart* was to let those characters from *Rosie* finally grieve. Why is grief, the way you understand it now, different from how you understood it before? Why is it so important?

AL: Well, before, which is to say probably in my twenties, and most of my thirties, I was going along with a great palace lie that grief was to be gotten over as quickly as possible. All these people around me were having terrible losses and we're bucking up and having short periods of grief and getting on with life with a certain amount of dignity. And I was led to believe—my father's father was a Presbyterian missionary, and they call Presbyterians, "God's frozen people."

I grew up in a tradition where my father had never seen his father cry; he'd never seen his mother cry. They were missionaries in Japan. I never saw *my* father cry. I saw my mother cry twice, or three times. She's English. I'm in a twelve-step recovery program for children of the English. So on both sides I had the English who were like the Monty Python characters. I mean, no offense to the English people here. And then I had the Presbyterians. I mean, no offense to Presbyterians here. I'm a Presbyterian, but I grew up being told that you cry a little bit, that you get over it, that everyone's dealing with it, and that you do the best you can and that anything else is sort of self-indulgent, and that it's certainly inefficient. Especially for women, it so throws the mobile off balance when a woman just stops and says, "You know what, I'm actually too sad to do another load of laundry. And I'm too sad to make you any dinner. There's lots of food in the kitchen. Does anyone know where that is? Can I see a show of hands?"

It's very, very deeply inconvenient when the person who functions as the hub of a family, in the caregiving sense, has to stop. I had always been like a flight attendant for my family. I mean, my mother was a black belt codependent and I grew up to be one too. Like a geisha girl I was valued by how much use I could be to everyone else. I helped everybody else process their stuff. I distracted everybody else when they felt too sad. What you did if somebody was sad was you distracted them to get their mind off of it.

And you see people getting crazier and crazier trying to work harder and more feverishly. I came to feel when my best friend got sick, when I was thirty-seven, that we were, as a people moving forward, in a very isometrically tight way because we could feel the abyss opening at our heels and we thought if we stopped producing, nurturing, laundering and enabling the entire world to stuff down our real reaction, that the abyss would open up and swallow us. I came to feel that it was only the grief and the crying that was going to give us ourselves back, and that we were like dried gardens until then. And that if we began to cry, it was going to wash out years of calcified, stuffed down feelings, and that if we began to cry, it would water the ground at our feet. Christianity is *totally* the *wettest* religion imaginable. It's all wetness. It's all baptism. It's all "ye who thirst, come to the water." It's all about being wet. It's about being cleansed. It's about feeling that all the world has to offer is going to lead you ultimately to being very dehydrated spiritually.

The redemption in my work—which is a lofty word I don't usually use—people stop and life conspires and it builds up too many things. Like Elizabeth in *Crooked Little Heart* has stayed one step ahead of dealing with the fact that when Rosie was four years old, her father died violently. She was drunk and Rosie pumped her out of it, and when Rosie was sad Elizabeth pumped her out of it. Everything that Elizabeth has done has kept these things homogenized and kept the pond as calm as it could be. But the price that Elizabeth has paid by the time *Crooked Little Heart* begins is that she hasn't gotten to find out who she is. She hasn't gotten to dance. She's like the set designer and the makeup person for everybody else.

I wanted to push her so hard that she started to crack. Rosie had *never* laid down and sobbed with her mother because her daddy got snapped away from her.

There's that wonderful Leonard Cohen song that says, "there are cracks in everything, that's how the light gets in." It's a song about transformation. It's a song about—if you're English, hypothetically—you get some cracks on the exterior of the vase and you start to spackle like mad. You want to cover up those cracks so that no one can see that there are cracks in your family. They're cracks in your being; they're cracks in your heart. Jesus gets into the cracks, the Holy Spirit gets into the cracks. My first thought is, "spackle, spackle! Paint! Caulking that! We need some caulking stuff!" What Elizabeth finally got to was the point where there were too many cracks, and the light started getting in, and she started feeling things, and it was every bit as awful as her subconscious had told her it was going to be. And she got there, and she had a friend and a husband, and a child who somehow could hold the space for her to break down into those cracks. And then, to end there, to see this mosaic that's come crumbling down and to start picking up the mosaic chips in the tile, and to start to know them for the first time: who am I? What am I? Where did I spring from?

Ray Bradbury

DN: In many of your books, there have been religious themes, with many biblical references. You rewrote the Last Supper scene in *Graveyard for Lunatics* where you said actually it wasn't that last supper up there in the upper room. There was another place. You have another book coming out for burned-out preachers and rabbis and priests. What about those religious themes?

RB: All of our writing is religious. If you care about living at all, you don't have to make up a religion, you don't have to invoke the biblical things you learned in Sunday School. You don't have to be technical about it. If you are celebratory, the Jews say "to life," a proclamation. People have often said to me, "do you believe in Darwin's theory?" I said yeah I believe in that. Do you believe in Genesis, the first book of the Bible? Yes I believe that. They said, "how could you believe both?" I said because nothing is proven. Nothing is proven. So there's room for religious delicatessen. I'll take some of these, some of those, and some of them. Because we just don't know. Have you seen these various documentaries on TV the last few years? Tonight, you're gonna find the secret of life. How did life come on the earth? What makes the sun burn? Etcetera, etcetera, etcetera. Well you tune in and hell, they don't tell you that. They don't know. The earth came out of the sun, took a billion years to cool. The rains fell, the first primitive plants came up. The ponds of scum created amoeba like creatures but there was no life here. Lightning struck. The chemistry of the world. The inanimate minerals decided to live, How come? How come? We don't know. We don't know. It just happened. That's not much of an explanation is it? It just happened? That's really scientific, is it? That's what the scientists say. It just happened. Well hell, give me some lightning, I'll go make my own life.

The thing is, there's room to believe it all because you are the inhabiters of a miraculous world. Why have we been put here? The question is asked time and again. Shall I give you the answer? Have you been waiting for the answer? I've got it for you.

There is no use having a billion stars. There's no use having a planet earth if there isn't someone here to see it. You are the audience. You are here to witness and celebrate. To witness and celebrate. And you got a lot to see and a lot to celebrate. That's your business. You put it in your work. You put it in your stories. Otherwise get the hell out and get out of our way and let us live. If you're gonna be a cynic, if you're going to be a pessimist, there's no hope for you. I can't help you. You got to help yourself. But we are here as an audience. God cries out to be saved. Whatever God is, we have various names. We make him much too anthropomorphic. That's not what it's all about. Creation, the universe,

Jehovah, you name it. It's all mysterious. But we are here to be the audience to the miraculous. You are privileged. You're going to be alive once. You're never coming back. Think of that. You got one chance to pay back. You owe. You owe to the universe. The burden of proof is in your lap and in your writing and you gotta pay back. I demand it. Now you get the hell out of here and do that and you're going to have a good life. What in hell was the question?

DN: I don't remember either.

RB: He's afraid to ask me anything else.

Garrison Keillor

GK: I grew up in a fundamentalist evangelical sect called the Plymouth Brethren, which arose out of a revolt against the formalism of the Anglican church in England in the 1820s. They were fundamentalists. They believed in the literal truth of every word of scripture. They were evangelical. They believed that those who did not accept Jesus Christ as their personal savior were condemned to everlasting hellfire, damnation. They were non-hierarchical, they did not have ordained clergy. They had brethren who felt called by the spirit to be teachers and preachers. But they were strict. Because they interpreted scripture as they did, there was no dancing, there was no movies, no television, no alcohol, no tobacco, and gambling and profanity.

To outsiders it looked very prohibitive. To those growing up in it, it was a very warm and a very loving atmosphere because your whole family was there. They're easy to make fun of and I certainly have done my share, but I'm done with that because when you come to a certain age you realize how blessed you were to grow up among people who abstained from alcohol, because it means the children grow up absent the sort of weird moods that alcoholics are prone to and so you did not have to deal with the immature anger of your parents. Your parents were very level, for the most part.

Growing up among people who believed in literal interpretation of scripture meant that literacy was crucial, because everyone had to read the Bible and understand it. And because they believed in the priesthood of all believers, you were responsible to God for your understanding. It was not enough that you should simply fall in line behind the others and trot along and be obedient. It had its problems, of course. If you believed in literal interpretation of scripture, then legalism is ever a peril, and it certainly was in this group. It leads to schisms, so they divided. This group, once powerful in my childhood, which 150 years ago was once large and powerful and influential, became scattered and disappointed. Now it's like some tribe of Ojibwe, sent off on a reservation.

But the assets that were gains, even without knowing it, growing up in this faith. I'm sure the Nazarene church or whatever evangelical church you may come from are powerful assets for a writer. And of course you use that. You use everything at your disposal. And when it comes to English prose style, one could find worse models than the King James Bible. I don't know if the Nazarene church still holds with the King James, but it's there in your library.

There's a really interesting tension. I'm not a theologian, so it's not easy for me to talk about this, but living within the traditions and the ceremonies of the organized church can do tremendous damage to one's faith. One becomes, you know a little soldier, and one easily becomes sort of robotic. You learn to say the right things and to use the language of that culture and then one day you look at yourself and you think, do I really think that? What do I really think? A person, I think, in this tradition, a Christian, needs to have some sense of peace, but if you do not have mystery in your life, then what is faith for? That's my feeling, but I don't know any more about it than you do.

Chris Hillman (Interviewed by Karl Martin)

KM: There's a strong influence of gospel music in The Flying Burrito Brothers, with imagery from gospel songs, songs of the church, specifically in "Sin City."

CH: "Sin City" was a special song that Gram Parsons and I wrote. We were putting The Flying Burrito Brothers together and sharing a house. We were so close working as brothers at the time. Gram had this great love of country music as I did, so we immediately hit it off. "Sin City" was sort of a tongue-in-cheek look at the culture at the time. We were going on about Hollywood, "this old town is filled with sin, it will swallow you in if you've got some money to burn. Take it home right away, you've got three years to pay, and Satan is waiting his turn." So what did we do? This wasn't thought out ahead of time. It was inside of us and we both drew from the gospel, the old Baptist hymns, and using that terminology but in a contemporary setting. We go on through the chorus of "this old earthquake's gonna leave me in the poor house." Each verse touches on something in Sin City.

I truly love "Turn, Turn, Turn," and I didn't write it. King Solomon wrote it. Not sure if his heirs are getting any money for that. I love that song. Roger McGuinn, the lead singer in the Byrds, sang it at my wedding thirty-two years ago. It's a charmed song. I've sung it at funerals. It's such an interesting verse out of Ecclesiastes three. It's so black-and-white. He's saying "to everything, there is a season, turn, turn, turn." That part was added by Pete Seeger. It's a wonderful summary of the whole thing, but it was all black and white. There's good and there's evil, there's right and wrong, there's rich and poor, there's weak, there's strong, and it was all just as it lies. As you get older, there really isn't much gray area in a lot of these things in life. It is such wisdom, and that song never fails to get me.

Jane Smiley

DN: The first part of *13 Ways* is some of the best writing advice I've ever read. It was really helpful and clear. In there, though, you make some mention of having some sort of a spiritual awakening. Did that help or hurt your writing?

JS: It helped. What happened was, I found my current husband, and he was a follower of *A Course in Miracles*. I didn't grow up in a religious family, and I've never been a follower of anything, but he really liked it. So I thought, "OK, cooking him dinner's only gonna go so far, if he's really interested in this, I'll see what I think."

There's a bunch of lessons. Then there's a kind of re-writing of the Bible. When you first open it, you think, "This is a bunch of gobbledygook." But as you get into it, certain things seem true. One of the things that stuck with me all these years is one of the principles of the course, which is "I give everything all the meaning that it has for me." That's a novelist's precept if ever there was one. Because that's my job as a novelist—to take the world around me and give it meaning and put it on the page. So I accepted that.

I finally thought, "OK, maybe I can participate in this sort of religion thing," after having no religion in my life. And then they started having these huge arguments about who owned the text and who got the money," and I thought, "there they go!"

DN: Yup. Just killed it.

JS: Killed it. They're being like all those other religions. It's about who says the right things and who gets the money.

Christian Wiman

DN: You wrote a poem when you were seven. That's really what launched you, right?

CW: That's what launched my career, yes. We were attending the First Baptist church in Dallas which at the time was the largest Baptist church in the world. It took up four city blocks. They had a bowling alley, gyms and all these multiple services on Sundays with thousands of people. We would go there and at the end they had an altar call. One day when it came time for the altar call, I slid out of my pew and my parents thought that I was going to be saved—that's early for Baptists—I was eight or nine. I slid out and went all the way down front. It was like a mile down to the front of the auditorium and gave my piece of paper to brother Chriswell who was the minister, who was the head of the Southern Baptist Convention. And it was a poem.

DN: Had you just written it in church that day?

CW: Oh no no. I assume I had written it earlier and brought it to church, like this was going to be my offering. Some people offer their soul, I offer a poem. I mean it's so metaphorically apt, at the altar call I give a poem instead of myself. But the poem was "I love the Lord and he loves me, I will not forget and neither will he." It's genius huh? Then he published it in the Southern Baptist newsletter, which is an enormous publication. My biggest publication was in a Southern Baptist newsletter at eight years old.

DN: There's some clarity to that poem.

CW: Exactly. Then it was a long dry spell after that.

DN: Wouldn't you say that you spent a long time trying to reclaim that clarity?

CW: Yeah. I mean that poem haunts me actually.

DN: Why?

CW: Because I do forget. I love the Lord and he loves me. I will not forget and neither will he. I forget all the time. I forgot for twenty years.

DN: You did go through a dry spell later on in terms of writing poetry, where you felt like you couldn't write.

CW: I went three years without writing anything

DN: Do you know why?

CW: I guess I would answer in different ways. I had reached the end of one kind of writing and had nothing else to say. That's the easy answer. The harder answer is I think God said—stop. Stop. You're going in the wrong direction. You're desecrating your gift. So I had three years of not being able to write and it was excruciating for me. I mean that's how I had defined my life, as a poet, that's what mattered to me. And then I had three things happen in quick succession: I met the one I'm now married to, and I got very sick with cancer—that happened shortly after we met—and then one day we walked into a church together which was at the corner of the street where we lived in Chicago.

It was a United Church of Christ. We just walked in, I didn't even know what that was, and we just walked in because it was at the corner. It just happened to be the church on the corner. It was a little church, there were about forty people in there, and the preacher was a young guy who had gone to Yale Divinity School.

DN: But it was a total random thing.

CW: Completely random. I walked out of that first service and went home and wrote a poem and it was my first poem in three years and I wrote it in an hour and it was the title poem of one of my books. I would say that moment changed my life. Everything I wrote after that was different, it was quite dramatic.

DN: On the one hand, for those three years you felt like poetry was taken away from you, like there's some force—God or whatever—took poetry from you. Then you fell in love and that opened you up and you started writing again. Love did that?

CW: I definitely think that's the answer. I mean I think that human love does, it contains or catalyzes, the love of God. It wants to be more than it is. It's always moving through us, it's not something we possess, it moves through us, and wants to be more. So yeah it really was like an electric shock in my soul. It was powerful.

DN: One of my favorite statements I ever heard you say is "love is always on the move." Because it moves through you.

CW: It moves through you, and I think it moves the sun and the stars—as Dante says. That's the wonderful thing. There is a terrible aspect to love. God's love also includes all the destructiveness of the world and that's sometimes hard to comprehend. The vision that God gives Job at the end of the book of Job is a vision of predation. Creation, but also violent predation, blood. He feeds the animals, he feeds the raptor its meat, and this is God doing this. I think that is love too. I think God's love is incomprehensible to some extent. It's quite intimate and comprehensible in the realm of human love, but it's also incomprehensible and it includes our destruction and that's something we resist.

DN: What does our destruction have to do with love?

CW: Well, we all are going to die, and we're dying because of God's love. It is the action of love that includes all of creation, and that's a lot of destruction.

DN: One of the things you've said poetry does is that it connects you with ultimate reality, which would include—I guess—death.

CW: Absolutely. It's connecting you with both of those things at the same time—ultimate life and ultimate death at the same time.

DN: When you got your diagnosis for cancer, which just amazes me that that was left for you as a voicemail, and you were told that this was going to be fatal, at some point did you say: "Oh I've got to write about this, I've got to fully engage this and fully inhabit this?"

CW: No, but it was very natural the way it happened. I did get it as a voicemail—

DN: Isn't that just a little galling, to get something like that as a recording?

CW: I've had a doctor throw a disc—he couldn't get it to work on his computer—he threw it across the room and hit me in the throat. I've had a doctor draw me a graph, showing me when he thought I was going to die. I mean I've had some really cruddy things done. Some wonderful things on the other side, more wonderful, many more wonderful than those examples.

DN: You are still alive.

CW: Exactly, exactly.

DN: So there's that. But did you think, "I want to try to capture what this feels like?"

CW: Well, I wrote an essay about it. And that poem that I was mentioning was probably one of the first things, which was pure celebration. Pure praise.

DN: Why praise? Why not condemnation? Why not rage?

CW: I was enraged, but I felt the love of God. Christianity doesn't promise any supernatural relief from suffering, a remedy from it. But it does give you a supernatural use. Christianity promises that there is meaning. It is a mystery to me. I was enraged, I was in love, and it looked like I was going to die and I felt the love of God *very* intensely. Very very intensely. So there was a kind of joy. It was joy. I was terrified and furious and full of lament, but I was also joyful. It is quite mysterious to me. That's why I think that you have to seek both sides of creation and destruction. These things are happening at the same time at every instant and reality is awesome as in—terrible. It doesn't hug you exactly. But another answer is that when I needed to write something about it, I turned to prose and I wrote this essay which went kind of viral. It went everywhere.

DN: Is this the American Scholar essay?

CW: Yeah. I published it there but I never put it into a book or anything. It was just a short little essay about stopping writing poetry and getting a diagnosis. It was short—maybe six pages. I initially wrote it for the church newsletter. They asked me to write something for their Christmas newsletter, and I started to write something and was like: well, this is what I'm thinking about. I was going to do it in one hour and I couldn't. So I thought, well, I'm a professional, I have to go and write something and so I really wrote something, and it turned into that.

DN: Which, because of the popularity of it, turned into *My Bright Abyss.* So the essay and then the reader response . . .

CW: A church newsletter first.

DN: A church newsletter. Well, it's just a continuation of the early church newsletter from when you were nine. I can say with confidence that the book, *My Bright Abyss*, is the most beautiful and profound expression of the mystery of suffering that I have ever read. I found it startling how beautifully written it was. Even though I knew you had written it, I thought you were going to die at the end of the book.

CW: That would have been a trick. But I wrote it thinking I was going to die. I finished that book in the hospital as I was getting a transplant. I put it together as I was getting a transplant and I put it all over the room. I had it spread out all over the hospital room and I was working on it and I was quite lucid even though I was blasted with chemo and stuff. But yeah, I put it together in those circumstances.

DN: Why did you feel so compelled to write about it? Why not just; "I gotta survive this. I gotta get through it," or "I gotta give up and I gotta die." Why would you want to try to record all this?

CW: I wasn't trying to record—there's not that much about cancer in that book. I was trying to record the experience of God. I'm a writer. I was trying to survive too. Trying to keep my mind alive, I was trying to give form to all of these things. It would have been impossible for me not to write when all that was going on.

DN: I think one of the most amazing lines out of it said: "When my life broke open, I knew very well I believed in something. Exactly what I believed, however, was considerably less clear." So was that what drove you? You believed in something because you felt this joy and this love?

CW: I wanted to try to articulate it. That book circles around a big question mark or hole or something. It doesn't answer the questions that it poses at the outset. How could it? No one else has managed to.

DN: That's one of the reasons we write, isn't it? To just pursue those questions as far as we can?

CW: Yeah, to have the questions be alive in us. Every generation needs them differently. They need to be reformulated for us again and again. The question of how God exists—I think God's existence needs to be reexperienced again and again. The way we experience God is not the same way they experienced it 1,000 years ago or 2,000 years ago. It's always changing.

DN: You have used the term "accidental theology." What does that even mean?

CW: I teach a course at Yale Divinity School called Accidental Theology. I use different kinds of art or different kinds of writings, I've used some movies, even works of art in a museum. A lot of the best theology, the truest theology these days, is being done outside of the field of theology and is in the work of artists or thinkers of other sorts.

I find it in poetry all the time. My understanding of God is enlarged by people who would not claim to have any belief in God. So accidental theology is when I see this happening. Partly it's to answer a need. I think my students are hungry for this. They are getting theology in their other classes and they're really hungry to see it in these other forms. It gives me a way to read anything I want to read. You can put anything on a syllabus and call it accidental theology.

DN: You once said, "I always have this sense that something is going to resolve my spiritual anxieties once and for all. That one day I'll just relax and be a believer." How's that working out for you?

CW: Really well (*laughing*) it's going great.

DN: You got it all nailed down now?

CW: My fate is to be in agony. There's no doubt. But that is my fate with poetry too. My relationship with my own work is antagonistic. I'm not fond of it. I get no pleasure out of reading it. I take a lot of pleasure in other people's work. I love it. I can get very excited by it. But my own work—I can do without it. I can't stop writing it, but it leaves me cold.

DN: Why is art so much better at theology than theology?

CW: Maybe it's not in all times, but maybe there's certain times where we need God expressed differently. Maybe we've looked away or maybe we've looked in the wrong place. I mean I think Protestantism has really neglected art to its own detriment, sort of calcified because it doesn't admit to its mystical experience and doesn't believe in a natural theology or the sacredness of the creative world. I grew up learning about the fallen world. The world is something you have to escape from. The world is something that needs to be transformed. I think art is a way of understanding God lavishing his love on the created world. And so that's why.

Some of my best friends are theologians, but theology has done what so many of the humanistic disciplines have done and worked itself into a tiny little corner of jargon and kind of group speak, where they are speaking to each other. Not all of them. I love some Rowan Williams. There are theologians where I have learned an enormous amount from. But the field in general can be frustrating.

DN: You could say the same thing about the study of literature or poetry.

CW: That's right. I think there's a direct analogy

DN: We study it to a point where we've sucked all the life out of it.

CW: Think of all the Ph.D. students in literature that hate literature.

DN: Why is that?

CW: For that very reason. You go into it because you love reading the books. You love responding to it. And suddenly you've got to use these formulas to figure out what's wrong with all these books or what they've done wrong. And it becomes tedious.

DN: Regarding your reconnection with your faith, I'm reminded of that Mary Karr description, "I decided to start acting like I believed in God even though it seemed like horse dookie. I just needed to." Was that the same for you when you and your wife went to church? You just started acting like it?

CW: No. The way that it happened was that she initiated it. It's the way most things happen in our relationship. She said let's go and I went. But from that point on it was urgent and immediate and very very real. I was not acting. I know what Mary means, and there are times where you need to simply act as if you believe in God and then some kind of response often will come. But at that time, that's not the way it was for me.

DN: One of the things that I love about what you write about is how a person's soul gets confused with the self. What's the difference between a person's soul and a person's self?

CW: I think of the self as an aspect of a person, it's the personality that we're expressing all the time. It's us meeting each other, it's the way we interact. Occasionally you meet someone's soul and you are aware of that, but that's pretty rare. I think of the soul as being our inner life. Now, whether you can share that—I asked a class of Divinity School students the other day, we were reading Nietzsche and he says that "the greatest suffering of humans is the fact of their loneliness" essentially. That's not the way he puts it, but it's that essentially we are sealed off and that one's consciousness is sealed off from another and there's no way to broach that ultimately.

You can pretend you are—we have language and you know, you can make love, you can do all of the things that we do to try to meet each other, but ultimately, you're sealed off. I asked the class of Divinity School students: so is this true? Is this the greatest suffering? Do you agree with Nietzsche here? Every one of them said yes. They do. Every single one of them. Now, I don't believe that quite. I believe that love makes possible a connection with another person's soul and not simply romantic love either. I mean love in all of its various forms makes a kind of ultimate communication possible. That is ultimately a form of faith, I guess. I have no proof of it. But it's a form of faith. And I do believe it.

N. Scott Momaday

DN: You have spoken of the sacred nature of the creative act, whether it's about the land or about ancestors, or about the human spirit. What do you mean by the term sacred?

NSM: An understanding that the earth, the environment, nature is composed of spirit. I wrote a book called *Earth Keeper* fairly recently, where I tried to indicate that if we're going to save the earth, we're going to have to understand it's not enough to understand the crust of the earth on which we stand, we have to understand that it is supported by spirit. So, that's sacred. And much of the experience of the Native American is sacred and so it's a great thing to write about. It's endless.

DN: But by sacred you mean something other than the material, what we're standing on, this chair. There's another dimension, correct?

NSM: Yes. That's what I mean. The Earth is composed of spirit. There's something spiritual about our existence we don't understand enough about it.

DN: You've got this great line that says, "The sacred is not a discipline, it is a dimension." I think that's a theme pretty much in everything that you write, that you want to enter into that dimension. Is that accurate?

NSM: It is. I do want to get to that. That it's there and it should be not be exploited, but made use of.

DN: Do you have to come to a place in your own spirit before you can actually get there, or as soon as you start creating you're in that kind of cloud?

NSM: I don't know how to answer that because on the one hand, you come into the world possessed of spirit. You come in completely innocent and your whole being comes from a source that you have nothing to do with and that is hard to recognize, but it is essential to your being. And that is an understanding of the spiritual nature of the Earth. I don't know that that can be taught so well. You can't go and take a class in it.

DN: That's why it's not a discipline.

NSM: Right.

DN: But when you sit down to write or paint, do you just collect yourself and say, "Okay, I need to tap into something," before you get going?

NSM: That's a fair statement, I think. When I write or paint, I'm working with something inside myself, I'm expressing a dimension of my experience that is sacred, that is spiritual. That's very important. I couldn't work without that understanding.

DN: On this same theme you've said, "To encounter the sacred is to be alive at the deepest center of human existence." When you're writing and when you're painting, you're coming alive, aren't you?

NSM: Mhmm, in a sense, yes. I feel more alive I think when I'm working, creating, expressing myself at the deepest level.

DN: I would love to hear your account of you trying to climb down a rock wall and you found yourself at the bottom. You call that a sacred experience, correct?

NSM: Yes, because I didn't understand how I got to the bottom. I lost consciousness and I was in this situation where I was in great danger. I was suspended in a rocky shoot on the side of a cliff. It was an impossible situation because I knew that I couldn't stay there very long. I was pressing my arms out against the wall and they were shaking.

DN: Were you thinking "this is it?"

NSM: Yeah. I'm just thinking, this is surely it. I'm not going to get out of this. The next thing I knew, I was on the ground looking up at this place which was very high above me. Something intervened in my existence and saved me. I don't know what it was, but it was an interesting experience, a profound experience.

DN: How did it change you?

NSM: It gave me a greater sense of myself, a greater appreciation of life because I came very close to the end of it. But there it was, and there it is. It was a transforming experience. I don't know much more than that about it.

DN: You just know that something happened?

NSM: Something happened. I can't tell you what, I don't know how I made that distance from the shoot to the ground. I was sitting on the ground looking up, regained consciousness.

DN: Imagine all the possibilities of what happened there.

NSM: I have no explanation for it.

13

The Importance of Reading
What Writers Inform Your Own Writing? What Role Do Libraries Play?

The classics are the classics for a reason. They talk about eternal themes and real human emotions and problems and real psychology. It doesn't change.

DON WINSLOW

When I lived in Detroit, I wanted to know how to work on my car. I didn't know the first thing about engines, other than that model V-8 I assembled as a kid, but there was an older guy in our community who had worked on cars for a living, and I asked him if he'd teach me. It was glorious. Before long, he gave me some of his old tools and let me do the work while he observed. I learned more than how to change the oil. I learned how to adjust the timing, how to fix a carburetor, how to diagnose a problem. Mostly, the guy was an encouragement. I never got good enough, or had the desire, to make any money at it or get professional training, but I learned enough to do a lot of my own work and help a few others who knew less than me.

That's what reading does for writers. Reading gives us desire to write more, to take risks in our writing, to develop discernment for what works and what doesn't. To use a different kind of metaphor, reading fills the well. Imagine that writing is a kind of exhaling. When we write we deplete our writerly lungs, empty the literary tank. Reading is a kind of inhalation, where we take on more words, and put something back in the tank.

These aren't perfect images, but every writer I know says you can't be a good writer unless you're a reader. Something about reading awakens the language gene in us and gets us moving toward getting words on a page.

Some writers take this a step further and memorize poems or prose passages. When those words and patterns get inside you, they give you a kind of scaffolding for the writing that you'll produce.

When we had the poet Christian Wiman at our Writer's Symposium, we had a dinner for students, faculty, and local writers. There were about fifteen of us sitting around the table, and I asked each person to tell of a poem or other piece of writing that meant something to them. One student said there was one poem in particular that she learned in high school, but couldn't remember all of it. She began to recite it, and after a few lines stopped and said, "That's all I can remember. But that poem shaped me when I first began writing."

For some strange reason, I turned to Wiman and said, "What's the rest of that poem?" I barely got the question out, and he began reciting the rest of it, including several more verses. His well was full.

For many of us, it starts with imitation. Eventually, we develop something other than the voices that shape us. We become our selves.

Libraries are part of this equation. What function do they serve today? Are they vestiges of our cultural past? They still have books in there, right? But what else do they have? It's an argument in my town during every budget cycle.

All you have to do—even in today's electronic era—is go to one of those libraries in your town and see the beehive of activity going on there. Books, research, children's section, archives, storytime, shelter from the storm—both literal and metaphorical. It's a place to gather.

And how worried should we be about each new technological development? Will we even need these collective spaces in the future? Will we need writers? What will change and what will remain necessary?

Where will we turn for our collective wisdom?

Nick Hornby

DN: What was it about Anne Tyler's writing that got your attention?

NH: I went to Cambridge in England, and it pretty much killed me in terms of alienated me from literature, from writing, from everything. And I spent . . .

DN: That's what a college education does, right?

NH: Yeah. I spent three years avoiding my tutors because I hadn't done any work. A lot of time going to secondhand record shops and talking about and playing football. When I look back on it, it was probably my first two books were the result of my Cambridge education, but not perhaps in the way that Cambridge had hoped.

Afterwards, I knew I wanted to write, but I couldn't see how to do the third-person English prose where there's a distance and an omniscient narrator. I tried writing screenplays instead. I didn't know what form they were supposed to take; I didn't know anyone in the film industry. One day I was in a bookshop looking for something to read, still feeling a bit alienated post-university from reading, and I picked up *Dinner at the Homesick Restaurant*. It had a voice, first of all, that I recognized as a voice, which again, I hadn't been reading very much of in my classical education or the traditional education. She was speaking. She spoke to me, and I thought, "Whoa, you can do that?" And then you look at the back of the book, and it says, "Greatest living novelist" and "Winner of the Pulitzer Prize," and you think, "Wow, not only can you do it, but you can win prizes doing it just through talking to people?" And then you look at the bestseller list in *The New York Times*. She's Number 1; you think, "You sell books as well?"

DN: Sign me up.

NH: Just sign me up. But it was like a jolt of electricity. The realization that if you use your speaking voice and as much elegance and wit and soul as you can while doing it, that amounts to something, that means something to people.

DN: And yet Charles Dickens is still your guy.

NH: I never thought I could write a Charles Dickens novel. That was the difference. With Anne Tyler, it wasn't like I thought I could ever be as good as Anne Tyler, but I thought that's something I can pitch for. I can pitch for that. That is a runway that I can get on the beginning of. It felt to me like everything I consumed just came out as a direct copy. But Anne Tyler read High Fidelity, and she knew that I talked about her work a lot, and she read it and wrote me a letter about it and said, "I have no idea what it has to do with my work, but I really love it." And I thought, "Well, that's maybe how influence should be. You don't know how much you had to do with it."

Mary Karr

DN: Poetry had a big influence on you.

MK: Oh, it just kept me alive.

DN: Your mom read poetry to you, you read poetry to your mom.

MK: I read poetry to my mom. Even my father, who'd never read anything but a sports score in his life, we read poems out loud, we memorized poems, we said poems to each other. Even my sister who even then wanted to be a Republican and join the country club and marry somebody rich, she would just get misty eyed. It was a very powerful medium. She's *still* one of the great readers. My mother's dead, so she hardly reads anymore.

DN: And she never calls!

MK: *Never* calls!

DN: You wrote that poets were your first priests, and poetry itself, your first altar.

MK: For me, it's eucharistic.

DN: Why?

MK: You take somebody else's suffering, their passion, into your body, and you're changed by it, you're transformed. You're made more tender, or more human. You're more alive to your fellow human beings. I can literally read a poem and lift my head from the page and look out and my heart would just be softer.

DN: And yet your junior high principal said what about poets and prostitutes?

MK: I was doing really badly in algebra, and he called me in and gave me this lecture where he said, "You need to learn about mathematics." I said, "I don't want to know anything about mathematics. I want to be a poet." I knew this guy was an idiot when I was twelve. And he said, "But you'll need to be able to multiply fractions to do recipes when your husband's family comes over and to—"

DN: He really knew how to reach you, didn't he?

MK: ". . .To sew your dresses," and I said, "Yeah, I'm not worried about that. I think I'm gonna be a poet." And he said, "if you continue . . ."—this is an actual sentence—I remember the sentence because I said it to my mother, and my mother went nuts and called the school. "If you continue down this path of wanting to be a poet, you will wind up no more than a common prostitute."

I was twelve years old! I weighed like sixty pounds, you know?! What an astonishing sentence for a grown man to say to a child! I just can't even imagine the mentality of the man when I look back on that place where I grew up! That was a high school principal!

Joseph Wambaugh

JW: You can't be a good writer without being a good reader. I was reading all my life. I went to libraries when I was a little boy. I read Jack London's *The Call of the Wild* ten times before the age of twelve. I loved that book, and I just kept reading it over and over.

DN: Who do you read now?

JW: I read anything that comes my way now. I like Tom Wolfe. Do you know Tom Wolfe?

DN: Heard of him.

JW: He's not bad. I've come to know him. Becoming a writer has given me the opportunity to meet people like that. Truman Capote was very kind to me. Gave me a good jacket blurb for my book *The Onion Field.*

Billy Collins

DN: A lot of people have compared you to Robert Frost. You actually had dinner with him?

BC: Lunch, yeah. We didn't speak. I went to a Jesuit college in the '60s, and he was invited to read and speak at my college. He was quite old—he would be dead within three or four years. I was on the literary magazine, so just as a student representative, a few of us were invited to have lunch with him in this little faculty or priestly lunch room. It was made clear, not through words but through looks, that we weren't to speak. Because it could only go downhill.

DN: So you just sat there and watched him eat?

BC: The reputation of the college was at stake—in jeopardy. He was talking with a few Jesuits at the head of the table, and we just watched him eat. Or tried not to watch him eat, was more like it. We didn't want to stare at him. But I technically had lunch with him. It's not the kind of lunch you would imagine having with anybody.

DN: You wrote a poem about splitting wood in the winter, and the first line of that poem is, "Frost covered this decades ago, and Frost will cover it again tonight." And I assume you're talking about the weather, but you're also nodding at him, right?

BC: T. S. Eliot talks about this, and others, that every major poet, Frost certainly, Yeats, they take up a space that no one else can occupy anymore. It's like they control a certain ground. You can't have two people on the same base at the same time. I think, like, *The Swan,* I don't think you can write about swans without Yeats in the background. He did the swan. This poem came about—I have a house up above New York City, and there's woods in the back, and I love splitting wood. It's great exercise, and they say he or she who splits wood, warms themself twice. You warm yourself while splitting the wood, and then you are warmed later by that which you are splitting. I'm looking for a metaphor, and I thought there must be some metaphor possibilities in splitting wood, but I thought, "well, that's Frost." You can't go into that area, it's like police tape around the woods, because that's Frost's area. It kind of bugged me, and finally I wrote this poem called "Splitting Wood," but I nodded to Frost in the first line. It starts capitalized, it's the first word in the sentence. It says, "Frost covered this decades ago, and Frost will cover it again tonight, the leafy disarray of these woods." And then it just goes on. But I was nodding to Frost. So that's sort of a negative influence, you know.

DN: Because it's taboo?

BC: You feel like you're trespassing. Or it's like when you're covering someone else's song, making a cover of a song that that person possesses. If you sang "I Left My Heart in San Francisco," you're covering Tony Bennett. Now, do you want to cover him disrespectfully? Is it an homage to him? Or are you misinterpreting it? There's lots of types of relationships you can have with the predecessor. So it complicates writing. If you *read.* If you don't read, you're immune from any of these anxieties.

DN: How big of an influence on your poetry is Bugs Bunny?

BC: Well, large. What are you basing this on?

DN: I'm basing this on a statement that you're more influenced by Bugs Bunny than you are Emily Dickinson.

BC: Oh, OK, well, that was a rare moment. A number of writers were asked by the *Wall Street Journal* to write something about some obsession or habit or odd thing about themselves that readers would be kind of surprised to find out. So Junot Diaz, for example, wrote about his obsession about the video game, *Grand Theft Auto.* He wrote about how he just couldn't stop playing it. So I wrote an essay about how one of my influences is Warner Bros. Cartoons. Looney Tunes and Merry Melodies, and how I was not a Disney guy at all. Because Disney was very bourgeois. I mean they're married—Mickey and Minnie. And Donald and Daisy. You know? It's just too settled. But there could be no

Mrs. Daffy Duck, you know? He's beyond the conventions of marital love.

But I did talk about how it really helped my imagination to be in a very pliable world where everything kind of morphed, and you could pull a refrigerator out of your pants, or something. And you weren't even *wearing* pants! Just that crazy, pliable world. I thought it probably had some influence on the plasticity on the imagination and how the laws of gravity are suspended quite nicely as they are in poetry.

The day it came out in the *Wall Street Journal*, it was Saturday, and they did this incredible graphics job, you know? On the front page of the *Wall Street Journal*, up where the banner is, there were all these Looney Tunes characters, and they're all in drag because they're dressed as muses, and Bugs Bunny was a famous cross-dresser anyway. I held this thing in my hand, and said, "I can die a happy man—I put Bugs Bunny on the cover of the *Wall Street Journal* above the banner!"

DN: You have some harsh things to say about how poetry is taught. You've said that high school is where poetry goes to die. And you even have a poem about this.

BC: If you have the right teachers teaching the right poetry, it doesn't have to die there. I'm as guilty of this as anybody, but I think one of the reasons that people lose interest in high school is not the fault of teachers, it's the fault of adolescence. One of the things about adolescence, at least how I experienced it, is that one is interested in acceleration, and speed—whether it's car speed, or today, it's computer speed. Texting or messaging. Everything has to go fast. And poetry, obviously, is an appeal to slow down. That's one reason that poetry comes in lines. The effect of that is that it asks you not to rush through it as you could with prose. Stop here and come back in the poem. Every time the poem does not go out to the end of the line, the poet is there for a sort of prose avoidance system—we have to stop it before we turn into journalists or something.

DN: Careful there!

BC: So the line ends, and then you go back in the poem. The shape of the poem is always telling you, "come back in, come back into the body of the poem. Rejoin the field of words that are in this poem." That's that powerful nonlinear recurrent thing that's going on in poems.

The tendency of classrooms is to put a disproportionate emphasis on interpretation. You know, what does the poem mean? In poetry, the language is used in such a way that it's not to be brushed aside in order to find a meaning. The language puts resistance against that sort of dismissive substituting meaning for what the poem is actually saying.

When Frost was asked at one point to explain one of his poems, he said, "oh, you want me to say it *worse?*" I just said it—that's what it means. To start talking about it would produce an inferior text, and not only that, but you wouldn't know if his explanation was true or not. Then you'd have someone interpreting his interpretation. Then you just have this hall of mirrors of interpretation after interpretation.

DN: It does seem that a lot of schools do that to literature, to poetry, instead of literature we call it "textual analysis." We do all these things. And it just seems that it just takes the fun out of reading.

BC: Well also, there are just so many pleasures that don't require teachers. I mean, not *all* those pleasures but *literary* pleasures. I wrote an article once called "Poetry: Pleasure in the Hedonist Reader," and I think it's maybe seven pleasures you get out of poetry. The pleasure of metaphoric connection, the pleasure of imaginative travel, the pleasure of rhythm, the pleasure of sound, and the seventh and last pleasure is the pleasure of meaning. Because I went to graduate school—if you don't have a head for challenging text, there's no real point in being in graduate school. You can look at my copy of the collection of Wallace Stevens or Piers Plowman, you will find just marginal comments all over the place. I have a real taste for it, but I don't write that way, and I feel that the teacher almost imposes him or herself between the poem and the student by choosing poems that require interpretation. Because if you choose poems that don't require your intermediacy, then there's no class, really.

I always think that poetry classes should be taught chronologically backwards. I know in survey courses, you start with Chaucer. That's a ridiculous place to start! You know? If you start with contemporary poetry, you know, hook students on that, then you can walk students chronologically backwards into modernism and even into the nineteenth century.

DN: What about hip hop or spoken word-type things? Would you include that in how poetry could be taught?

BC: I don't know! I mean, I gave a reading just a few weeks ago, and this rather elderly gentleman came up to me and said, "what do you think of hip hop music?" And I said a few things about it and then I said, "do you listen to hip hop music?" And he says, "well, at intersections I do!"

Joyce Carol Oates

JCO: I was reading the comic books maybe at an early age. I probably stopped reading when I started reading Wittgenstein in high school.

DN: Seriously? Wittgenstein in high school?

JCO: Seriously? Of course. If you're reading Wittgenstein in high school, you're serious. I mean, by definition, you're not fooling around. Mad Magazine stayed with me a little longer. That was a really revolutionary and very exciting, subversive magazine. Little did we know that it was just casting a mirror, turning a mirror on life. I thought it was an exaggerated comic book—not at all.

DN: It's some pretty significant satire.

JCO: Stendhal said the novel is a mirror on the roadway. And it's sort of what Mad Magazine is in terms of the United States.

DN: Didn't you also read Edgar Allen Poe when you were younger?

JCO: Well, I read a lot of different things. When I was fairly young, I read Henry David Thoreau. I think that helped along with Lewis Carroll to form my personality, such as it is. And Edgar Allen Poe is a little different. Poe has different voices. One of them is a very contemporary kind of voice in *The Tell Tale Heart*. It almost could be written today. I wouldn't say that Poe was a strong influence. But I always did really much admire Henry David Thoreau.

DN: The reason I asked about Poe is I just wondered if his writing had some impact on some of the topics that you choose and some of the things that you have people thinking about in their head and in their heart. It looks like those could be linked.

JCO: Well, influences are myriad, especially for somebody who's read a lot. One can be influenced by any number of like 1,400 books, and it's hard to say. We're also deeply influenced by our experiences. The deep emotional experiences of our lives are what shape us as people and as writers. And the literary influences may be formal, they may show you a way of organizing your material. But it's these deep experiences, these unconscious—these sort of resonances, unconscious, that determines what we will write.

Carlos Ruiz Zafon

CZ: I wouldn't dare to step into Ray Bradbury's shoes, especially because when I was working on *The Shadow of the Wind*, I would see Ray Bradbury very often around Los Angeles. He was not a driver. He was a native Angeleno. He rode the buses at the time, he was in good health, and I remember seeing him very often standing at bus stops in this kind of safari gear. He was always wearing khaki shorts and these long socks, and he was standing there with his glasses and you'd be driving, and say, "oh my God! It's Ray Bradbury!"

Jane Smiley

DN: *The New York Times* said that your ability to master all genres drives other writers crazy. We're a jealous bunch, Jane!

JS: That's what Charles McGrath said. I'm not sure that he took a poll or anything.

DN: Maybe it just drove *him* crazy.

JS: Well, I apologize for driving anybody crazy.

Nnedi Okorafor

NO: I started writing these strange stories, and I wasn't seeing anything even remotely like what I was writing. I just kept on, because that's what you do, you just keep on. I loved writing and that wasn't going to stop me. I was at the Clarion Writers' Workshop at Michigan State University, where I did my first master's degree. I was there for this six-week workshop on science fiction and fantasy. That workshop was phenomenal for me because it was the first time where I accepted what I was doing, where I really accepted that I was writing this speculative fiction and it was ok.

Until then, I've had only creative writing classes where all my professors were telling me that writing science fiction and fantasy was bad. If you wanted to be a real writer, you weren't writing that kind of stuff. It was not real literature. I was told that point blank by professors that I respected and that I learned from even after they told me that. So I was already having this mind-blowing experience at the Clarion Writers' Workshop and one day, they took us to the bookstore and I was going through the science fiction and fantasy section, and I stopped because there was a book in that section that was something I had never seen before. There was a Black woman on the cover, and it was in the science fiction and fantasy section. I never seen that before. I bought it because of that, no other reason. It turned out to be Octavia Butler's *Wild Seed.*

DN: You'd never heard of her before. But you saw a Black woman on the cover of a book and said that's for me.

NO: Yes, yes, yes. Exactly. That's why book covers are very important. Octavia Butler is one of the finest science fiction writers in general, but she's also the first high-profile African American science fiction writer, and I just happened to pick up her book. *Wild Seed* starts off in Niger—pre-colonial Nigeria, the main character's name is Ebo, it's Anyanwu. I knew exactly what her name meant, and so I opened this book and I started reading. This woman is a shape-shifter who has been alive for over three hundred years, and she ends up meeting another African immortal from Egypt. We follow them all the way through the white man, slavery, going through the middle passage to the United States. So for the first time you're seeing that whole thing through the eyes of a character that's lived the whole thing. It was just extraordinary. She writes in this clear, very engaging way. You read the first paragraph of *Wild Seed* and you will not put that book down. You have to finish it. That's how she writes.

I read that and my mind blew because this was a speculative fiction narrative where some of what would be considered magical elements, like shape-shifting, are explained in a scientific way. She heals people in a scientific way. She can go into her own body and heal her own self, so she can heal cancer. It's just an amazing amazing book. And I was like "Oh my gosh this is actually the first time I'm seeing this kind of narrative with these kinds of characters." It was this validation that I didn't know I needed until I found it.

DN: This is what you're doing for other people who are saying, "What about this kind of writing?" That's gotta be kind of a kick to think you're having that same impact on a lot of people who are reading your stuff.

NO: That's a powerful thing. Possibly one of the most powerful things of being a creative because you're adding to—you're becoming part of the fabric. That's an amazing feeling.

Christian Wiman

DN: When you first started writing poems, you wanted to write a poem that would last forever. And then a poet that you knew personally, and one that I have admired from afar—Donald Hall—disavowed you of that notion. Do you remember what he said to you?

CW: We were having hamburgers in Chicago. He said he was thirty-eight years old when he realized not a word he wrote was going to last. He said it just as casually as he took a bite of his hamburger. I was thirty-eight years old at the time, which Don obviously knew, and he was giving me a little hint. The miracle is, if you think of Don at the age of thirty-eight having the realization that nothing he wrote was going to last—he went on to write another fifty years. That's the really miraculous part and a paradoxical part. If you know something is not going to last, I think he might be wrong about that actually, with his own work. But if you think that and most writers do suspect it, even T. S. Eliot suspected of his own work—why persist?

Alice Walker

DN: I love this essay that you wrote about Flannery O'Connor where you got mad at her. You read her growing up, and you got mad at her, or at least the people who said she was the only southern writer worth reading. Apparently there were no Black writers where you were reading. And then you came back to her, and you appreciate her, right?

AW: This is very long ago, but I love Flannery. And actually, Faulkner, for most southern people, would have been head and shoulders above O'Connor as the southern writer.

DN: But then, as a result of asking "were there no black writers," you started writing stories that you thought you would've wanted to read when you were young. And you read Zora Neal Hurston. I started reading her because I was visiting Haiti a lot and I was interviewing Voodoo priests. She helped me understand Voodoo in a way that no other writer helped me. But you rediscovered Zora Neal Hurston. Everyone had kind of forgotten about her. So thank you.

AW: You're welcome.

DN: But what made you want to resurrect her?

AW: Love. But also I was writing this story about my mother. This is a story about during the depression—my mother was very good looking—and she dressed up to go get some food from the commissary. This was a period during the depression when people didn't have enough food to eat. She had received some cast-off clothing from the North, and she put them on to go get some food, and she looked really great. The white woman who was in charge of giving out the food refused to give her food because she looked so great. I was so angry with this woman who had shamed—well she couldn't really shame my mother because she had a great big heart and everything, but she had insulted her. Years later I decided that I was going to take this woman on. Now this woman had died many great moons before this. But anyhow, as a writer I get to settle a few scores.

What could I do to this woman? She died when I was in college. So I decided that I would Voodoo her, but that meant that I would need the real deal. So I went to the white anthropologists to find out about Voodoo from Black culture. And do you know what one of them said? He said he didn't think Black people had a large enough brain. So I said to hell with him, and I turned and I found Zora. Then I found the story about how you actually Voodoo someone. That's what I put in my story. So if you ever want to know how to Voodoo someone, just read this story and you're on your way!

DN: Was it effective?

AW: Of course it was!

DN: You tried to find where Zora was buried—

AW: I did find it!

DN: I know you found it, but you had to pose as her niece.

AW: I did!

DN: But you're not her niece!

AW: How do you know? Okay I lied.

DN: It was worth it.

AW: This is what you do to deliver a gift. Zora was on her way to delivering this novel to you, I want you to know. She had done her work, she had written this novel, she was virtually penniless, she was ill, but she was writing this novel and she was going to get this novel to you down the generations. The least I could do is help her.

Margarita Pintado

MP: Lorenzo Garcia Vega is a remarkably unknown Cuban writer, and the reason he's so unknown is because he was heavily censored by the Cuban government. I'm writing a book on him and I'm getting very excited because more people have been finding him and reading him. This is our Latino American Beckett, he is our Proust, and he remains completely under the radar. In the late seventies, he wrote an extraordinary book called *The Years of Origenes*, it's in Spanish, *Los Anos de Origenes*, and exposes everything that is going on in the Cuban Revolution, and the way that the regime is treating artists and how they are being forced to exile. Why Lorenzo? I knew my topic of dissertation, but I didn't have an author. My advisor thought of Lorenzo. He was alive and we became good friends. I went to Miami and visited him and we formed a friendship that lasted for about three years, and then he died. He changed my life and he changed the way I think about poetry. I became a poet for him.

He read my stuff and he approved. He wanted to do a blog with me and we did a blog together. It will be published soon as a novel. He was a brave man. He was a bag boy in a Publix store in a supermarket in Miami. But he was also this huge figure that people knew. People would go to the supermarket to say hi to him. This is a Cuban national.

DN: And he's bagging groceries in Miami.

MP: With a lot of dignity. He wrote a whole book about his experiences as a bag boy. It's a work of art. He proves that poetry can emerge and, it's everywhere; you don't need a formal job, the things we associate with success. He wrote about failure in such an honest way that I was drawn to him.

I also go back to poets like Mary Oliver, those great classics that help me stay centered, focused. I'm reading a Puerto Rican poet, Manuel Ramos Otero, he died from AIDS in the early '90s, I'm writing a paper on him so I've been reading those very hard poems on the illness. Unfortunately, many of the poets I read have not been translated into English, and I'm trying to do something about that, which is not easy.

Don Winslow

DN: In your book *City on Fire*, you connect to one of the oldest stories there is. Was the influence of the Iliad and other ancient Greek myths an intentional thing, or was it a revelation after you started writing?

DW: That was a kind of genesis of the idea for the book. Back in the early '90s I realized how ignorant I really was. I had this very narrow education in African history, which I loved. I was very well grounded in Shakespeare because I was working directing it a lot. But for the rest of the body of world literature, I was really, really dumb. In college I was selected for this special areas program and that's all you did. I got one of those Great Books lists, and I thought, I'm going to read my way through this list. It took me seven years. But early on, of course, in that list are the Iliad, The Odyssey, the Greek tragic dramas, the Aeneid. So I'm reading the Iliad, and the precipitating event that allegedly caused the Trojan War was an argument over a woman. A beautiful woman.

In the New England crime wars that I grew up in and around, one of them started on a beach in an argument over a woman. The parallel just smacked me in the face and I began to think, huh, are there others? If I read through these classics, are there other parallels to real, contemporary crime? And crime fiction. Yeah. A lot. And so I conceived this idea, let me start with the Iliad, although I see it through the point of view of Aeneas, and carry that through two more books. As American crime moves west, the characters move west. And follow the characters from the Iliad, the Aeneid, all of those, through the saga.

DN: What it made me think of was that you're retelling the first story that has been passed on through civilization, and you're retelling it in a contemporary setting. But what I thought was amazing is, the story still works. The story matters. It's about a woman, but it's also about the nature of evil and human nature and mixed motives and all these things. And you're tapping into what feels like mankind's original story.

DW: The classics are the classics for a reason. They talk about eternal themes and real human emotions and problems and real psychology. It doesn't change. The circumstances change, some of the details change, but that sort of gut material doesn't. That was what was so exciting.

DN: Your main character wants to be a better dad than he had. He wants to have a better family than he was raised in.

DW: Right. Which are basic human desires. If you go back into mythology, go back into the Aeneid and find out about Aeneas's childhood, that's what it was. Abandoned by his mother as an infant and raised by a neglectful father.

N. Scott Momaday

DN: You went to Stanford to be a poet. You edited a collection and studied Frederick Tuckerman. Why Tuckerman? He was known primarily for one poem, right? Cricket?

NSM: He was known for that poem, which was late in being discovered. I think it was in the middle of the 1900s, 1950 maybe that publication was put out by Covington Press. My mentor at Stanford, Yvor Winters, wrote something about it in which he said, this is the greatest poem in English of the nineteenth century. So I got interested in Tuckerman and I edited his work because he was not well known, but he was an excellent poet. I had to do something about that. I read first on microfilm at Stanford and then I went to Harvard and read his manuscripts and put them altogether.

DN: What impressed me about his writing was his ability to describe landscapes, which I think is also one of your great gifts. Do you feel maybe that influenced your ability to describe what we're seeing in the land ahead of us. He seemed to be really good at that.

NSM: I think that's an accurate statement concerning Tuckerman, but it's not a landscape that I write about. He wrote about Greenfield and the Connecticut valley and so on, which is a wonderful thing to write about, but it's not what I do. I write about a different landscape entirely.

DN: True, but it was his ability to draw a picture with words that impressed me. Yours is a different landscape, but you do the same.

NSM: Well, I hope so. He was primarily a sonneteer. He wrote 106 sonnets or something like that. They were brought out by Witter Bynner in the 1930s, I want to say. That was the only publication that was available to modern readers. He did publish a book of poems in 1860. It was well received, he sent copies to Hawthorne and Melville and the literati of his time. He traveled to England and met Alfred Lord Tennyson, who gave him a copy of Locksley Hall. In his lifetime, he was known well enough, but he became obscure very quickly. Very few people of my generation knew of Tuckerman. So, I'm pleased that I edited his complete poems because they deserve to be there. He fell again into obscurity, can't help that, but at least his work is in libraries.

DN: And then you went to study Emily Dickinson's poems. What did she teach you as you immersed yourself into her creative genius?

NSM: I don't know how to answer that. I think her impression on me was very great, but it would be hard to pin down. I think she's probably the greatest American poet of all. She's beyond imitation. You can't imitate her, but she's a wonderful poet. Her view of language, so wonderful, so compelling. She wrote about 1,700 poems, my goodness. And I read all of them in manuscript. I spent a year at Amherst, which was her hometown. That was very moving to me. I got to see the Pelham Hills, which she saw and got to see where she had her garden. She's a great writer.

Amy Tan

AT: The very first essay I wrote was called, "What the Library Means to Me."

DN: We study it here in our Great Works course.

AT: Yes, especially that opening line: My name is Amy Tan. I'm eight years old.

DN: We were riveted.

AT: But it's the ending, I realized, where you have to wring their hearts or wring their wallets.

DN: I'm misting up just thinking about the ending.

AT: I missed the library so much. I gave 18 cents to Citizens of Santa Rosa Public Library and it was my entire allowance or my entire life savings at that point. Of course I knew that it would cause people's hearts to melt to think that this little child had given all her money and that would cause other people to give money to the library. So they made me the winner. I won a transistor radio, and today I'm in a rock 'n' roll band. So it's all connected.

Lysley Tenorio

LT: Every Wednesday in elementary school was half day, so my father would pick me up and take me to the library to pick my books out for the week. That was where I really started enjoying reading and realizing that books were kind of an escape and a refuge from daily boredom or whatever stresses an eight-year-old could possibly be suffering from.

DN: What were those stresses at eight?

LT: Hamster crisis and things like that.

DN: What were some of those early books that got your attention when you were little?

LT: The Beverly Cleary books, Ramona, some Judy Blume, like "Tales of Fourth Grade." Not the scandalous ones like "Tiger Eyes." And then books like "From the Mixed Up Files of Mrs. Basil E. Frankwiler," the brother and sister who ran away to live in the Metropolitan Museum of Art. They're just so vivid to me in my mind, even now.

Jeannette Walls

DN: As bizarre as your family was, they were readers.

JW: Voracious readers.

DN: Your dad would read the dictionary. If he disagreed with the definition it gave . . .

JW: He would disagree and say, "That's wrong!" and he would send letters to the dictionary.

DN: Then you and your siblings would write letters.

JW: And he would start up a correspondence. They would respond and he'd write back, and then they'd eventually get a little bit tired. But he was one of those cranks who was all the time calling up and disputing things about the way that something was done.

DN: You always had books.

JW: Always, always. But I have to tell you, and I don't even know if I wrote about this, but I didn't go into my first bookstore until I was in my early twenties. It was always libraries, and I will always be indebted to libraries. It was weird walking into a bookstore. This is kind of like a library except you pay the fine before you get the book.

Wherever we lived, our houses, our cars were always filled with books. Sometimes it was because we didn't exactly return them. We just always had books. Always.

DN: Do you remember when you saw a television program for the first time? I think it was the program Lost in Space. And you came back and told your mom about it.

JW: I couldn't believe anything was so amazing as this television that this friend's family had. These amazing programs would appear on it. I ran back and told mom the plot of it, and she was suddenly, "Oh, that's trash." She took out some H. P. Lovecraft and Edgar Allan Poe and started reading it. And I thought, "Dang, mom's kind of right. That danger, danger stuff was pretty exciting. But wow, mom's actually right."

DN: You have talked about the book *A Tree Grows in Brooklyn,* and said you read when you were ten. *That's 440 pages*. You read a book that long when you were ten?

JW: Oh yeah. I cannot remember not being able to read. When I was three years old, my parents were baffled. My father was convinced I could read, but mom didn't know whether I'd memorized most of the Dr. Seuss books or could read them. I can recite most of the Starbelly Sneetches to this day. I was reading books without pictures, as we called them, from a very early age.

DN: But back to *A Tree Grows in Brooklyn,* this is about attempts to eradicate the tree, to stamp it out.

JW: There's this wonderful description she has of this tree that grows no matter what. It's considered a weed tree. And it grows through cracks in the sidewalk; it grows when there's not enough water, and people hate it because it's so common. But if it weren't so common, people would think it was beautiful, and of course, it was a metaphor for the main character.

DN: And for you.

JW: I really related to this girl who was not popular, not pretty; she didn't have a lot of friends, but she loved books, and her love of reading. Oh, and she loved her drunken old daddy. Those two things rescued her, they got her out of that situation. She was my best friend. She was my only friend.

Nnedi Okorafor

DN: So many times in your books there's a callback to ancient wisdom, and that wisdom resides in books. You're really celebrating reading in all of these stories because you're saying that the wisdom's already there. You're telling people to go to the library.

NO: Yes. In the Akata series the library is the most important, most powerful place—the librarians are the most important and powerful people. I mean, it's knowledge. Libraries are powerful and I think people forget that or take that for granted. For me, being a professor but also a student, I mean I have a bachelor's, two master's, a PhD—that's a lot of school, and that's why I keep saying it. I understand profoundly, the power of libraries. I've been around them for so long and I've seen so many different types. And I've explored them just for fun. The things you can find in libraries are indeed magical and powerful. I always tell students, especially in universities and colleges, not to take that for granted. You won't always have access to that university library. There's so much knowledge in there and there's so much power and there's so much access to the past, present, and future in those libraries. My obsession and my love of that come through in my work.

Don Winslow

DW: My dad was a sailor who loved books, and my mother was a librarian who loved to sail. I grew up in this little New England fishing town on the coast of Rhode Island. The book is set there. This little library where my mom was an assistant librarian, was a fourth the size of this room, built in the 1870s. I would go to that library as a kid, which meant I could go anywhere in the world. I discovered not only could I travel in space, I could travel in time. I could go to Paris in 1798. I could go to Africa in 1403. From that little town where, frankly the expectations of us were not high, I learned to love the world, to be excited about the world, to be excited about reading. We always had books.

We often forget how essential to democracy libraries are. Think about it. Prior to the free lending library, the only people who had access to written knowledge were the rich, the aristocrats. You had to have a certain income to be allowed into those libraries. Libraries like that still exist. But then the free library comes around and everybody has access to newspapers, magazines, books, pictures, whatever they want to learn and to grow and participate in society. To improve themselves or just to enjoy themselves.

Anthony Doerr

DN: In an age of artificial intelligence, Amazon and the internet, do we even need libraries anymore?

AD: Woah! Dean, come on! Where we live, and it gets cold out, the library is the last place you can use the restroom without buying a $7 latte. Let's just start there.

DN: We start with the biological function.

AD: It's warm. You can sit there and read *Time Magazine* if you don't have anywhere else to go. If you're an older person whose kids are like, "Hey, can you take the grandkids today?" And you're like, "Uh, okay; what do they like?" Go to the library. It's the best place for that. If you're a young person and you want to meet your friends and you don't know a place that anybody will approve of, you go to the library. So it is a functioning public, open, free community space for everybody. Forget about the stuff that's in there.

Then, if you want to interact with our government or apply for a job, still huge portions of the United States don't have regular access to the internet. It is an incredibly equalizing tool to be able to go use a free computer. Those of us who have computers in our pockets, I take that for granted—but that's not the case for everyone. As the pandemic showed in my kids' high school in Boise, one-third of the kids didn't have regular access to the internet at home. Libraries are an enormous tool for that.

Then, let's talk about the preservation of human wisdom and access to information. I know you use librarians; I go in and ask them stuff. They help you in so many different ways. So to have access to go study the work of the masters for free, to learn how to take that home and care for public property—it's one of the last ways that we all share the common green, that you get to bring home *The Phantom Tollbooth* and spill chocolate milk on it and apologize and deal with fees and late fees—you're participating in our community and in culture. Libraries are so unbelievably essential, and those book-banning attacks are so off. There's all these challenges right now, like they're trying to criminalize certain acts. If librarians hand out "obscene," who's deciding what's obscene? It's like one book from 1990 with one page on masturbation or something. And they're trying to make it a misdemeanor for librarians to hand all these books out. Anytime you see a librarian, you should be like, "Thank you so much. Here's some money; here's a latte."

14

Words of Wisdom

What Advice Do You Have for Aspiring Authors?

A real writer, a real artist, never really wants any advice at all.

JOYCE CAROL OATES

When we ask writers for advice, what are we really asking for? We wonder if there is a secret that has eluded us, or if there is some special incantation they do before the muse descends, or if they light this kind of incense, or drink this kind of tea, or if they're just so much more advanced than us that we can sit back and accept that we will never achieve their level of genius, so we might as well go back to playing video games.

Maybe.

But we could also be asking for little nuggets that will help us get going, keep moving, stop listening to the devil on our shoulder that whispers (or shouts), "You suck."

In writing seminars that I have given, I usually go through a list of things beginning writers do that might keep them from getting where they want to be. I wouldn't call them mistakes, necessarily, but they are definitely impediments to writing well, in my opinion.

Here are a few of them:

1) Rookie writers don't write regularly. This must be part of your diet as a creator. It's almost impossible to sit down and knock something out that's really well done if you do it only once a month. Can you just decide, "This morning I'm going to run a triathlon?" I didn't think so. Or, "Tonight I'll sing in my city's opera." It's all about practice. Even if it's a blog post, a diary entry, a letter to a friend, practice is part of what will improve your writing.

2) Rookie writers spend *way* too much time on first drafts. This is a huge problem with college students, in my observation. They inch along, word by word, thought by thought, phrase by phrase, going back, deleting, working until it's perfect (in their view), and they turn it in and assume it's great. I don't know where this perfectionism comes from, but I think it kills the creative juice. Instead, spew it out. Give yourself a cerebral enema. I know someone who, when she writes, she equates it to vomiting, and then, exhausted and dehydrated, she imagines God holding her forehead over the toilet and rubbing her back, saying, "There, good. Is there any more?"

   This goes against the nature of the anal retentives, but this is the best way. Once you get it all out there in what Anne Lamott calls a shitty first draft, *then* you can look for the nugget, the part that's worth writing about. There's a good chance that you had no idea what this piece was really about until you backed the truck up and emptied it all out there. Don't spend too much time on first drafts.

   I had a student recently tell me that she edits as she goes, so the "vomit draft" I just described to the class didn't really apply to her. I've seen her writing. I disagree.

3) Rookie writers don't revise. This is related to the point above. They think what they carved out is a pearl and they send it in. But good writing takes several passes and some time away to reflect on it. Social media and blog posts might be a little different in this regard, but even then I suspect a lot of people wish they had reflected a little more before they hit "Publish." Mary Karr's book "Lit" was 300 pages long. But she wrote 2,000 pages. Wallace Stegner said, "Hard writing makes for easy

reading." The main character in the movie "Finding Forester" said, "You write your first draft with your heart. You write the next draft with your head." Don't turn in your first draft.

4) Rookie writers sacrifice clarity for what they think is "artistic." Cutting out the adjectives was good enough for Hemingway, and it's good enough for you. The reason Mary Oliver's poetry is so beautiful is that it's so simple. Same with Billy Collins. You don't have to sound smart. You just have to tell the truth. And you can do that when you stop trying to impress people.

   When my son was in high school, he asked me to read a paper he had written. I crossed out all the unnecessary stuff and said he didn't need it. He protested: "Teachers love this kind of crap," he said. He was probably right. But you're not in English class any more. You've already taken the AP exam. Don't focus too much on the art of what you're trying to say. I had a young writer contact me and ask what some of my favorite words were—she wanted to sound more impressive in her writing, she said. In her case I told her my favorite word was "Don't."

5) Rookie writers don't offer anything new or fresh to the discussion. At its worst, the work just perpetuates stereotypes, re-affirms assumptions, and removes the need to think. Good writers complicate your thinking. Don't insult your readers.

6) Rookie writers try to ride a particular market. I was at a writers conference where hopeful writers could talk to a panel of acquisition editors, and the question came up—"What is hot right now?" Some editors said that books about the Amish were popular, and they were buying manuscripts on that topic. Others were looking for books that involved vampires. I got to work on a manuscript involving Amish vampires immediately. Kidding. There's nothing wrong with trying to capitalize on the market's interest, but my recommendation is that you write what's interesting to you, what you would have liked to have found. Asking "Will it sell?" is a question for later. The more important questions are "Is this anything?" and "Did I tell the truth?" Also, if the editors are telling you what they're acquiring now, by the time you write

your version of it, something new will have bubbled up. It's hard to hop on the popularity train when it has already left the station.

7) Rookie writers try to be cute. Don't try to draw attention to yourself. Get out of the way. Just tell the story.

So what *should* you do?

1) Keep a journal. George Plimpton told me that one of his regrets as a writer was that he didn't keep a journal. Of course he kept one when he was doing participatory journalism, such as when he was working out with the Detroit Lions football team (he kept a small notebook in his helmet), but he didn't keep a broader journal of people he met or ideas he had or things he overheard. I keep a journal when I'm traveling (Anthony Doerr's book *Four Seasons in Rome* is the result of his keeping a journal), going through something significant in my life (my book *New Father's Survival Guide* is the result of my keeping a journal the first year of my son's life), and when I read something noteworthy or possibly worth stealing. I was watching a hockey game on television and heard a commentator describe the confusion of a goaltender on a particular play, "He didn't know whether to wind his watch or to steal second base." I reached for my journal for that one. I don't know when I'll use it in my own writing—wait. I just did.

2) Related to the above about keeping a journal with examples of good writing, pay attention to how writers describe things. Specifically look at how they use figures of speech—metaphors, similes, ways they compare certain things to other things. Taking note of how writers make comparisons will free up your own creativity in description. Instead of saying "She was as quiet as a mouse," a collection of good descriptions could allow you to use instead, "She was as quiet as a Navy SEAL slipping below the surface of the water." The first one is a cliché that will not move the reader. The second one might.

3) When you're done writing for the day, don't wait until you finish a section or complete a thought. Stop in the middle of an idea. Better yet, stop in

the middle of a sentence. You aren't going to feel like writing tomorrow because of all the inertia you will have to overcome again (remember how reluctant you were this morning when you tried to write?). But if your first task in the next writing day is to finish a thought, a sentence, a section, then you're already in motion, and you'll more easily move into the work for that day. It's a bit of a psychological trick to play on yourself, but it works.

4) Have a reading group. Maybe. Many of my writer friends feel that they benefit from having a read and critique group. Everyone in the group is obligated to bring in pages they've written, and members of the group give feedback. But I have just as many writer friends who feel that they work better in isolation, and the only feedback they need is from their agent or editor. Writers in the early stages often don't have agents or editors, so the read and critique groups are their primary source for helpful response. This is where writing classes can be helpful, but even then you have to have a thick skin.

When we workshop students' stories in my writing classes, I give fairly strict guidelines as to what are helpful comments and what aren't. I tell them to avoid statements such as, "I liked it." That's too vague and not helpful. What, specifically, worked? What didn't? And I remind them that everyone is going to have a turn on the hotseat, so be mindful of one another's feelings. I also try to have something I have written for the students to critique. Believe me, it is humbling to have a twenty-something who has never published anything tell me that my description of a scene "doesn't work," and that I should "show, not tell." But that's part of the deal in a reading group. It takes some humility to expose your ideas to others.

Here's some final advice from me—well, actually from people I have read over the years. Muriel Rukeyser ends her poem, *The Speed of Darkness*, with these lines:

"Who will speak these days,
if not I,
if not you?"

And this, from Steven Pressfield's book *The War of Art*:

> Creative work is not a selfish act or a bid for attention on the part of the actor. It's a gift to the world and every being in it. Don't cheat us of your contribution. Give us what you've got.
>
> (P. 165)

But enough from me. Let's hear advice from some of the greats.

Joseph Wambaugh

JW: Learn to type. It's helped me throughout life.

DN: What about joining something like a police force?

JW: I don't think you have to be a cop to even write about cops. I could possibly write about ballet if I knew something about ballet. I'm not sure about having direct experience in a profession or vocation or a job is all that necessary. You have to have a storytelling heart, and be able to communicate emotion and don't be afraid to do it.

Anne Lamott

AL: I have a problem with writing conferences that I get asked to—and I used to do a lot more—where a lot of other writers, and agents, and editors are getting a very lovely week at a very beautiful place to fill people with the belief that if they work harder, and type their manuscripts just right, and master the art of the query letter, that they will probably get to be writers, and that getting to be writers will fill them up and make them well and whole, and that if they become published writers, that the world will validate their parking ticket. Well, none of it's true.

The one fly in the ointment is that the writing is the only thing that works. It's a paradox that discipline is the only way you find freedom, creative or otherwise. Soul freedom is in the discipline of sitting down and being in a relationship with yourself, like you would be with somebody that you really love, another person, where if somebody came to me and said, “I love literature so much, I find a direction, I find illumination, I find solace, and I feel it’s a calling to read great literature, and I love to write, and I want to play!” I wouldn’t say, “Oh, for God’s sake, well, that’s *ridiculous*! You have a job, you know, you’re not actually fun. I don’t think you’re that interesting.”

I wouldn’t do that. With a friend, I would say, “I don’t think there’s anything more important than that you figure out a way, by prearrangement with yourself, to get a little writing done every day.”

DN: So it’s about writing. It’s not about publishing.

AL: It is about writing. I don’t think that people should not publish for the sake of not publishing. I don’t think there’s anything more corrupting about publishing than there is about the rest of the world. But it’s a lot of false hope. It’s the great belief that there’s something out there that’s really going to do it for you. I have a lot of students over the years, who have banded together, and it’s very touching to me—writers groups of three and four people, five people, and they meet *every* Wednesday for coffee, and it’s a form of benevolent pressure because you have to show up with something to read, or pretty soon, they don’t invite you back. So you need to bring three new pages, there’s four of you, you’re going to read them out loud, and you pass them out, you *work* on them. Maybe you’ve gotten fifteen pages done, but at least you’ve gotten your three done. The most important advice I could give you is that the great lie, if you asked me, is that you have to do it alone and suffer or we can’t really count it. That’s the American way. And I will not name the gender that came up with it, because that will sound angry, but I don’t buy it for a second.

If you can find people who can function as midwives and birth coaches, say, “You want to write a book so that your grandchildren will know what it was like for you in Tokyo in 1930? I so entirely support you, that I will meet with you every week, and let’s give this three months and see what it’s like.” And to avail yourself for their calls, when they’re not doing well, when they want to give up—because you know the Lamott theorem of creativity is that if you make enough calls, someone, somewhere is going to be doing all right. If there are five of you in your writing group, one person's doing fine, they're just riding along, they're not thinking too much about whether it's going to be an Oprah Book of the Month.

They're doing it because they can't not do it, is what it boils down to. You call that person, and that person says, "I was gonna give up too. And last week I wrote 300 words." That's my advice: 300 words a day is one typed piece of paper, without very good margins. And it's *one* page today and my students go, "Oh, no, I'm quitting my job." And I say, "Oh, please don't quit your job. Please, please don't quit your job." "No, I am gonna quit my job. I'm going to write for eight hours a day." I go, "Don't quit your job. Don't work for eight hours a day. It's not going to work. It's not going to happen. Write one page a day." "No, I'm committed. I'm gonna quit my job." I'm a little codependent; I feel frantic about the family surviving. And then I see them three years later, they go, "I was in your writing group at Book Passage." I go, "Oh, how'd your book go?" They go, "Oh, I haven't gotten started yet. But my last child is leaving high school and I'm going to really be able to bear-down then. I'm gonna be able to write six, seven hours a day." I go, "Don't write for six, seven hours . . .

DN: Write one page a day.

AL: Write one page a day." Taking time off for major holidays and bodily breakdown, it's probably 300 pages a year—a sloppy first draft.

DN: That's a good year.

AL: It's a great year.

Chitra Divakaruni

DN: What's your best advice for writers?

CD: I tell my students often: One, read widely. Two, steal even more widely.

DN: Is there a third? Or can we just rest on those two?

CD: The most important thing is really to believe in yourself and keep writing. Writing takes a lot of work. This has been my experience, and you have to throw away a lot of things you write, and sometimes we are so attached to what we write, we can't bear the thought of having to throw it away. I tell my students, "Don't be afraid to throw things away." And if you *really* can't throw it away, get an empty shoebox, and put them in there, and don't take them out for a long time.

DN: And then throw that away!

CD: Exactly.

DN: Your advice, "read widely." Only read good writers, acclaimed writers, read everything?

CD: We read for so many different purposes. When we are reading in order to improve our writing, we should really be very careful who we pick and choose. We should read people whose work we can learn from, whose work inspires us, whose work reminds us why we wanted to become a writer in the first place.

Peter Matthiessen

PM: You really have to write. You can't wait for the muse. You've got to get your ass on that seat and get to it. You do! Then the good moments will come and you're very grateful for them. But if you wait till you feel like writing: "Oh, no, I don't . . ." Forget it. It comes in the process. That's how you learn. The other thing, of course, is the reading. You have to read, really. Hemingway had an excellent piece of advice: "Don't hit an easy patch and then write it and get done and say 'Ah, okay, now it's time for the dry martini.'" No, you shouldn't do that. You should save that easy one to get you cranked up in the morning. That is *very* valuable, because sometimes getting cranked up in the morning is very hard.

Greg Laswell (Interviewed by Karl Martin)

GL: My writing mentor when I was going to college was Dean Nelson. I took his class twice. The most valuable thing that I took away from being able to interact with him, while I was trying to learn how to write, was if you're not at least a little bit afraid of what you write, then you may be lying to your audience. So if you're not showing them everything, that means it's a waste of their time, especially within the singer-songwriter genre where the most important part of that interaction between the listener and the writer is communication and honesty.

I remember calling Dean one day because I had written an album, and I woke up and hated everything on it, and I saw *way* too much of myself in it, and I panicked. So I called him and I'm, like, "Are you ever afraid of what you write? Or do you ever hate while you write?" And he told me, "I hate everything that comes out of my mouth." That enabled me to know you don't have to be a fan of the way you sound or, or what you write. Your only job is to communicate honestly. Sometimes I feel like I'm writing a letter to someone in class, and then the teacher picks it up and reads it to everyone. And so it's a little embarrassing.

Christopher Buckley

DN: What kind of advice would you have for people who want to write?

CB: I think it's a tremendous thing to do. I'm glad I didn't know, when I graduated from college, what's involved, because it's probably like many, many other fields: it's hard to make a good living out of it. If you enjoy nice French wines and fancy restaurants, you might consider law school.

This may be either a truism or a cliche, but you've got to give it absolutely everything you got. Having said this, I realized this is probably true of practicing medicine or going into politics and becoming governor, running for president. But it's true from what I know of writing that you got to give it 110 percent. My great hero was Tom Wolfe. He was sort of the guy who made people in my generation want to be writers, because reading his prose was like nitrous-injected English language. You just didn't realize the English language could perform this way. I remember being horrified in my twenties. I got to know him a little bit when he told me that he thought it took ten years to learn how to write. I thought, "ten years?! Who's got ten years?!" Now I've been at it, into my third decade, I would say it takes maybe twenty. It depends on how much talent you have. I had to work. I was not the classic "A" student; I had to work out. But if you want to do it, go for it.

But in the end, you either write or you don't write. An elderly, distinguished British director, a friend of mine, said something that I thought that was very telling. When he's talking to a young person, he can tell by the way they phrase it, whether or not they're going to be writers. The ones who say, "I want to be a writer," as opposed to "I want to write." It's the ones who say, "I want to write" who are probably going to give it the energy that it takes. A lot of people think there's something romantic about being a *writer*. Well, look at me! Do I look romantic?

Amy Tan and Sandy Dijkstra

SD: It all starts with reading. Nobody could be a good writer who is not a good reader. The very first thing is to be a reader. But then it's about somehow finding your voice and finding what it is that you do best. Amy could make a lot of money at being a business writer, but it was not who she was. Amy found what was in her bones and that was largely her childhood and her family story. Especially for fiction writers, it's about finding your story.

Now this doesn't exactly answer your question, because you asked a crasser question about how you get an agent.

DN: The crass commercialism stage is where I'm at right now.

SD: But you've got to have the goods to get an agent, you know? Agents are always looking for talent. What you do is you write articles. We read magazines. We come chasing you. You publish reviews that are absolutely breathtaking and they're dazzling in the writing and it says at the bottom, I'm working on a novel. And we chase you. I always say that it's best to be in the group whom we are chasing, and that's by taking the first few steps yourself, getting into this little fiction magazine which made my agent feel like you were a writer. Get your local bookseller to know who you are. Get into a writing group with people whose work you respect. There are many different steps you could take. But it all starts with finding out who you are, what it is you have to say that the world should care about. Without that, it won't happen.

AT: I would say similar things, but on the very practical level, I would say go to places like this. Go to conferences. Go to symposiums. Go to workshops and look at a magazine called "Poets and Writers," and you'll see a listing of all kinds of resources for writers and poets from conferences to fellowships to grants, retreats, and stay in the company of writers, serious writers. That will fuel you and keep you going. The other is, if you're serious about making your craft better and you're not sure where your voice is, join a writer's group. Start one and read your work aloud and critique it. Know who your good editors are who your bad editors are. Not all the people in your writer's group are going to be your ideal readers.

DN: You did this.

AT: I did. I wrote my first two books in a writer's group, so I found it enormously helpful until I could have my own sense of my editorial voice in my head. If you could find one voice or two readers who you can really trust whose opinions on your work seem pretty much on target with your intentions, do that. But gradually it's nurturing yourself as a writer. Improving yourself, and then of course making those connections, knowing how it works. Start getting your stories published in little magazines. Don't aim for the *New Yorker*, believe me. Now that I'm there, I see how almost impossible it is to get into the *New Yorker* if you're a completely unknown writer. They have contracts with people like me, and if I send them stuff, they'll publish it occasionally. Get published in a little magazine and your chances are better at getting noticed. They like to discover you there. Those are practical things, but I think the big thing is really find your voice and your real reason for writing. If it's to get published, you have a long, hard road ahead of you because everybody wants to get published. Your reasons have to be a lot stronger than that to simply stay at the writing.

Garrison Keillor

GK: In just one paragraph, this is all I know about writing, and I pass it on to you free of charge: It is never done. It is never finished. It is something that you can, if you wish, spend the rest of your life working at. The possibilities for improvement, for clarity, for elegance are endless. You can occupy your entire life doing this and still feel challenged and stimulated by what is left to be done. This is not true of football. It's not true of tennis. It's not true of mathematics or about playing the violin, but it is true of using the English language.

The second thing I would say is that it is the single most useful tool that you have, no matter what you do with your life. Whether you become a teacher, whether you go into business, politics, whatever you may do, your ability to use this gorgeous language that we have inherited is the single most important tool that you have. Spoken, written, whatever you do with it, this is something that is crucial to you. Math, you can live life without it. They won't tell you that, but it's true. And the other things, you know, history and the humanities, you can pick up as you go along in life and you will. But that's what I know about writing.

To young people, what I would pass on to you is the fact that elderly people are your readers. By which I mean, people over twenty-five. And to them, you are mysteries. And so you begin with this advantage. They want to know about you, and you are mysterious. You are the future. And they really want to know about you. They want to know even more about you if you are an immigrant, if you come from an oppressed group, if you are from the wrong side of town, wrong side of the tracks, you come from a disadvantaged background. The reader is terribly curious to know about you. This is a democratic enterprise—

the writing of literature—and includes nonfiction in that. This is a democratic enterprise. This is an enterprise that has offered equal opportunity to women long before anything else did. Women were writing novels in the early eighteenth century, about the same time the novel came about, so there are no advantages here for wealth and power and having graduated from Harvard. None. Zero. The field is wide open for you. There's a world that wants to hear about you. And if you come from an evangelical background, all the more so. We're going to sell your book. We're going to sell your book to all those Catholics and Anglicans

Chris Hillman (Interviewed by Karl Martin)

CH: Anybody who is a songwriter or is embarking on a career in music or just playing music, listen to the old music. Listen to the masters in all genres. Jazz, country, and rock. None of them had a blueprint. You listen to early Elvis Presley on Sun Records, and he's coming out of left field and he's so good. Here he was, absorbing a lot of gospel music, a lot of early blues and R&B in his music. There's all of these Wonder Years of rock and roll, from '55 to around 1960. Study that music. Study the old country music and how they formed a lyric and how Hank Williams would take the simplest chord changes and add these beautiful lyrics, and Lefty Frizzell and of course Merle Haggard. Everybody from that era. And old jazz, bebop. My lyricist hero is Johnny Mercer. Johnny Mercer's written so many beautiful songs, pop standards. At my age I am listening to the music my parents listened to.

We had a wonderful guy functioning as a manager who gave us the greatest advice we ever got. He said, "Go for substance and depth in these songs. Make music that you'll be proud of in forty years." What great advice, as opposed to grabbing the quick hit that you think might get on the radio real quick.

Billy Collins

BC: Be respectful of the reader. Or at least reader-conscious. Realize that self-expression itself is wildly overrated as an activity. As Zadie Smith said, "if you want to express yourself, just go out in the backyard and ring a bell." The whole idea for me, as bourgeois as it is, is to capture the reader. Capture. You capture the reader, and you do it through strategies. You do it through seductive technique, which sounds rather demonic, but a seductive technique is a heavy and clear title on the poem, and not writing a poem that's deflective of entry, a poem that just welcomes the reader into it, and is not obstructive in any way.

I'm writing to myself, really. I'm writing to someone who's like me. Or maybe I'm writing to other poets. Poetry is a mixture of clarity and mystery. It's very important to know when to be clear and when to be mysterious. That's something that's very hard to teach; you can only learn it by reading other poetry. It's knowing what cards to turn over and what cards to leave face-down. If you turn all the cards over, the poem is simple-minded. But if you leave them all face-down, there's no game either. You can't play with impenetrable obscurity. This is about apple picking with your mother? Why didn't you say so! Or name it "Apple Picking with My Mother."

Now, how you *feel* about your mother, that's a mysterious card. That's something that's probably fraught with ambivalence and not to be simplified, or trivialized by overt statement. So leave those cards down. But at least we have to know you're in an orchard. There's no secret there. Almost every poem that's not working is usually guilty of one of those two sins—being clear about something you can't be clear about, or being mysterious about something that should be obvious, should be a given.

Lysley Tenorio

LT: If you are writing fiction, something I tell my students, and it always seems to devastate them for the first class, I say, "Just because it happened to you doesn't mean it's interesting." That can sound really brutal, but the reason I say that is because my students, especially my freshmen will write these stories and critique them as a group and we'll say, "I didn't quite understand why or I didn't believe it that there was a burglary on page seven." And the student will say, "That's how it really happened so it has to be there." But that doesn't matter. What matters is the story. If you want to be a journalist, if you want to write nonfiction, great. But if you want to write fiction, what matters is the story, not what actually happened. Nothing in life is inherently interesting. It's only the way it is presented that makes it interesting.

Destin Daniel Cretton (Interviewed by Karl Martin)

DDC: I always get a little bit uncomfortable talking about how to make it in an industry, or how to get to a certain place in filmmaking or storytelling, partially because there is no clear route. Everybody talks about that, and it is the wrong reason to do it. If you go into it with the idea of this step is going to help me make it in this industry, I promise you will be disappointed all the time. You still might get there eventually, but it's going to be this really disappointing voyage. It's never going to go as you expect it to go. This is something I am continually learning. This idea of why do I do this can be applied to anything, I suppose.

For me, I do this because I love doing it. I don't do this to have a career, to make money or to get to a certain point, or to get an award. I'm not going to lie—those temptations come in all the time. But I have to remind myself everyday to not think about that, because then what comes out when you're writing is this just weird, forced, concoction of what you think other people want or what will win an award. That shouldn't be the reason for writing things or for making something. For me, it should come from a place of processing through something, of trying to learn about something about the world, of trying to learn to get better at this craft.

The awards and accolades are wonderful, but the idea of creating something for the sake of creating it is for the sake of learning something and working with other people, learning something about myself, becoming a better person in the process of work. Those are things that I try to cling to.

Joyce Carol Oates

JCO: A real writer, a real artist, never really wants any advice at all. I mean, what advice would you give Picasso? What advice would you give Hemingway? I think people pretend to want advice: "I'm a young writer and I want advice." It's just sort of like you're being friendly or courteous or something. Secretly you're thinking, I don't really need any advice. But the most general and harmless advice you can give a young writer is to do a lot of reading and talk to different people and let people talk. And have a lot of different experiences. The bedrock of writing is having experiences and listening to people. There's no particular secret to it.

Nikki Giovanni

NG: You're trying to tell your story as you see it, and you hope other people see it. I present my story as I see it, and I present it in love. If this was a meeting of the Klan, and you came in here with the hoods, I would've read the same poems. Because that's all I know how to do. But then I came from Nat King Cole who stood on a stage in Alabama when they attacked him for singing "I love you for sentimental reasons." If Nat can do that, I can read those poems.

You have to read something every day. I really believe that. Other than that, when you go to Singapore, go first class.

Robin Jones Gunn

DN: You told me something not long ago that you got some advice for you as a writer, and that is to listen to good poetry. Why? What does that do?

RG: Years ago, Bodie Taney told me that because she was so dyslexic and couldn't read—her mother would read to her Sir Walter Scott novels and all this classic British literature, and it put in Bodie this love for words and how the English language fit together. I really love poetry, so I downloaded some fifty best English poems and things that are really easy to find, and I would listen to them over and over because those masters of our language were able to weave the words in such a melodic way that you just could feel it resonating. The harmony. This is *our* language; English is beautiful! I became so much more appreciative of how to craft an economy of words to just simply craft that description. That helped me a lot in writing.

I felt like I would absorb the lyricism of the poems so that when I would sit down and write, I'd have that meter, that rhythm around. I've only got English, so I might as well really study it, and master it, and love it.

Write and pour your whole heart into it, and work at it very hard and not give up. We give up too easily, and there's plenty of ways in our western culture to get the training. Take a class, go to a writer's conference, get training through an online program. The fascinating thing about this art, like other arts, is that it will outlive you; once you're gone, what you've written will go on. If you take that work seriously and do the hard work, it can have immense value.

Jane Smiley

JS: First of all, you have to be good with language. You have to know how to punctuate, you have to know how to write the sentence, you have to know how to spell. Because if you aren't good with language and don't teach yourself to be good with language, than all these little mistakes are like a pebble in your shoe. They'll make the whole thing much more of an effort than you want it to be.

DN: But what if you're not good at those things?

JS: Then you have to learn. You have to practice and learn. This is the pyramid of the novel: the bottom of the pyramid is language, and that's where the door is. You have to be able to walk in that door and be at ease in there. One of the best ways is read, read, read. When you're reading, you become much better at writing, too, because the language goes into you and comes out.

DN: Read *anything?*

JS: The Bobbsey twins. Anything. The other thing that you have to have is patience. You have to train yourself to be patient with yourself and know that your main job is to just finish this novel. Once you finish the novel, or whatever the book is that you're going to write, and toss it out into the world, you don't know what's going to happen to it. You *hope* something good is going to happen to it.

My third piece of advice is you have to find pleasure in the process. Which means putting together the plot, putting together the characters, putting together, looking around, putting the setting on the page—those things have to please you, and you have to enjoy those. Those are the only lasting pleasures. Every award you get, every book review you get, [brief spitting sound effect] it's gone! But if you sit down at your desk every day and you get involved, even the book that I had the hardest time with, the one where I decided that I would commit suicide so they would publish it . . .

DN: You can only do that once!

JS: I'm only half-joking! But I had real problems with it, and when I would sit down and go over it, I would feel frustrated, but I couldn't help myself. I would feel fascinated by, "How am I going to fix this, how am I going to fix this? How am I going to make it right?" And I couldn't keep myself away from it. So that turned out to be a pleasure—a frustrating pleasure, but also a pleasure. Because I just couldn't leave it alone!

DN: Which book was it?

JS: I'm not telling!

Anchee Min

AM: Anybody can be a writer. It's not about what to write, it's about how to write, and that takes two things. One is determination. Commitment to what you want to do. Second is craftmanship. I am determined not give people crap. If they pay $30 for my book, I want them to walk away with something, so they don't feel cheated. I would feel cheated if I read a book that doesn't give me nothing. I wanted them to know China and know the part of the world, to enrich themselves.

DN: Do you write those sometimes even though you think this might not ever get published?

AM: Oh, every one I write, I think it—that's how you begin. You say, do I do it if I don't get published? If it sits under your pillow forever, would you do it? If the answer is yes, I do it. When I start writing *Red Azalea*, I was very, this raw voice.

Nnedi Okorafor

NO: My advice is always to don't talk about writing. Don't sit there and dream about it, actually do it. Just sit down, and if you want to tell that story, tell the story and don't be afraid of telling your story. That voice, and this is something I often hear from new writers, asking, "Who's going to be interested in the story that I have to tell?" Just shut that off, and go and write. Also, I don't believe in writer's block. I don't believe that writer's block exists. There are natural pauses in writing, and it's okay to take that pause if it comes. You don't have to write every day. I know Stephen King said it, and I think Stephen King is a great writer, he's one of my favorite writers. But I don't believe you have to write every day. You just have to want to write and that you have to do it. If there's a day where you can't write, don't feel guilty. A lot of times that feeling or that need of "okay, I have to write everyday," is what will cause you not to do it because you're putting a lot of pressure on yourself. For me, I write every day, but I don't feel like I have to write every day.

DN: Do you think writer's block might really be a sign that you're working on the wrong thing?

NO: There's always a reason. If something just isn't coming, maybe you need to go outside and chase some grasshoppers. Go do something else. That's always my solution.

DN: Really, that's what does it for you?

NO: That's what does it for me. It doesn't take much. But there are all sorts of reasons that you need to locate what the reason is as opposed to saying "Oh I have this condition called writer's block and that's gonna be my excuse for not writing." No, there's typically something that's going on. Just figure that out and don't panic. Pressure is one of the things that stops a lot of writers at the door.

Also, when you've never written a story and you think "Oh I have this book in me," and you sit down and start trying to write a whole novel? You might want to start with something shorter. Novels are a whole beast in themselves. If you wanna write something, start with something short. If you're stuck with the story, just write a scene in that story, the scene that is most interesting to you. Then see what happens.

DN: Didn't you start by writing about an outhouse?

NO: Yes, exactly.

DN: There you go, start there. Everybody has an outhouse experience they could write about.

NO: That's an interesting way to put it. But yeah, my first story was about an outhouse.

Christian Wiman

CW: You have to be a reader. No one was ever a great writer without being a great reader. You have to really love reading. That should be the first love. Another piece of advice that might have helped me when I was young is to find someone, or a group, someone with whom you feel a great kinship and can share work and can sustain each other in that way so that you can encourage each other. Particularly if you are inclined to solitude. You can drive yourself crazy in that kind of interiority, so find some support. That's actually very good advice for a person of faith as well. I find that solitary faith, any faith that remains completely solitary becomes despair. There's always an urge, always an effort, a need to share it or to understand it in translation with someone else.

Alice Walker

AW: Find meaning. It's all well and good to want to be a writer, to think that you can write. It's a label. But without meaning, it is pointless. And if you don't feel any joy in doing it, don't do it.

It's wonderful when you feel great—it's a little like being a part of creation. You're doing your part, you're writing the part of creation that is yours to write. I have written so many things in absolute bliss while I was just weeping like a crazy person, and it was just incredibly wonderful. I hope that for you. What I don't hope for you is that you just sit there and you keep trying to make something happen, and it's not happening in your heart, and it's not happening in your spirit. Don't do that.

Also, I don't believe in writer's block. You don't have writer's block. You should just go do something else.

Don Winslow

DN: You've got some pretty strong feelings about who should be in your writer's group.

DW: Yeah. No one.

DN: I know that's how you feel, but when you say if you're going to be in one, who should be in them?

DW: People who know more than you do. I chose those words deliberately. I worry about writers in writer's groups of their peers because it gets political, and it gets personal. It gets less honest but also, I don't mean to be insulting, I'm probably hurting people's feelings here but, you want to have someone who's done more of it. Who is better than you at that moment in time to be looking at your stuff? So I'm extremely selective about who I show any material to.

DN: Do you show it to anybody?

DW: My agent and my editor. That's it.

DN: Any other advice?

DW: It's going to sound glib, and I don't mean it to. Writers write. Before it's a noun, it's a verb. The mistake a lot of aspiring writers make, myself included, is to bite it off into big chunks. This year I'm writing that book. Maybe not. How about Tuesday you write two pages? And Wednesday you write two pages. And maybe two pages is too much. People have lives. I had seven published books in my career before I could quit my day jobs. It was a side gig for me.

DN: You were writing while you were on stake outs as a private investigator.

DW: Yeah. It made me pretty lousy at stakeouts.

DN: While you were doing these side jobs did you keep a journal?

DW: No. I don't journal. Listen, I'm not interesting. I'm sure we've learned that by now.

DN: There's nobody left in the audience. They were all too bored. But seriously, you were working on anti-terrorist stuff, leading hikes in China, directing Shakespeare . . .

DW: I've never been tempted to keep a journal. I want that energy and that time going into trying to tell good stories.

Anthony Doerr

DN: You draw this parallel between science and storytelling, where you say, "Instead of writing what you know, you write to know, and that's what scientists do too. They do experiments to know something, and that's what you're doing when you're writing." You don't know everything about electromagnetic waves. You're writing to find that stuff out, right?

AD: Absolutely. The writing advice that you'll often get if you go to a workshop is "write what you know," and I understand where that comes from. I think fundamentally, that's good advice if it's about writing about falling in love, or writing about having your heart broken, writing about feeling lonely and isolated, writing about feeling lost. Those are things we've all felt. Some people, of course, more than others, but if it comes to, say, "Write about a violin maker in the 1600s who's falling in love," that doesn't mean because you haven't made a violin before, you can't write that. It means you might have to do a bunch of work. I'd go talk to a couple of violin makers—might be really cool, you might learn a lot. But that's where the energy in writing comes from. If you already know something, you don't want to write about it because the reader won't feel that electric energy of discovering stuff along with you.

And read widely. It's okay if the first time they give you Virginia Woolf or Sandra Cisneros, and you're like, "I don't get this," try again five years later. Keep trying those things. There's a reason people are still reading the Brontës and Melville; give that stuff a chance before you die. I think just because you want to be, say, a jazz pianist doesn't mean you shouldn't listen to Simon & Garfunkel. Listen widely; read widely. You can learn as much from talking to somebody or just being open to like, "Oh, sure, I'll read this article Grandma sent me even though it seems boring." Just stay open all the time, and your curiosity should lead you.

DN: Do you have a writing group? I know Shauna, your wife, is one of your first readers. Do you have others who you trust?

AD: Well, I have my editor. The problem is you get to a certain point where too many voices would frighten me. I think writing groups are phenomenal, so find people who support you because it's a crazy thing to do to, like, make worlds with words in your bedroom—that seems weird. So have people who are doing that with you to support you. But in my case, I don't know if I've outgrown it, but I've got so many critics screaming in my own head as I wake up and read through my own work that by the time my wife gets through it and then my agent, the time it gets to my editor, I don't think I want too many other voices telling me things. I'm too afraid.

N. Scott Momaday

DN: A mentor told you to imitate people you admired, and one of the people you started to imitate was Robert Frost. Why Frost? There are a lot of great poets, and he's one of them, but why Frost?

NSM: He's very accessible, for one thing. He writes in a very plain style and it's easy to read him, and he can teach you a lot about poetry. I think you may be referring to a priest who was at Jemez Pueblo when I was there. He was the postmaster. Great poet, Fray Angelico Chavez. I used to go down and when the mail was distributed, I'd corner him and talk about poetry. He said don't be afraid to imitate writers that you admire, because you will eventually find your own voice. I think that's true. It was good advice.

DN: You said about your own writing that you write about the significant moments and then you try to cast everything else away. Would that be part of your advice as well, is look for those moments, moments that say, this changed me, this marked me, this transformed me in some way. Would you advise people to start there?

NSM: If you can, yeah. If you can center upon a moment or a group of moments that are transforming, that's a good start. That just gives you a way to enter into writing or painting.

DN: You have this great exchange in *The Bear's House* where Yahweh and this Bear are discussing, and Bear says, "Can you teach me to write?" Do you remember what Yahweh says?

NSM: He says, "I can teach you to write, but I can't teach you to write Moby-Dick."

Nick Hornby

NH: The first thing I would say to any writing student is, "Are you reading?" Are you reading everything that you can get your hands on? There's a terrible tendency, I think, where everyone wants to be a writer, and no one wants to read. Apparently, with poetry, that's absolutely true. There are way more poets than there are readers of poetry books or poetry magazines. No one's very interested in anyone else's poetry, but they want you to read theirs. It's an interesting thing about writing that one of the processes of growing up, all of us, is understanding and accepting that we're not special. So, these things start to fall away.

The one thing that never falls away is writing. Everyone thinks they can write because they can. If you're literate, you can write. And there are so many different kinds of books. We all know if we go into a bookstore, we're looking at books on those shelves, you're thinking to yourself, (*points to imaginary books*) "That person cannot write for shit, and their books are everywhere. *Points to another imaginary book.*) "That person's a genius," right next to the person who can't write for shit. So, it's a very difficult medium to be prescriptive about.

Even writing well or writing badly doesn't make any difference. But if you read, first of all, you find stories. There are stories everywhere.

There's no shortcut with agents or publishers. People say, "What is the name of your agent? How do I get an agent?" Well, I say, "Don't worry about that stuff. If you've written something brilliant, you're not going to worry about who the agents are because they'll be coming to you."

So, it's write every day, read every day. That's it.

Amor Towles

AT: The only advice I can offer, which is what my experience was: read, write, repeat. That's it. We as writers educate ourselves by reading all different kinds of storytelling and seeing and being amazed by what Márquez is doing in magical realism, to see what Whitman and Melville were doing as they were inventing the American discourse from nothing. Go back to read the Deep South writers, or the Beat guys and I love the French writers of the Second World War era because they're all crazy. There's no plots. The characters don't have names. You can't make head nor tails of it, but I love it because it's just a different way to tell a story.

That's the mission. You just keep going on a hungry basis, reading through different approaches to storytelling and then forcing yourself to try your hand at not copying, necessarily, but being open to trying to tell different stories in different ways as often as possible to master your craft.

Index

9/11 terrorist attacks 171–3
13 Ways of Looking at the Novel (Smiley) 173, 275, 300
The 40 Days of Musa Dagh (Edgarian, Balakian and Werfel) 211
100 Years of Solitude (Márquez) García 288

About Grace (Doerr) 81, 157, 180, 218
accidental theology 306
Akata Witch (Okorafor) 245–6
Albee, Edward 33
Alice in Wonderland (Carroll) 58
All the Light We Cannot See (Doerr) 81–2, 84, 157, 283
The Ancient Child (Momaday) 23, 219, 285
"Aristotle" 236
Armenian genocide 37
Arranged Marriage 95
art 51–75
The Atlantic 13, 204
Atonement (McEwan) 115
At Paradise Gate (Smiley) 62
At Play In the Fields Of the Lord (Matthiessen) 161

Balakian, Peter
  The 40 Days of Musa Dagh 211
Barn Blind (Smiley) 62
Becoming Madame Mao (Min) 213
Beerbohm, Max 29
believability 240–1
believable characters 238–40
Bell, Rob 293
"The Belly of The Whale" 247
Bennett, Tony 319
Berger, John 42
Berryman, John 43
Bible, King James 299
The Big Short 159
Bird By Bird (Lamott) 14, 91
Blackmur, R. P. 43
The Blind Side 159
Boccaccio, Giovanni 171
Bohjalian, Chris 37, 199
  on believability 240–1
  ideas 115
  rejections of manuscripts 212
  The Sandcastle Girls 37, 115, 189–92, 211
  The Sleepwalker 190
  on stories 37
  subject matter 115
The Bone Setter's Daughter (Tan) 260
The Book of Phoenix (Okorafor) 119
The Boston Globe 180
Bradbury, Ray 6, 53, 77, 160, 233, 250, 258–9, 291, 296–8, 323
  cafeteria-style faith 291
  Graveyard for Lunatics 296
  ideas 96–7
  The Martian Chronicles 77
  subject matter 96–7
Brooks, Gwendolyn 47
Buckley, Christopher 5, 256, 346–7

Buckley, William F. 5
"Buffy the Vampire Slayer" 104
Butterfly 16

cafeteria-style faith 291
The Call of the Wild (London) 317
Campbell, Joseph 132
Capote, Truman 318
Carpenter, Karen 104–5
The Carpenters 104–5
Carroll, Lewis 58
    Alice in Wonderland 58
Castro, Fidel 215
The Cemetery of Forgotten Books (Zafon) 111–12
chapter length 252–3
Cheever, John 59
Chesterton, G. K. 20
Christian faith 91, 291
Christianity 295
Christie, Agatha 53
    James Bond 53
Christy Miller (Gunn) 114, 209
Christy Miller book series 7, 114, 209, 238
The Christy Miller Series (Gunn) 7
Chronicles of Narnia (Lewis) 292
City on Fire (Winslow) 177, 194–5, 248, 328
Clarion Writers' Workshop 324
Clifton, Lucille
    "Homage to My Hips" 127
Cloud Cuckoo Land (Doerr) 77, 83–5, 157, 196, 252
Coates, Ta-Nehisi 125
    The Water Dancer 125
Cohen, Leonard 296
Collins, Billy 28–30, 52, 60–1, 150–2, 162–3, 199, 205, 318–22, 351
    ideas 101–3
    on imagery 236
    "Splitting Wood" 319
    on stories 28–30
    subject matter 101–3
The Color Purple (Walker) 45–7
The Complete Works of Thomas Mann 64
conflict
    importance of 236–7
"The Contortionist" (Pintado) 127–8
Cooper, James Fenimore 199, 205
Cosmopolitan 212
A Course in Miracles (Schucman) 301
Cretton, Destin Daniel 266–9, 352–3
    ideas 105–6
    subject matter 105–6
Crooked Little Heart (Lamott) 92, 294–5
Cuban Revolution 328
cultural heritage 132–3
cultural imagination 124
Cultural Revolution 40
culture 33–4

David Copperfield (Dickens) 38
Defoe, Daniel 51
    Robinson Crusoe 51
DeMent, Iris 10
"Desert Rose" 101
Detroit Free Press 207
Diaz, Junot 319
Dickens, Charles 38, 64, 315–16
    David Copperfield 38
    The Pickwick Papers 39
Dickinson, Emily 33, 43
Dijkstra, Sandra 145–50, 154–5, 347–9
Dillard, Annie 14, 256
discipline 231, 256, 270, 342
    humanistic 307
    mental 265
Divakaruni, Chitra 27–8, 54, 232–3, 257–8, 288–9, 344–5
    ideas 93–6
    Mistress of Spices 27
    Sister of My Heart 93–4, 187–8
    on stories 27–8
    subject matter 93–6
The Diving Bell 16
Doerr, Anthony 48–9, 71–3, 77, 157–8, 178–81, 195–7, 218–19, 282–5, 335–6, 359–61
    About Grace 81, 157, 180, 218

All the Light We Cannot See 81–2, 84, 157, 283
on chapter length 252–3
Cloud Cuckoo Land 77, 83–5, 157, 196, 252
Four Seasons in Rome 157, 282–4, 340
ideas 81–5
Memory Wall 157
Molluscs 71, 178
The Shell Collector 157
on stories 48–9
subject matter 81–5
Dubliners 208
Duplicate Keys (Smiley) 62
Dylan, Bob 10

Earth Keeper (Momaday) 309
Edgarian, Carol
The 40 Days of Musa Dagh 211
Rise the Euphrates 211
Eliot, T. S. 318
emotional songwriting 100
The Emperor of All Maladies (Mukherjee) 48
Engaging Father Christmas (Gunn) 210, 211
The English Patient (Ondaatje) 115
English romantic poetry 28–9

faith 49, 99, 182, 292, 358
cafeteria-style 291
Christian 91, 291
traditional 291
The Faith of a Writer (Oates) 31, 107
Faulkner, William 107, 166, 206, 326
fiction 17
literary 103–4
reason to write 19–49
Finding Father Christmas (Gunn) 210, 211
First World War 37
Fitzgerald, Scott 166
Fleming, Ian 53
James Bond 53
Foreman, Jon
ideas 98–9
subject matter 98–9
"Four Dead in Ohio" 10
Four Seasons in Rome (Doerr) 157, 282–4, 340
The Fragile Species (Thomas) 21
Frank, Anne 200
Frost, Robert 42, 318–19

Gass, William 25
A Gentleman in Moscow (Towles) 222–3, 226–7, 229–30
A Gentleman Moscow 158–9
Gerwig, Greta 6
Gilbert, Bil 135–6
Gilbert, Elizabeth 17
The Signature of All Things 292
The Snow Forest 201–4
Giles, Molly 146
Giovanni, Nikki 35–6, 169–70, 289, 353–4
ideas 112–13
on rhythm 237–8
on stories 35–6
subject matter 112–13
The Glass Castle (Walls) 267
God Hides in Plain Sight 13
"Gospel of The Bleeding Woman" (Manning) 126
Grand Theft Auto 319
Graveyard for Lunatics (Bradbury) 296
Greenlanders (Smiley) 39, 62
Grisham, John 5
Guest, Judith 8
Ordinary People 8
Gunn, Robin Jones 7, 36–7, 52, 66–8, 208–11, 256, 271–4, 289, 354
on believable characters 238–40
Christy Miller 114, 209
The Christy Miller Series 7
Engaging Father Christmas 210, 211
Finding Father Christmas 210, 211
ideas 113–15
on stories 36–7
subject matter 113–15

Hamlet (Shakespeare) 23, 111
Hard Laughter (Lamott) 293
Heaney, Seamus 61
Heifetz, Jascha 258
Hemingway, Ernest 140
Hillenbrand, Laura 7
Hillman, Chris 150, 263, 299–300, 350
ideas 100–1
songwriting 235
subject matter 100–1
Hitler, Adolf 37
"Homage to My Hips" (Clifton) 127
Hornby, Nick 219–20, 230–1, 315–16, 362
ideas 87–8
subject matter 87–8
House Made of Dawn (Momaday) 155–6, 181–2, 219
"How I Measure Your Body" (Manning) 247
How to Write Short Stories 179
Hughes, Langston 141
humanistic discipline 307
Hurston, Zora Neal 326–7

"I Am Not a Hipster" 267
The Ice Storm (Wiman) 174–5
Icke, David 216
ideas 77–133
Bohjalian on 115
Bradbury on 96–7
Collins on 101–3
Cretton on 105–6
Divakaruni on 93–6
Doerr on 81–5
Foreman on 98–9
Giovanni on 112–13
Gunn on 113–15
Hillman on 100–1
Hornby on 87–8
Keillor on 100
Lamott on 89–93
Manning on 125–7
Matthiessen on 98
Momaday on 131–3
Oates on 106–11
Okorafor on 115–22
Pintado on 127–31
Tan on 99–100
Tenorio on 103–5
Towles on 85–7
Walker on 124–5
Wambaugh on 88–9
Wiman on 122–4
Zafon on 111–12
"I Love My Sweet Desert Rose" 101
importance of conflict 236–7

Jackson, Jenny 241
James Bond (Christie and Fleming) 53
Jarell, Randall 42
Joyce, James 208
Joy Luck Club (Tan) 145, 147–8, 260

Karr, Mary 316–17
Keillor, Garrison 52, 59–60, 79–80, 161–2, 261–3, 298–9
on getting published 262–3
ideas 100
"Local Family Makes Son Happy" 162
subject matter 100
The Kellys and the O'Kellys (Trollope) 38
Kesey, Ken 288
Sometimes a Great Notion 288
King, Stephen 5, 17, 65–6, 256, 276, 349–50
King Lear (Shakespeare) 61, 78, 111, 242, 244
King Solomon 300
Koertge, Ron 151
Krall, Diana 5
Kwan, Michelle 255

Lamott, Anne 13, 14, 17, 164–5, 291, 293–6, 342–4
Bird By Bird 14, 91
Crooked Little Heart 92, 294–5
Hard Laughter 293
on her first novel 205–6

ideas 89–93
subject matter 89–93
Lanham, Andrew 267
Laswell, Greg 345–6
Le Guin, Ursula K. 145
L'Engle, Madeleine 20
Letters to an American Lady (Lewis) 271
Letters to a Young Poet (Rilke) 200
Lewis, C. S. 256, 271
Chronicles of Narnia 292
Letters to an American Lady 271
Lewis, Michael 159
Liebling, A. J. 59
"light verse" 163
The Lincoln Highway (Towles) 222–3, 229
literary fiction 103–4
Lit World Conference 36
"Local Family Makes Son Happy" (Keillor) 162
London, Jack 210, 256
The Call of the Wild 317
Longley, Michael 236
Lopate, Phillip 126–7
"Portrait of My Body" 126
Lovecraft, H. P. 333

Macbeth (Shakespeare) 111
MacDermots of Ballycloran (Trollope) 38
Madame de Lafayette 172
Mademoiselle Magazine 152
Mad Magazine 322
Mailer, Norman 207
Man Made of Words 24
Mann, Thomas 64
Manning, Katie 125–7, 279–80
"Gospel of The Bleeding Woman" 126
"How I Measure Your Body" 247
ideas 125–7
subject matter 125–7
"Tasty Other" 127
on thinking visually in poetry 247
Mao Zedong 199, 213
Marche, Stephen 200
On Writing and Failure 200
Márquez, Gabriel García 288
100 Years of Solitude 288
The Martian Chronicles (Bradbury) 77
Martin, Karl 98–101, 105–6, 266–9, 299–300, 345–6
Masekela, Hugh 150
The Matrix 82
Matthiessen, Peter 20–1, 54–5, 136–8, 160–1, 199, 233–4, 345
At Play In the Fields Of the Lord 161
ideas 98
on stories 20–1
subject matter 98
on writing novels 204–5
Maugham, William Somerset 64
McCord, David 53
McEwan, Ian 115
Atonement 115
McGuinn, Roger 300
McPhee, John 283
Media Associates International 36
Melodies, Merry 319
Memory Wall (Doerr) 157
mental discipline 265
"The Middleman and Other Stories" (Mukherjee) 62–3
Miller, Christy 238–9
Min, Anchee 40–1, 73–4, 154–5, 199, 356
Becoming Madame Mao 213
Red Azalea 154
on stories 40–1
Mississippi Valley Review 154
Mistress of Spices (Divakaruni) 27
Molluscs (Doerr) 71, 178
Momaday, N. Scott 21–7, 74–5, 131–3, 285–6, 309–11, 330–1, 361
The Ancient Child 23, 219, 285
cultural heritage 132–3
House Made of Dawn 155–6, 181–2, 219
ideas 131–3
pilgrim's journey 132
on stories 21–7
subject matter 131–3

Moneyball 159
The Morning News 283
Morrison, Toni 35, 103
Mouradian, Khatchig 190–1
Mr. Rogers' Neighborhood 40
Mukherjee, Bharati 62
  "The Middleman and Other Stories" 62–3
Mukherjee, Siddhartha 48
  The Emperor of All Maladies 48
My Bright Abyss (Wiman) 44, 305

Nacho Libre 291
narrative songwriting 100
Nash, Ogden 163
National Geographic 59
Netter, Gill 267
The New Centurions 140, 204
New Yorker 52, 141, 162
The New York Times 96, 109, 202, 207, 218, 315, 323
Now Is the Time to Open Your Heart (Walker) 279

Oates, Joyce Carol 31–4, 58–9, 152–3, 269–70, 322–3, 353
  The Faith of a Writer 31, 107
  ideas 106–11
  The Sacrifice 108, 206
  on stories 31–4
  subject matter 106–11
  Them 109
  on writing in college 166–7
O'Brien, Tim 20
  The Things They Carried 20
O'Conner, Flannery 146
O'Connor, Flannery 3, 9, 326
The Odyssey 253
Okorafor, Nnedi 41–2, 70–1, 77, 276, 324–5, 334, 356–7
  Akata Witch 245–6
  The Book of Phoenix 119
  ideas 115–22
  on stories 41–2
  subject matter 115–22
  Who Fears Death 77, 119–20, 122, 244
  on word choice 244–6
  Zahrah the Windseeker 244
Old Testament 9
Oliver, Mary 7, 328
Ondaatje, Michael 115
  The English Patient 115
The Onion Field (Wambaugh) 318
On Writing and Failure (Marche) 200
The Opposite of Fate (Tan) 161
Ordinary People (Guest) 8
Ortega, Daniel 215
Otero, Manuel Ramos 328
Othello (Shakespeare) 111

Parsons, Gram 300
Pascal, Blaise 292
Pereira, Fernando 167
Perlman, S. J. 59
The Pickwick Papers (Dickens) 39
Pintado, Margarita 127–31, 280–1, 327–8
  "The Contortionist" 127–8
  ideas 127–31
  "Still Life" 128
  subject matter 127–31
Plath, Sylvia 152
Plymouth Brethren 298
Poe, Edgar Allan 333
Poe, Edgar Allen 322–3
  The Tell-Tale Heart 322
Poetry Magazine 205
"Portrait of My Body" (Lopate) 126
Possessing the Secret of Joy (Walker) 124
Potok, Chaim 19
Powers, Richard 84
A Prairie Home Companion 79
Pressfield, Stephen 80
  The War of Art 16, 80
Pressfield, Steven 16
The Princess of Cleves (Madame de Lafayette) 172
Publisher's Weekly 205

quilting 55–6

Rago, Henry 205
Reader's Digest 59
reading 2, 7, 34, 363
  habits 277
  importance of 313–36
  as inhalation 314
  as mental activity 252
  and writing 48
Red Azalea (Min) 41, 74, 154
Rilke, Rainer Maria 130, 200
  Letters to a Young Poet 200
Rise the Euphrates (Edgarian) 211
Robbins, Harold 64–5
Robinson, Roxana 78
Robinson Crusoe (Defoe) 51
Rolofson, Kristine 69
Rowling, J. K. 200
Rukeyser, Muriel 341
  The Speed of Darkness 341
Rules of Civility (Towles) 139, 225

The Sacrifice (Oates) 108, 206
The Same River Twice (Walker) 47
The Sandcastle Girls (Bohjalian) 37, 115, 189–92, 211, 240–1
Savages (Winslow) 177
Scott, George C. 145
Seeger, Pete 10, 300
Sendak, Maurice 9
  Where the Wild Things Are 9
The Shadow of the Wind (Zafon) 111, 153–4, 167–9, 323
The Shadows (Zafon) 63
Shadowspeaker (Okorafor) 41
Shakespeare, William
  Hamlet 23, 111
  King Lear 61, 78, 111, 242, 244
  Macbeth 111
  Othello 111
The Shell Collector (Doerr) 157
"Short Term Twelve" 105, 267
The Signature of All Things (Gilbert) 292
Silver Pavements, Golden Roofs 95
"Sin City" 299–300
Singer, Isaac Bashevis 17
Sister of My Heart (Divakaruni) 93–4, 187–8
The Sleepwalker (Bohjalian) 190
Smiley, Jane 37–40, 61–2, 154, 170–3, 274–6, 300–1, 323, 354–6
  13 Ways of Looking at the Novel 173, 275, 300
  At Paradise Gate 62
  Barn Blind 62
  on creating characters 242–4
  Duplicate Keys 62
  Greenlanders 39, 62
  on stories 37–40
  Ten Days in the Hills 171
The Snow Forest (Gilbert) 201–4
Sometimes a Great Notion (Kesey) 288
songwriting 235
Sontag, Susan 33
Southern Baptist Convention 302
The Speed of Darkness (Rukeyser) 341
spirituality 196, 201–2, 291–3, 295, 300, 307, 309–10
"Splitting Wood" (Collins) 319
Steele, Danielle 5
"Still Life" (Pintado) 128
stories 19–49
  Bohjalian on 37
  Collins on 28–30
  Divakaruni on 27–8
  Doerr on 48–9
  Giovanni on 35–6
  Gunn on 36–7
  Matthiessen on 20–1
  Min on 40–1
  Momaday on 21–7
  Oates on 31–4
  Okorafor on 41–2
  Smiley on 37–40
  Tenorio on 30–1
  Walker on 45–7
  Wiman on 42–5
  Zafon on 34–5
storytelling 17, 22–4, 34–5, 46, 48, 54, 64, 131, 352
Styron, Bill 33

subject matter 77–133
- Bohjalian on 115
- Bradbury on 96–7
- Collins on 101–3
- Cretton on 105–6
- Divakaruni on 93–6
- Doerr on 81–5
- Foreman on 98–9
- Giovanni on 112–13
- Gunn on 113–15
- Hillman on 100–1
- Hornby on 87–8
- Keillor on 100
- Lamott on 89–93
- Manning on 125–7
- Matthiessen on 98
- Momaday on 131–3
- Oates on 106–11
- Okorafor on 115–22
- Pintado on 127–31
- Tan on 99–100
- Tenorio on 103–5
- Towles on 85–7
- Walker on 124–5
- Wambaugh on 88–9
- Wiman on 122–4
- Zafon on 111–12

Summer Promise (Gunn) 238
"Sunday Bloody Sunday" 10
The Swan 318
Switchfoot 98–9

Table For Two (Towles) 85
Taking the Arrow Out of the Heart (Walker) 279
Tan, Amy 140, 145–50, 259–61, 331–2, 347–9
- *The Bone Setter's Daughter* 260
- ideas 99–100
- *Joy Luck Club* 145, 147–8, 260
- *The Opposite of Fate* 161
- subject matter 99–100

"Tasty Other" (Manning) 127
The Tell-Tale Heart (Poe) 322
The Temple of my Familiar (Walker) 277, 278
Ten Days in the Hills (Smiley) 171
Tennyson, Alfred Lord 330
Tenorio, Lysley 30–1, 62–3, 140–1, 152, 165–6, 263–6, 332, 352
- ideas 103–5
- on importance of conflict 236–7
- on stories 30–1
- subject matter 103–5

Them (Oates) 109
The Things They Carried (O'Brien) 20
Thomas, Lewis 21
- *The Fragile Species* 21

Thompson, Hunter S. 14
Thoreau, Henry David 322
A Thousand Acres (Smiley) 242, 244
"Time Between" 150
Time Magazine 335
To Build a Fire in Honolulu (London) 210
"To Hell With Dying" (Walker) 141
"Top of the World" 105
Towles, Amor 52, 53, 136–9, 158–9, 362–3
- comparison to Andre Agassi 228–9
- *A Gentleman in Moscow* 222–3, 226–7, 229–30
- ideas 85–7
- *The Lincoln Highway* 222–3, 229
- *Rules of Civility* 139, 225
- short stories 223–5
- subject matter 85–7
- *Table For Two* 85
- on writing 197

traditional faith 291
A Tree Grows in Brooklyn 333
Tribune 102
Trollope, Anthony 38
- *The Kellys and the O'Kellys* 38
- *MacDermots of Ballycloran* 38
- *The Warden* 38

Trump, Donald 289
Tunes, Looney 319
Twain, Mark 14
Tyler, Anne 315, 316

Unbroken (Hillenbrand) 7
Updike, John 33
Urrea, Luis Alberto 56–8, 145, 188–9, 221–2, 234–5

Vega, Lorenzo Garcia 327
Vonnegut, Kurt 33

Walker, Alice 45–7, 52, 55–6, 124–5, 141, 175–7, 213–17, 277–9, 326–7, 358
  banning/censorship of books 213–14
  The Color Purple 45–7
  on David Icke 216
  on forgiveness 194
  ideas 124–5
  Lyme disease 176
  Now Is the Time to Open Your Heart 279
  Possessing the Secret of Joy 124
  The Same River Twice 47
  on stories 45–7
  subject matter 124–5
  suicidal thoughts 175–6
  Taking the Arrow Out of the Heart 279
  The Temple of my Familiar 277, 278
  on violence and writing 192–3
  The Way Forward Is with a Broken Heart 47, 279
Wallace, Alfred 293
Walls, Jeannette 17, 267–8, 332–4
  The Glass Castle 267
Wall Street Journal 202, 319–20
Wambaugh, Joe 256
Wambaugh, Joseph 54, 139–40, 144–5, 232, 256–7, 317–18, 342
  on being pessimistic and cynical 186–7
  ideas 88–9
  New Centurions 204
  The Onion Field 318
  subject matter 88–9
The Warden (Trollope) 38
The War of Art (Pressfield) 16, 80
Washington Post 120
Wassermann, Jakob 64
The Water Dancer (Coates) 125
The Way Forward Is with a Broken Heart (Walker) 47, 279
Webb, Jack 144
Weeks, Edward 140
Werfel, Franz
  The 40 Days of Musa Dagh 211
Whale Road Review 279
Wharton, Edith 181
Whedon, Joss 104
Where the Wild Things Are (Sendak) 9
Whitman, Walt 33
Who Fears Death (Okorafor) 77, 119–20, 122, 244
Williams, Lucinda 151
Williams, Miller 151
Wiman, Christian 42–5, 122–4, 301–9, 314, 325–6, 357–8
  cultural imagination 124
  The Ice Storm 174–5
  ideas 122–4
  on memorizing poetry 276–7
  motivations for poetry 123, 173–4
  My Bright Abyss 44, 305
  on stories 42–5
  subject matter 122–4
Winslow, Don 68–70, 177–8, 185–6, 281–2, 328–30, 334–5, 358–9
  City on Fire 177, 194–5, 248, 328
  on word choice/description/structure 248–52
Wolfe, Tom 14, 317
word choice/description/structure 248–52
writers 1–5
Writer's Digest 154
Writer's Symposium By The Sea 4, 6, 16
writing 5–10
  as act of creation 10
  bearing witness 6–7
  co-creators 10

reasons for not 10–16
as way of becoming more whole 10
as way to express outrage 10

Zafon, Carlos Ruiz 34–5, 63–6, 270–1, 323
The Cemetery of Forgotten Books 111–12
ideas 111–12
The Shadow of the Wind 111, 153–4, 167–9, 323
The Shadows 63
on stories 34–5
subject matter 111–12
Zahrah the Windseeker (Okorafor) 244

About the Author

Dean Nelson is an award-winning journalist who has written for the *New York Times*, the *Boston Globe*, dozens of magazines and news organizations, and has written fifteen books. He is the founder and director of the journalism program at Point Loma Nazarene University in San Diego and the founder and host of the annual Writer's Symposium By The Sea. His fifteenth and most recently published book is *Talk to Me: How to Ask Better Questions, Get Better Answers, and Interview Anyone Like a Pro.*

www.ingramcontent.com/pod-product-compliance
Lightning Source LLC
Chambersburg PA
CBHW060251250826
50388CB00003B/31